TROPICAL DREAM PALACES

ODILE GOERG

Tropical Dream Palaces

Cinema in Colonial West Africa

OXFORD
UNIVERSITY PRESS

OXFORD
UNIVERSITY PRESS

Oxford University Press is a department of the
University of Oxford. It furthers the University's objective
of excellence in research, scholarship, and education
by publishing worldwide.

Oxford   New York

Auckland   Cape Town   Dar es Salaam   Hong Kong   Karachi
Kuala Lumpur   Madrid   Melbourne   Mexico City   Nairobi
New Delhi   Shanghai   Taipei   Toronto

With offices in

Argentina   Austria   Brazil   Chile   Czech Republic   France   Greece
Guatemala   Hungary   Italy   Japan   Poland   Portugal   Singapore
South Korea   Switzerland   Thailand   Turkey   Ukraine   Vietnam

Oxford is a registered trade mark of Oxford University Press
in the UK and certain other countries.

Published in the United States of America by
Oxford University Press
198 Madison Avenue, New York, NY 10016

Library of Congress Cataloging-in-Publication Data is available
Odile Goerg.
Tropical Dream Palaces: Cinema in Colonial West Africa.
ISBN: 9780190089078

Printed in India on acid-free paper

CONTENTS

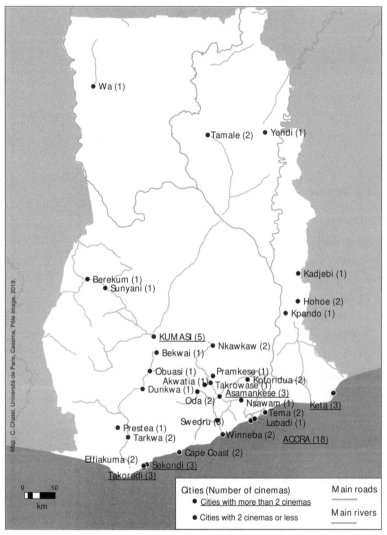

Cinemas in Ghana, early 1960s

Source: AMPECA, West African Report, 3 December 1962.

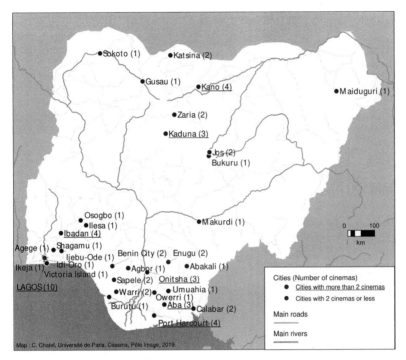

Cinemas in Nigeria, early 1960s

Source: AMPECA, West African Report, 3 December 1962.

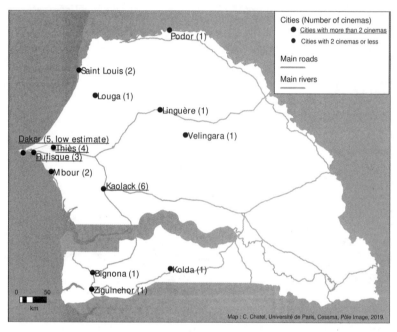

Cinemas in Senegal, around 1958

Source: *Guide AOF*, 1958 (*Les Guides bleus, Afrique de l'ouest, AOF-Togo*, Hachette, 1958).

LIST OF ACRONYMS

To refer to the countries, I use colonial terms: French Sudan for present day Mali; Gold Coast for Ghana.

BFI	British Film Institute
CFU	Colonial Film Unit (founded in 1939)
CO	Colonial Office
COMACICO	Compagnie Marocaine Cinématographique et Commerciale, founded in 1933, then Compagnie Africaine Cinématographique Industrielle et Commerciale
CPP	Convention People's Party, Ghana
FOM	*France d'Outre-Mer*
FWA	French West Africa (also AOF, or *Afrique occidentale française*)
NEA	Nouvelles Éditions Africaines
RDA	Rassemblement Démocratique Africain (African Democratic Rally)
RG	Renseignements généraux (Intelligence service)
SECMA	Société d'Exploitation Cinématographique Africaine (founded in 1936)
SFIO	French Socialist Party (Section française de l'Internationale ouvrière)
SLWN	*Sierra Leone Weekly News*

INTRODUCTION

Less than fifty years ago, West Africa's towns were full of cinemas, known then as 'dream palaces'. Mobile cinema vans also traversed the countryside. A highly popular urban leisure activity—also popular in rural areas when villagers got the chance—until the 1970s to the 1980s, cinema offered spectators a break from their daily routines. Even though not all countries were equally well equipped, the cinema presented images which resonated well beyond the four walls of the movie theatre. Watching a film today, at the start of the twenty-first century, is far easier and often instantaneous thanks to internet streaming and mobile phones, but, as a result, the culture of sharing that accompanied public screenings in Africa has also gone. All that remains is a handful of buildings which have been converted into warehouses or churches, and the nostalgia of those who lived through this period. 'We just followed the vibe; we didn't know we would be questioned about it,' said Soumaïla Coulibaly, who was a fervent film-lover in the 1950s.[1]

Cinema spread rapidly in Africa. All over this vast continent, just like everywhere else, people were attracted to the novelty of the moving image, to its promise of escape, and to the messages it conveyed. From Zanzibar to Brazzaville, from Johannesburg to Dakar, the first film showings were a huge hit with the initially limited turn-of-the-century audiences. Cinema continued to grow from then on, becoming the predominant urban leisure activity on the eve of Independence.

The chance meeting of cinema and colonization would not have had the same impact without the presence of dynamic local economic actors and enthusiastic spectators. While the demand for images was immediate, supply, on the other hand, was subject to complex processes. This was due to conflict between the entrepreneurial desire to develop a profitable activity on the one hand, and, on the other, the concern of the colonial administration, certain entrepreneurs, and the political and moral elites not to rock local societies by introducing foreign images that risked weakening colonial domination and upsetting social and gender relations and representations of both others and the self. A place of escape, as the expression 'dream palace' illustrates, and a place where spectators' awareness could be raised through education, cinema was indeed potentially subversive for populations whom the authorities sought to control, and also offered subjected peoples a breathing space.

It is this history of both expansion and censorship that *Tropical Dream Palaces* seeks to trace, filling a historiographic void with regard to West Africa, while at the same time looking further afield to Central Africa and its different models. Bar a few exceptions, swathes of the continent indeed remain unstudied in this field, even though cinema took off there actively, albeit at varying rhythms and to different degrees.

Historiographic perspectives

The past few decades have seen the publication of a growing number of works devoted to African cinema created after Independence, or to cinema in Africa. The list is now too long to offer an exhaustive overview, especially as approaches vary according to historiographic trends and time. After the first general studies of films made in Africa by African directors—notably *Le Cinéma africain des origines à 1973* by Paulin Vieyra (1975), 'Focus on: African Filmmaking Country by Country' by Nancy Schmidt (1985), *Le Cinéma africain de A à Z* by Férid Boughedir (1987), and *Twenty-Five Black African Filmmakers* by Françoise Pfaff (1988)—studies have focused on the conditions of the emergence, then the development of these films, placing the emphasis on directors, national productions, film genres, or the ways in which cultures are formed by the representations constructed in these films. Other research has explored distribution mechanisms and institutional aspects, post-Independence state policies, and the development of festivals, notably the FESPACO (Pan-African Festival of Film and Television of Ouagadougou), set up in Ouagadougou in 1969. While incorporating historical reflection, and taking the colonial legacy into account, the existing research does not develop these perspectives further. This reflects the variety of disciplines that focus on cinema—from anthropology to film studies, communications studies, and cultural studies.[2] The huge success of the Ghanaian and Nigerian video film industries, regrouped under the nebulous neologism 'Nollywood' (from Nigeria and Hollywood), has encouraged a questioning of audience preferences, the cultural roots of visual representations, and the distribution mechanisms of films that circulate well beyond their zones of production.[3]

Since the 1990s, film analysis theories and their implications have been amply explored in relation to Africa, but authors have rarely given voice to Africans regarding the films selected or produced for them. Sources are more loquacious about colonizers observing the colonized watching films than about the reactions of the latter group. The question of reception remains a complex one. Colonial films have been decrypted as vectors of imperial propaganda and representations of the colonized destined for metropolitan audiences, just as images of black people, Africa, and Africans have been in cinemas of the West, revealing the extent to which cinema plays a role in constructing and perpetuating stereotypes (Bickford-Smith and Mendelsohn 2007; Bloom 2008; Genova 2006; Slavin 2001).

There are many studies focusing on cinema in contemporary Africa. Rare are those, however, that focus on cinema as a new leisure activity: an activity that influenced several generations, shaped perspectives, and opened up spaces for dream, dialogue, or dispute. Renewed epistemologies and historiographies, which emphasize the context in which films were watched, have barely touched upon colonial histories; the same can be said of studies of film reception in the colonial period, notably for methodological reasons or for lack of sources. Contrary to anthropologists' analyses of other festive practices of the time, analysis of cinema as a social and cultural practice is still embryonic and rarely focuses on extended periods, such as the century in which cinema emerged. Few studies concern the organization of the film sector in the colonies; the mechanisms by which audiences are constructed and film cultures are acquired; the impact of screening foreign images on spectators in the colonial context; or the use that spectators made of these foreign images.

Southern Africa was the object of the first studies, partly due to the early establishment of bioscopes, but also, and above all, due to the specificity of segregationist policies imposed on African spectators (Powdermaker 1962; Nasson 1989; Bickford-Smith 2000; Ambler 2001). These analyses highlighted the development of racial theories which were contemporaneous with the introduction of cinema, and which questioned Africans' ability to understand moving images. These theories led to the drastic cutting of whole segments of films, often at the expense of the plot, or to the production of films 'for Africans'—that is, for spectators conceived of as illiterate and proletarian, and thus kept away from any image that might help raise their awareness. In *Flickering Shadows*, for example, James Burns evokes 'Southern Rhodesia's rather hysterical fear of the cinema' (2002b, p. 2). The limited vision of African audiences influenced the conception and organization of cinema as a leisure activity, notably in the mining compounds. Set up in the 1930s, the Bantu Educational Kinema Experiment (BEKE) and, later, the Colonial Film Unit (CFU) both embodied these policies, which were rolled out across the whole of the British Empire after the Second World War. Interest in segregationist policy and the existence of abundant archives have generated studies focusing on Central and Eastern Africa—Kenya, Rhodesia, Zambia, and Zanzibar most notably (Smyth 1979, 1983b; Kerr 1993; Ambler 2001; Burns 2002b; Fair 2004, 2018; Reinwald 2006). Dominated by the missionaries, the Belgian Congo's model has similarly been identified as one which promoted cinema as a means of acculturation, entertainment, and propaganda with a paternalistic, even racist, perspective (Ramirez and Rolot 1985; Convents 2006).

Northern Nigeria, where William Sellers, the first director of the CFU, was active in the late 1930s, has also received critical attention (Larkin 1998). Paradoxically, West Africa has otherwise not attracted the same level of interest, even though cinema developed early there, from Saint-Louis in Senegal to Accra. Initially from the salaried and educated classes, spectators all attended the cinema with the same enthusiasm. African, Lebanese, Indian, and European entrepreneurs enjoyed a wide margin of manoeuvre in West Africa, especially in British colonies. It was nonetheless not until the twenty-first century that the first studies emerged. Interested in cultural history, notably in urban spaces, I was struck by the lack of research into this leisure pursuit, which is frequently mentioned by older witnesses in their memoirs.

This account looks, for the first time, at both French and British territories, at their similarities and differences during the colonial period.[4] It will demonstrate that on-screen images met with the same success in both. Historically rooted divergences depended more on social category—the best examples of which being the reticence of the Krio in Sierra Leone and the progressive disaffection of the Ghanaian bourgeoisie—and on the relative influence of religious factors in the spread of cinema, whoever the colonizer. The range of films varied little, with a fraction more onus on Egyptian films here or on Indian films there, but all with a shared Hollywood base that was particularly strong in the British Empire, where American films did not need to be dubbed. Specific administrative policies came into play, be it France's centralizing logic or Britain's unifying imperial policy, whatever each colony's degree of autonomy. Ultimately, however, censorship models were comparable. After Independence, the hitherto relatively similar situations diverged as national models imposed themselves more firmly. Until recently, no works on this subject existed, other than research on Northern Nigeria (as seen above), an article on Ivory Coast (Retord 1986), and a Master's dissertation followed by a doctoral thesis on Dakar (Seck 2003–2008). More recently, added to these were a dissertation on Togo that I supervised (Zimmermann 2008), and a doctoral thesis on Ghana (McFeely 2015). Yet, to date, many areas have still not been looked at in detail: Senegal (beyond its capital); The Gambia; southern and central Nigeria; Sierra Leone (which was more resistant to cinema); Dahomey (Benin); most of Ivory Coast; and the colonies of the Sahel.[5]

All research takes place over a long period of time—in this case, more than a decade. It is enriched over the years with new perspectives that arise from the evolution of historiography. This study is thus inspired by developments in film research. There has been a progressive movement from film history to aesthetic analysis to a history of cinema as a social practice, in keeping with the renewal of film studies initiated by Douglas Gomery (1992) and Robert Allen (1990) on both methodological and thematic levels. It is this approach, reflecting the recent epistemological shift, that I apply to cinema in the colonies. While until the 1980s film history favoured the analysis of films as texts, research now focuses on the study of practices, of 'shared pleasures' (Gomery 1992), and of the economic, cultural, and social environments of cinema. Various works highlight the need to consider the constantly changing contexts in which people go to the cinema and in which given audiences, but also individuals, watch films.[6] Research now also focuses on other culturally dominated zones—be they in the Maghreb or the Mashriq, in Central Europe or the Middle East.[7]

Certain studies have thus documented the relationship between imperialism and film production (Chowdhry 2000; Jaikumar 2004) and between nationalism and cinema, for example in countries formerly belonging to the Ottoman Empire (Drieu 2014). Others have analyzed the USSR's international policy, especially after Independence (Chomentowski 2016, 2019), notably from the angle of transnational or trans-imperial circulations, or funding and training policies. Elsewhere, analyses of cinema in Africa highlight the local success of certain films or the specific impact of film genre on spectatorial behaviour. The success of Indian cinema, which was more popular than Hollywood on the east coast from Kenya to Zanzibar, stemmed from both the dynamism of the subcontinent's entrepreneurs and the obvious proximity of sensibilities (Fair 2004,

2009, 2010, 2018; Reinwald 2006). Some studies look at the figure of the cowboy in westerns as a new model of masculinity in Central Africa (Ambler 2007; Burns 2002a; Burton 2001; Gondola 2009, 2013, 2016), while others have (re)evaluated the local reception of Hollywood films outside the United States (Stokes and Maltby, eds, 2004) or studied the role of missionaries and institutions such as the Carnegie Foundation (Burns 2002b, 2013; Reynolds 2015).[8] Laura Fair's book *Reel Pleasures: Cinema Audiences and Entrepreneurs in Twentieth-Century Urban Tanzania* (2018) superbly illustrates the importance of studies focusing on one country: it benefits from the new questions and knowledge which have accumulated with cinema's development in an increasingly globalized context; ranges from the colonial to the contemporary; and examines different local, national, and transnational scales and circulations.[9] The present book is situated within this perspective.

Drawing on multiple sources

As Laura Fair points out, research conditions have evolved over the past decade, enriching our understanding of this area of study. While it was previously difficult to access the films that spectators watched in Africa from the 1930s to the 1950s, most of them are now accessible in digitalized forms online. Similarly, cinemas' rapid closure often led to the destruction of their archives, as neither the owners' families nor researchers were interested in them at that precise time, but other documents have since emerged. This work makes use of extremely varied sources to paint a broad picture of the cinematographic landscape.[10] *Tropical Dream Palaces* draws on the archives and the accounts of African and European spectators, administrators, and observers. It also turns to the press, and to the one-off studies that are available. There is no 'cinema' category in the archive collections; the documents are classed by theme or period under the headings 'police and security', 'teaching', 'subsidies', 'general administration', and so on. The hazards of source conservation and archival classification reinforce the geographic eclecticism of the approach, especially regarding the early, pre-1940s days of cinema, for which data is patchy, dispersed, and scarce. Piecing together these elements, it has been possible to reconstitute gradually the beginnings of cinema. Its expansion during the final decade of the colonial era helps to sharpen the perspective in places, thanks to the documentation available.

Produced by diverse metropolitan or local administrative services, the colonial archives shed little light on colonized populations' experiences of cinema.

They do, however, help us to follow the creation of film policies via surveys carried out at strategic moments (when the talkies were introduced in the 1930s, for example, or when sociological surveys were conducted in the 1950s); to analyze the development of cinemas and distribution mechanisms; or to study models of censorship.

Spectators' voices are nonetheless perceptible, in all their diversity, but one has to be capable of discerning them and therein surpassing the filter of the colonial vision, which is tainted with prejudices and misunderstandings. Offsetting the biased analyses and fragmentary citations are the testimonies of these spectators, expressing themselves in written works (novels, autobiographies, the press, existing interviews) or oral enquiries. These sources give access to facets of spectators' experiences, and partially make up for the absence of official documents. However, recent oral enquiries and memoirs written after the event are shaped by the play of memory, and more easily reconstitute a general atmosphere than the specific impact of a given film or of censorship. Looking back, people also tend to embellish their youthful years. The press, for its part, detailed film programmes, and sometimes mentioned audience reactions to films, but largely covered events at well-to-do cinemas. To these sources may also be added iconographic elements (old postcards and photographs), which give a clear image of buildings that have since disappeared or been altered. Rare, however, are visual sources showing spectators in or around the cinemas, which would have better helped to reconstitute their attitudes and the atmosphere.

What does cinema convey?

Retracing the history of this key leisure activity in the colonial context—that is, within a complex relationship of domination and limited autonomy—means not losing sight of the fact that the colonial relationship determined cinema's political economy. This had an impact on the establishment of distribution networks, which were dominated by European actors and capital, even if African, Lebanese, and Indian entrepreneurs did also invest in this sector. The colonial relationship also influenced certain aspects of film policy, notably censorship.

Screening venues, audiences, and films themselves are the fundamental focus of this study. To these can be added those involved in film distribution: the film-lovers or entrepreneurs who capitalized on the lucrative potential of this economic activity. Indeed, the colonial authorities let the private sector run the enterprise. However, they rapidly perceived the ambiguous power of cinema, which is on the one hand a propaganda tool and an 'opium of the people', but on the other a form of entertainment, offering an escape from the burden of foreign domination, an insight into the wider world, and an alternative to colonial discourse. Indeed, for the colonial powers, cinema represented a threat to stability which had to be countered by the surveillance of movie theatres, the films that were shown, and audiences. For spectators, however, cinema was not primarily about dissent: it was above all an opportunity to escape, relax, or even learn about alternative ways of life. Cinema created dedicated recreational spaces and moments of community interaction. As a form of leisure, it broke with the practices of the past. Hitherto differentiated according to gender or age, and generally related to collective festivities or family events which marked the key stages of life or work in the fields, social gatherings and modes of relaxation took on a new tonality in towns, while conserving their collective character. Beyond this key pleasure aspect, spectators discovered an incredible reservoir of social or identity-based models in films that challenged their own representations. The cinema occupied a crucial position. It even came to define urbanity, according to the writer Tierno Monénembo: 'A town wasn't a proper town unless it had a cinema' (1998).

Yet in what conditions did the shift from moonlit storytelling sessions to a night out at the cinema take place? What were spectators looking for on the screens and in the darkness of the cinemas? To answer these questions, the atmosphere of the early days of film needs to be reconstituted, analysing audiences in all their diversity, discovering their favourite films, and looking at the forms of sociability that developed around this new leisure activity. Analysing cinema as a global experience summons a host of related questions that stem as much from social history (the diversity and hierarchical categorization of audiences in the colonial context), as from urban studies (the location of cinemas, travel within the town, buildings and infrastructure) and the cultural history of leisure activities—without forgetting, of course, the political contexts that above all other factors determined the population's margin of manoeuvre. All of the elements involved in a screening are fundamental: the journey to the screening venue; the wait while reels were changed; the animation in the queue or on the way out; and the advertising (posters, music, human billboards) that concretized cinema's presence outside the screenings, reaching the eyes and ears even of those who didn't go.

Commercial cinema is at the heart of this analysis, but one cannot totally ignore other forms of distribution, such as the patronage of the missionaries and screenings in schools, cultural centres, and mining centres, or on planta-tions. As autobiographical testimonies show, it was often through these that people were introduced to the moving image, an experience that they wanted to enjoy again and which pushed villagers towards the towns.

The aim, then, is not to write a history of African film, which was very rare in the colonial era, nor of the many ethnographic and colonial films destined above all for metropolitan audiences—the latter of which speak volumes about the clichés that Western representations of Africa and Africans con-structed, and which are still present in people's minds.[11] Yet the study of cin-ema as a social practice in West Africa does obviously involve the analysis of film programmes and the reception of the predominantly Western and later Arabic and Indian films. For although going to the cinema is not just a ques-tion of seeing a film, this is of course a major part of the experience.

We are rarely able to go back as far as the very first screenings, such as the 1908 one described by writer Amadou Hampâté Bâ (1967). Chapter 1 thus focuses on the interwar years to show how screenings travelled 'From Under the Starry Skies to the Confines of the Movie Theatre'. Progressing from the often perilous early conditions (fragile equipment, damage done by the humidity, lack of electricity, and so forth), the system gradually became more stable and a first generation of spectators emerged. Focusing on Southern and Central Africa, pioneering studies accentuate the importance of worker audi-ences, from the Belgian Copperbelt to the South African mining com-pounds; broadening the analysis to West Africa, however, highlights other models rooted in local societies.[12] The cinema attracted the most dynamic and cosmopolitan social groups. Civil servants, traders, and minor entrepre-neurs would gather to watch films in small spaces (courtyards, cafés) before the appearance of bigger, specialized venues that followed codified rules of their own. Thus, in the mid-1920s, a Ghanaian businessman, Alfred J. Ocansey, opened a chain of cinemas in the south of the Colony. This transi-tion, which gathered pace in the mid-1930s, introduced new opportunities for both spectators and investors.

While cinema was the business of private entrepreneurs, Chapter 2 shows how colonial authorities intervened in its functioning, first for reasons of security and public order, then for reasons of censorship. The transition to sound film ('talkies') forced them to pay closer attention to this new media, an attitude that, while retaining the same legal basis, became more stringent after the war. A more or less developed film policy was put into place, at times involving the local production of films for audiences considered to have their own specific character. This book thus explores the first informal, then legal forms of control exerted over the cinema, and the concrete mechanisms of censorship.

While cinema as a new leisure activity took off in the towns, rural areas were not totally neglected, even if travelling cinema entrepreneurs stopped by only randomly—usually once a year, if the villagers were lucky. Chapter 3 traces these entrepreneurs' itineraries throughout the colonial period. Mobile cinema vans targeted the biggest villages, or the richest agricultural regions, adapting to climatic and economic conditions along the way. They played a major role in spreading film culture.

The silver screen opened spectators up to foreign, often strange worlds, telling stories that were very different from those of their daily lives. This 'Window on the World' (Chapter 4) showed different places, different representations of romantic relationships, and different intergenerational dynamics. In a context of political and cultural repression, the cinema offered up images that were far from the stereotypes of the 'colonial mission', or the idealized vision of whites. Crooks, gangsters, poor people, adulterous men, and loose or violated women invaded the screens. 'The cinema is a life-long night-school', said Ousmane Sembène (2005). It demonstrated to adolescents behaviours that were far from their own norms, and a new repertoire of signs (gestures, fashions, imitations). For them, westerns were the archetypal new model, and this genre participated in the self-construction of young men in the Independence era. Over the years, the range of film genres diversified, as did their provenance, with Egyptian and Indian films coming to compete with the productions of the West. This book thus broaches the circulation of film policies and models from the metropolises to the colonies—at times from the colonies to the metropolises—but also between the colonies, whether or not they were part of the same empire.

After 1945, cinema rapidly spread both geographically (in terms of the number of towns concerned and the equipping of suburbs) and socially. Its influence grew, as testified by the opening of many screening venues and the emergence of distinct audiences—processes analyzed in Chapter 5. In this context, spectators were sometimes able to pick between movie theatres as well as films, and thus enjoyed a range of markedly different experiences, from luxury first-run cinemas to the most downmarket venues.

While the colonial situation limited individuals' autonomy, cinema quite inadvertently gave them a political arena fostered by the darkness of the theatres and the unpredictability of audience reactions, which the censors could not always foresee. Paradoxically, cinema thus became a space of freedom, a potential social disruptor, and a vehicle for subversive ideas. This was particularly true in a late colonial context, and in that of the anti-colonial struggle. Chapter 6 demonstrates how the screen could play the role of mediator between different social groups, but also between audiences and the authorities, or between a society and the outside world in its transmission of alternative forms of modernity. Censorship was instigated in the 1930s and particularly active after the Second World War, when the expansion of cinema was such that it now reached all sections of the population—from the richest to the poorest, from the city centres to the peripheries. The overt surveillance of screens and movie theatres thus coincided with the rise in anti-colonial demands and the expression of nationalism, which found elements of inspiration in films. Colonial authorities had to adapt, for fear of provoking still more violent reactions. The emerging African political elites, who often backed the authorities, pursued other objectives: training responsible youths and laying the foundations for the coming nations. The divide between the political and moral elites on the one hand, who thought themselves invested with a mission, and the rest of the population on the other continued after Independence. Cinema remained the leading leisure activity for another two decades; in this sense, therefore, as in others, Independence did not signify a rupture.

Thanks to its variety of different sources and to its broad range of questions, this work presents a global history of the cinematic landscape, beyond the obvious specificity of each town, each cinema, or even each film show, which would all be fascinating to analyze.[13] Thinking on a regional scale—that of West Africa—has its ambiguities, of course, given the extent to which cultures and contexts vary, but by cross-referencing both written and oral documentation, it is possible to suggest the impact of this new media on spectators, to reconstitute the atmosphere in the cinemas, and to reveal the traces of censorship. Let us prepare, then, to follow the spectators beneath the stars or into the dark movie theatres for an episode of *Tarzan* or *The Lone Ranger* in their company.

1

FROM UNDER THE STARRY SKIES TO THE CONFINES OF THE MOVIE THEATRE

THE INTERWAR YEARS

Invented north of the Mediterranean, cinema soon crossed the sea and spread across the African continent, imposing itself as a new urban leisure activity. From the early one-off events as a result of individual initiatives, the cinema became an accessible and in some cases daily pleasure. Film distribution took varied forms. In major centres such as Dakar, the capital of *Afrique occidentale française* (AOF or FWA, for French West Africa), Accra in the British Gold Coast colony (now Ghana), and Lagos in Nigeria, film fans could choose between several movie theatres and film genres in the late 1930s, whereas smaller towns often had just one cinema and a single programme. Providing an exhaustive account of film distribution is thus quite a challenge, but it is possible to trace its main stages and modes. These depended on a number of factors, including the dynamism of individual entrepreneurship, the administration's attitude and legislative framework, socio-economic contexts, local culture, and so on. Everything depended on the identity of various actors—individuals, societies, institutions, missions, the administration—and on burgeoning audiences, eager for new screenings.

There are records of screenings as far back as the late nineteenth century both in the north of the continent in Cairo and Alexandria and the extreme south in Cape Town, shortly followed around 1900 by Tunis, Algiers, Saint-

Louis, and Dakar, then Lagos and Accra in 1903–4, Elisabethville in 1911, and Brazzaville, Lomé, and Zanzibar in 1916. In Zanzibar, a long-urbanized and cosmopolitan former sultanate, the populace enthusiastically embraced the cinema, easily integrating it into their existing range of leisure activities (Fair 2018). The first film projectors were imported to Brazzaville, Congo, by a Portuguese trader in 1916 to 'increase his café's sales', and later by a missionary in the 1920s for educational purposes. Documentaries were screened at Brazzaville's École urbaine in 1931, and hotels also began to screen films (Martin 1995: 86). Private and public initiatives, commercial pursuits and colonial propaganda, documentary and fiction thus existed side-by-side.

Cinema's transformation into a locally rooted, permanent practice is a complex phenomenon given the differing natures of screening venues, types of screenings, and images screened, but also the varieties of audience in the interwar years.[1] However, certain figures do give a measure of the medium's progression. Despite showing little initial interest in the cinema, the colonial administrations started to turn their attention to it with the advent of talking films. Several reports were indeed drawn up in the wake of the 1926 Colonial Office Conference and the 1930 British Imperial Conference. In the French Empire, studies were carried out in 1932 and 1937. The information compiled reports that in British tropical Africa—not including South Africa—in 1930, there were thirty-eight cinemas for an estimated population of 36 million inhabitants.[2] In 1939, the figures were a fraction higher in French Africa, giving an estimated total of forty cinemas for approximately 18 million inhabitants: thirty-five cinemas in FWA (or 15,000 places for approximately 15 million inhabitants), and only five in French Equatorial Africa (800 places for 3 million) (Lacolley 1946: 3). Calculating a ratio is fairly meaningless, given the huge contrasts between the different colonies and towns and the uncertainty of the demographic statistics. Generally speaking, however, the likelihood of seeing moving images remained low before 1945. But even though cinema was far from a mass pastime, it nonetheless played a growing role in the structuring of urban identities. Going to the cinema constituted one of the facets of urban life.

All film screenings, however simple, demanded a minimum amount of equipment. A screening could not be improvised in the same way that a village gathering could. The indispensable ingredients included a projector, a film, a screen, and darkness. Then came the spectators. Screening conditions were extremely variable, ranging from impromptu showings held in village squares to regular screenings in indoor or partially open-air movie theatres. The transition from one to the other was not automatic or linear, but depended on the vicissitudes of the entrepreneurs' lives and on the local socio-political context. Each community reacted differently to the arrival of this leisure activity, depending on its demographic make-up (social hierarchies, gender relations, age relations) and on specific religious or cultural factors, notably the existence of local theatre forms. These elements conditioned the format of the screenings. Other factors also had an influence. Some screenings were strictly dependent on the patronage of a dynamic entrepreneur and ceased upon his death, as was the case with Raphaël Fumey in Lomé. Economic vicissitudes could also bring an end to screenings. The durability, or otherwise, of a screening venue was rarely tied to public interest, which remained constant. It was the practical demands of screening that were more uncertain.

Early days: cafés, hotels and courtyards

To take lasting root, cinema needed to appropriate or create fixed venues. In the early days, it worked its way into dignitaries' social spaces, hotels, and community halls, and residential courtyards. Then buildings designed specifically for the screening of films gradually emerged from the late 1920s onwards. There was nothing particularly unusual in this, and the same process characterized the early days of cinema in the West: 'Early cinema had no fixed venues, but set out, rather, to meet the French in all sorts of places' (Bosséno 2002: 163).

In the early twentieth century, buildings devoted solely to leisure activities were very rare in the colonies. They indeed supposed the existence of a minority of wealthy Europeans or dignitaries, as in Senegal, the Gold Coast, or neighbouring Togo. Social venues that held screenings included clubs, community halls, hotels, and parish halls. The cinematic adventure began very early on in Saint-Louis, Senegal. As early as 1898, the town hall held screenings, charging three francs for a chair, two francs for a bench, and one franc for a standing ticket. Ten years later, Father Brottier of the Congregation of the Holy Spirit acquired a magic lantern to entertain fellow members. The Saint-Louis Cinéorama put on several screenings a week 'for the general public'; this provided an introduction to images, if not yet to cinema. In 1911, the Jeanne d'Arc parish hall, a rather spartan hangar, was fitted out to this end. From the 1920s onwards, screenings also took place in the back yard of a café on Rue Neuville, discreetly indicated by a sign marked 'cinema'. In 1927, the Colonial Council announced to its members a 'conference [on yellow fever] that will be accompanied by film screenings ... in the Café Rey cinema hall.'[3]

In many towns, hotels were the venues for early screenings: the Hôtel de la Poste in Saint-Louis, the Grand Hôtel du Palais in Dakar, the Grand Hôtel in Conakry, the Hôtel Ferrari in Kayes, the Hôtel Gariglio in Lomé, the Bayol Hôtel in Porto-Novo, the Sea View Hotel in Accra, the Hôtel du Plateau in Pointe-Noire, and the Hôtel Congo-Océan and the Assanaki brothers' restaurant, both in Brazzaville. In an effort to attract a European clientele, the latter two establishments—the first located in the residential Plateau neighbourhood, the second in the La Plaine administrative and commercial district—imagined an array of social and entertainment activities in addition to the film screenings, from gastronomic dinners to balls with orchestras, concerts, and so on (Martin 1995: 184–85).

The word 'hotel' alone is not enough to describe these screening venues, however, nor their atmosphere. The establishments' location in the European districts socially limited the clientele, of course, but their courtyards, where the screenings generally took place, sometimes had a separate entrance to distinguish between audiences. In Lomé, Aldo Gariglio held screenings in the courtyards of both the Hôtel Gariglio and, from 1928 onwards, the Luna-Park Hotel. The latter, which could accommodate approximately 100 people, above all targeted an African clientele. The former put on weekly screenings for fifty or so European and Lebanese spectators. Both the venues and their audiences were different, then, as were their ticket prices and film programmes.

The screenings organized in the early 1930s at the Buffet de la Gare, a hotel situated next to the train station in Bamako, took place outdoors in one of its courtyards, where there was also a dance floor and a restaurant. Almost fifty people regularly came to screenings. The station, which was a terminal of the Dakar-Niger railway, was a busy place of transit frequented by an array of people, including passengers and locals out to meet people or seeking new encounters. As a cultural crossroads and a melting pot, stations played a role in other towns such as Mamou, in Guinea, whose station featured an 'African bar-restaurant' and a cinema by 1948.[4] Indeed, this cinema is described in Tierno Monénembo's novel *Cinéma* as a 1950s social hotspot.

Private courtyards were also turned into venues for screenings. In Bamako in the same period, Madame Mähl operated a cinema in the spacious courtyard of her husband's printing plant, drawing a mix of European and African spectators. A photograph dating back to 1925 shows two types of wooden seats: chairs to the back, and benches to the front. A venue's characteristics alone are therefore not enough to determine its spectator demographic, given the many possible ways of dividing up spaces and audiences.[5]

In Lomé, the first screenings, which were organized by passing Europeans, periodically took place in the railway workshops (Zimmermann 2008). But in contrast to Mali, where Europeans had a bigger hand in the dissemination of cinema, in Lomé Togolese entrepreneurs, in liaison with partners in the Gold Coast, also participated in this adventure and organized screenings for their compatriots. As early as 1923, the renowned photographer Raphaël Fumey occasionally screened films in his own courtyard on Rue de Pêcheurs, for thirty to fifty spectators. His death in 1930 put an end to the screenings and his descendants got rid of his projector and reels of film, which, with the advent of talkies, had become outmoded. From July 1925 to May 1926, commercial employee Denis Tétévi Lawson invited twenty to thirty viewers, all of them African, to several screenings. Albert John Mensah added films to the activities put on at his famous Tonyeviadji café and dance hall, situated at the far east of the town on the road to Aného. He invited Alex Croydon Vomor, the owner of a cinema in Keta, a small town in the Gold Coast, to organize three open-air screenings for a public of some thirty spectators in August 1929, January 1931, and April 1932. Finally, the Empire-Ciné, also known as Kpelébé-Cinéma, was run by Ferdinand K. Anthony and operated out of his courtyard on Rue de la Gare. Here, he screened silent movies from 1932 to the 1940s.

This detailed information on the places and dates of screenings in a capital of under 15,000 inhabitants—350 of whom were European—is clear evidence of police surveillance of Lomé residents' activities in the 1930s. However, these screenings were not limited to the capital. In Kpalimé, a railway terminus of 3,000 inhabitants situated 120 kilometres from the coast, Michel Apaloo added the Central-Ciné to his establishment, which already offered a dance floor and meeting room, in 1937.[6] The multiplicity of these screenings demonstrates the elites' passion for cinema and its circulation beyond colonial borders, with disparate regions and populations connected by the same curiosity and culture.

Michel Anthony, born in 1916 and an important member of the community in Lomé, proudly declared: 'We were already familiar with cinema and all that!' (Marguerat and Pelei 1992: 23). However, these screenings only concerned a minority of city-dwellers, who heard about them by word of mouth. We can try to picture the atmosphere of these early screenings, enlivened by running commentaries and audience exclamations, but also by the ambient sounds of the city, the projector whirring, the yard inhabitants' comings and goings and children's interruptions.

The screening venues rarely lasted. The crisis of the 1930s, which coincided with the advent of the talkies—and thus the need to purchase new projectors and films—slowed down cinematographic activity. In the late 1930s, Togo's capital still had no real autonomous movie theatre. Screenings were still held in courtyards, at the Hôtel Gariglio, and in the newly built Hôtel de France, run by Maurice Archambeau, an entrepreneur who was to make his mark on the history of cinema in French West Africa.[7]

It can be added that, outside of areas on the equator, rains only fell for a few months, or even a few weeks, in the year, often predictably so, and that, depending on the latitude, the sun set between 6 and 7 pm. The darkness was not spoiled by public lighting, as this urban amenity was late in coming and was limited to certain streets in city centres. The moon was generally the only source of light pollution. In the late 1920s, screenings still frequently took place in the street: 'The facade of the [Palais] theatre on Avenue Roume housed the projection room for the open-air cinema, whose screen was set up on the opposite pavement. ... Raphaël, the guard, would chase off "squatters", or spectators sitting on the pavement behind the screen' (Diop 1978).

In this period, then, the cinema infiltrated both public and private, interior and exterior, organized and improvised spaces. At times, for that matter, the boundaries between these categories were unclear. A 'sheet' could well be strung up outdoors between trees, and the projector placed inside an adjacent café. That is what a certain Albert described on a postcard sent from Dakar in 1910: 'This card is of the top of the boulevard and the Poux Café. Opposite, the cinema screen is set up between the trees.'[8]

In addition to the courtyards and hotels, schools played a major role in introducing many colonial subjects to cinema. The École Normale William Ponty in Senegal, a teacher training college which had already adopted theatre practice as a pedagogical element in the 1930s, also popularized cinema. According to Doctor Sultan (see Chapter 3), in 1931, the school rented films which were screened by a former student trained to use the 35mm projector. The screenings took place in the presence of teachers, and a phonograph livened up the intermissions. The school encouraged students' passion for film by selling students tickets for the Dakar cinemas at a preferential rate: one franc, or one franc fifty, compared to the usual three to five francs. School screenings, whose objectives were both educational and propagandist, were also encouraged in elementary schools. Several initiatives were organized in the French Sudan (now Mali). Yet in the interwar period, few of these schools possessed the necessary equipment. In Togo, only the Aného school cooperative bought a projector—a Pathé Baby, the most common at the time. They purchased the projector in 1930, but only twelve screenings were organized due to the limited number of films available. Even though they remained marginal, film shows organized by schools, the authorities, or missionaries did introduce many pupils to this new media, which was a form of both leisure and knowledge.

Taking Root: the opening of the Rex, the Vox, Bart's, the Palace and the Empire Cinema

Over time, film developed its own specific venues, such as enclosed spaces, partially covered buildings, and completely indoor theatres—most notably where climatic imperatives made them a necessity, for example around the Gulf of Guinea with its abundant rainfall. While the press did announce their opening, precise descriptions of these cinemas are rare and photographers did not single them out as worth immortalizing, or as significant markers of the urban space, in the same way that they did governors' palaces or markets. It was usually by chance that a cinema featured on a postcard, such as the Sandaga or the Bataclan, both in Dakar. Yet the construction of these cinemas was not insignificant: it indicated the dynamism of a local or foreign entrepreneur, a sufficient pool of potential spectators to ensure profitability, and an entire organizational structure.

The majority of the screenings mentioned above were intermittent, and dependent on the purchase and arrival of films. Cinema's transition to a regular, stable activity was nonetheless smooth, albeit taking place in stages. The first imperative was to create an enclosed, delimited space, only open to those who had purchased a ticket. This meant securing a plot of land in the town centre or in a densely populated neighbourhood, and then proposing adequate, or even attractive, viewing conditions to the audience. The first cinemas built consisted of an area to the back protected from the rain by an awning and a much larger, completely open-air section. In the event of an unexpected downpour everyone would rush to take shelter at the back, but the screening would be called off if rain kept falling, or was forecast beforehand. The covered zone was fitted with chairs, while the rest of the 'theatre' offered simple wooden benches, introducing a division of the space and a hierarchy among audiences that existed in the West, but was adapted here to reflect colonial relationships.

A survey of the different British and French colonies reveals a diversity of approaches to cinema, in part due to contrasting modes of colonization, but also to local factors, such as commercial strategies, or the varying openness of African societies to outside elements. Let us first consider the dynamic Gold Coast, where cinema was almost exclusively the affair of local entrepreneurs in a context of cultural invention (highlife music) and economic innovation (the expansion of the cocoa industry).[9] Cinema was a big hit among the coastal populations of the Gold Coast, be they Ga, Ewe, or the descendants of freed slaves who returned from Brazil from the 1840s to the 1880s. It came to join existing forms of entertainment, including vaudeville theatre and concert parties, as a popular leisure activity. In Accra, the first screenings were held in community halls and centres, such as Azuma House (also known as the Cinema Theatre)—opened by Afro-Brazilians between 1904 and 1910 in the neighbourhood of Jamestown, one of the two ancient hubs of the city that developed around Fort James—and later Saint Mary's Church Hall. In 1913, a European trader, John Bartholomew, built the first cinema in Merry Villas Cinematograph Palace, a recreational centre. Bartholomew's Cinema rapidly became known simply as Bart's (Collins 2009: 228; McFeely 2015: 138).

Bart's remained unrivalled until the Ghanaian businessman Alfred J. Ocansey (1889–1943) invested in cinema. Born in Ada, east of Accra, and educated in a Protestant mission, Ocansey set up his own company in 1910, having previously worked in a British trading house. In 1918, he launched into selling cars and gramophones in Accra, asserting Ghanaians' place in innovative sectors, such as cocoa, as opposed to the big foreign firms. His nationalism also fuelled his creation of a publishing house (Palladium Press) and a newspaper, the *African Morning Post*, set up in 1934. It is unsurprising, therefore, that he soon saw cinema's potential, both in economic, political, and cultural terms, and as a form of entertainment and a way of circulating ideas. To this end, in the mid-1920s he built a chain of cinemas that spread beyond the capital: two in Accra (the Palladium and the Park Cinema), the Mikado in Nsawam, the Capital Cinema in Koforidua, and the Princess Cinema in Sekondi-Takoradi. Half of the ten cinemas registered in the Gold Coast in the 1930s belonged to him, even though his name does not appear in the official reports. The most famous of these was the Palladium in Jamestown, Accra. Was it the cinema admiringly described by the Governor of Togo as 'a vast, recently installed cinema theatre with all modern comforts'? No doubt, for the Governor went on to add: 'This cinema theatre belongs to a rich native who only shows audiences English and American films.'[10]

The Palladium was named after the London Palladium, a theatre that Ocansey had admired on a trip to London. Initially named the West End

Cinema Palladium, and located on Pagan Road near to Bart's, it was the first major commercial theatre. Its facade took its inspiration from its London prototype, which was similar to the neoclassical Afro-Brazilian architecture along the coast: a triangular pediment, pilasters, ornate volutes, and shuttered windows surmounted by semi-circular arches. All of Ocansey's cinemas put on music hall performances—emulating those of the London Palladium—in addition to film screenings, and they were sometimes frequented by Europeans. Ocansey sought to attract increasingly wide audiences with his accessible pricing. In the face of this competition, Bartholomew had to adapt and lower his prices by screening cheaper films (McFeely 2015: 153).

By 1932, the Gold Coast, which was a small country of 3 million inhabitants, had a total of ten cinemas located in eight towns. With the exception of Kumasi—the Ashanti capital and the Gold Coast's second largest town, located in the centre of the region with 35,829 inhabitants according to the 1931 census—these towns were all in the south. They were situated along the coast or the railway line, around the two poles of Accra and Sekondi (which had 16,953 inhabitants). The cosmopolitan nature of Accra's population and its demographic growth guaranteed the success of its three cinemas. From 1911 to 1921, the population grew from 18,500 to 38,000, reaching 61,000 ten years later. Keta (6,405 inhabitants) in the east was the most remote. Towns with a cinema were thus not the most highly populated, nor necessarily those equipped with electricity.[11] Ocansey's success was remarkable, as he took cinema outside of Accra and opened it up to lower-class spectators in zones boosted by the cocoa economy. However, his death in 1943 put an end to this enterprise. Rented out or sold off, his cinemas were incorporated into a wider network that began to develop in the mid-1930s. Indeed, in about 1935, Lebanese businessman Omar Captan built a cinema in Accra, marking the first stages of a new period that flourished after the war, in which the Lebanese and the Indians dominated cinematic activities.

In Nigeria, too, cinema was taking off, thanks to the investment of the African entrepreneurs who owned the eight active movie theatres which were unevenly distributed throughout the country in 1932. Most were in the south, with five in Lagos and just one in Jos in the centre of the country.[12] However, the Rex in Kano, the first cinema in the north, was built in 1937 by a Lebanese Christian businessman. Designed as an open-air, or garden cinema, it was located in Sabon Gari, the predominantly Christian district that was home to migrants from the south—outside the Muslim old town, whose conservative religious authorities were against cinema. It rapidly attracted a diverse clientele of both locals and migrants, who were already familiar with cinema from private or governmental travelling film shows.

One must nonetheless refrain from generalizing about the dynamism of cinema in southern Nigeria and the Gold Coast, and in Tanzania too. In some cases, once early curiosity had worn off, cinema did not supplant other forms of entertainment. Sierra Leone's outward-looking old city of Freetown, founded in the late eighteenth century and with a population of 45,000 inhabitants in 1921, did not undergo the same enthusiasm. In 1909, Freetown's Wesleyan Female Educational Institution alumni association did put on an event combining music and 'Cinematograph photographs', and various entrepreneurs occasionally proposed their services from 1912 to 1919, although none settled there.[13] In 1912, the press announced a visit from Culver's Cinema Company, which was awaiting a shipment in order that it could screen its films at the municipal Wilberforce Memorial Hall (WMH): 'The pictures will include Historical, Dramatical, Magical, Humorous and Topical subjects. Change of Programme every evening; Popular Prices: 1s, 2s & 3s'.[14] In 1913, another projectionist passed through, but only fleetingly, as did the British West African Cinema Company in 1915. The same year, a Sierra Leonean, N. D. Nicol, who had trained as an electrical engineer in England, presented a few films. His initiative was celebrated and people spoke of his success, but he disappeared from the public eye. Again, in 1919, the same West African Cinema Company sought a venue to set up in, on the proviso that there was popular demand. Their advertising boasted 'all the latest motor machinery and films, including pictures of Charlie Chaplin, Comics, Travels, Pictorial and Dramas'.[15] The screenings were held in either the Catholic Mission Boys' School, the Methodist school, or the WMH.[16]

It was not until 1922 that film screenings became more regular thanks to the perseverance of reputed Sierra Leonean photographers the Lisk-Carew Brothers, founders of the Freetown Cinema Theatrical Company. In 1920, they were offering two film shows a week at the WMH. To expand their potential audience, they invited along 'a good number of Tribal Rulers and their respective Santigees with a crowd of the aboriginal element' in 1921.[17] This information is interesting, as it highlights contrasts in the demographic composition of the town, which comprised freed slaves, known as Creole or Krio people (or Sierra Leoneans), who were initially in the majority and gave the town its character, and the natives. The press, run by the Krio people, strove to present the cinema as an enjoyable leisure pastime, and to target a literate clientele. Indeed, the Lisk-Carews' adverts boasted of the films' educational character, an effective selling-point for the Sierra Leoneans: 'To amuse is good but to amuse and instruct is better—so bring the children'.[18]

They were not alone. In 1921, a journalist noted that in the Gold Coast the government was subsidizing film shows for schoolchildren in Accra's three cinemas, and suggested that Sierra Leone did the same. This comparison attests to the circulation of information among the Creole diaspora, and to the Gold Coast's precedent-setting role (see Chapter 2). The Lisk-Carews' dealings with the municipality dragged out, but in 1922 they reached an agreement. Their screenings alternated short films and dance, thereby adapting to the technical conditions that changing reels imposed: 'These excellent exhibitions were interspersed with dancing till the program was exhausted.'[19] This initiative, which was officially but not financially backed by Governor Wilkinson, was deemed to be all the more worthy of support 'because it [was] an African venture'. Housed in the municipal building, the Empire Cinema nonetheless remained the only screen until 1948, as cinema struggled to rival ballroom dancing (the most popular activity among the public), theatre, and concerts. During the Depression, screenings nonetheless continued, and people attended to take their minds off the crisis with cheaply priced shows: 'Regardless of the hard-up days, men ... went to the Kinshu Cinema at the Wilberforce Memorial Hall run by a Mr A. Coroma and paid their two shillings and one shilling entrance fee' (Anthony 1980: 64).

In the French colonies, commercial cinema initiatives were the domain of Europeans, who opened venues at a time when screenings were disappearing in the African courtyards in Lomé, and African entrepreneurs were rare. What were the reasons for this stark contrast between the British and French colonies? Was it the result of a greater tolerance on the part of the British vis-à-vis African entrepreneurs and, conversely, the sidelining of native traders and tight controls in the French system? Was it a sign of the particular dynamism of the Gulf of Guinea traders, long turned towards the international world? At any rate, it does confirm the influence of local, cultural, and economic factors in the spread of cinema.

In French West Africa, there were two predominant personalities who shaped the cinema industry: Maurice Jacquin, who was from a family of Moroccan Jewish traders, operated in Dakar, while Maurice Archambeau, a trader and hotel-owner who had initially worked in Porto-Novo, expanded his operations to Dakar, Ouagadougou, and Lomé. In the 1930s, these two businessmen were responsible for French West Africa's two main film circuits: the Compagnie Africaine Cinématographique Industrielle et Commerciale

(COMACICO) and the Société d'Exploitation Cinématographique Africaine (SECMA) respectively. In addition to distributing films, they invested in building cinemas that they then leased out. Senegal was the most prolific colony, due to its urban expansion and the presence of numerous foreign communities, who reinforced local audiences. Dakar, the only city in French West Africa with 100,000 inhabitants before the war (6,000 to 7,000 of whom were foreign), soon had a varied range of cinemas, which came to compete with wrestling matches and dance as a popular leisure activity.[20] Birago Diop tells us that 'the first cinema in Dakar in the open-air: the Poux cinema' operated in the 1920s near to the Place Protet (now the Place de l'Indépendance); it is also mentioned on a postcard dated 1910 (Diop 1978).

In 1926, Jacquin opened the Rex. A few years later, the COMACICO was already running three cinemas on the Plateau, Dakar's administrative and residential centre: namely the Rialto, which opened in 1933 and was the most prestigious of the cinemas with its 1,300 capacity and comfortable seats; the Bataclan, opened two years later; and the Rex, the most lowly rated, which was near the port and put on reruns of films already screened elsewhere.[21] Subscription prices reflected the cinemas' hierarchy; entrance cost, respectively, forty-five, forty, and thirty francs in 1936.[22] For its part, the SECMA opened the Palace and the Alhambra in 1936. The cinemas were regularly modernized in order to cater to the needs of a well-off audience, made up essentially of Europeans and Lebanese. It was possible to reserve a seat in advance, and to relax in the café. That was not the case in cinemas intended for Africans, which were generally less comfortable, and even rudimentary. The so-called Médina cinema was 'a plot of land with a board on one side, in front of which benches and old metal chairs were set out' (Seck 2008: 68). The Sandaga was located at the bottom of the Médina district, near the hygiene services. Founded by the entrepreneur Louis Girard, it was a vast hangar, with a smart facade decorated with openings in a neo-Moorish style and brick cladding.[23] Its name was displayed in large letters, in both Latin and Arabic script. It targeted the clientele of this new district, designated in 1914, but it later shut down.

In Saint-Louis, too, cinema moved out of the cafés and into specially designed buildings. The Rex on the Place Faidherbe and the Vox on an inlet in the south of the town were built in the early 1930s. Both were vast and partially covered, with elaborate facades. The Vox reproduced Saint-Louis's architectural norms (arcades, light shafts above the entrance, and columns topped with cannon balls), while the COMACICO's Rex adopted an art-deco style, as can be seen in several photos of the time. The modernist facade extended onto a terrace overlooking the adjacent square, which accentuated the building's sense of gravitas. The ticket office was in a covered section, and a wall with an undulating top served as a screen. The building had an imposing air, with flags floating on top that could be seen from afar and neon lights which lit up the night. Cinemas stood out in the urban landscape, but it was rare that their architecture was so refined; the Rex demonstrates the high social status granted to cinema as a leisure activity.

Far from West Africa, in Eritrea, the Impero in Asmara was a fascinating example of the care put into these leisure buildings' architecture. Built from 1937 to 1938, it featured geometric lines, sober decoration and a porch to protect clients who were waiting for the show (Casciato 2006). In Tanzania, too, the 'cinematic entrepreneurs wanted architectural forms that were not just functional but attractive, innovative and inspiring' (Fair 2018: 12). In short, buildings needed to fascinate and attract a clientele.

In Abidjan, the entrepreneur Jean Rose inaugurated the Lugdunum, a 'talking and sound' cinema, in 1932, anticipating the official choice of the town as the new capital of Ivory Coast the following year, in place of Grand-Bassam. In 1936, Archambault and the SECMA opened the Rex in the Plateau district and the Vox in the Treichville district; subsequently, the Club and the Super Vox were built by his competitor, Jacquin (Lidji 1998: 64; Retord 1986: 11, 24, with a photo of the Rex in 1936). Local demand was strong, and in the same period Émile Dourlot, a mechanic who had started out organizing travelling screenings, joined forces with his brother to develop a range of cinemas. Also printers, they advertised to their wealthy and mainly European target audience by publishing *Abidjan-Ciné*, 'a bi-monthly journal of Abidjan and Ivory Coast's cinema news'; they printed 1,500 copies of the first edition, which gives an indication of the anticipated audience. In 1937, they announced the opening of the Plaza in Treichville, 'the COMACICO's no. 1 cinema, the most beautiful and most luxurious on the African Coast', which offered 1,000 seats and guaranteed parking. The Plaza had modern installations, in Cinemascope, and a programme which screened films 'at the same time as in Paris'.[24] Soon, Abidjan, which already had a population of 22,000 in 1939, was thus equipped with cinemas addressing different audiences, from the most wealthy to the working class.

In the less dynamic city of Bamako, the Soudan Cinéma, records of which date back to 1936, long remained the only cinema, alongside other rudimentary screening venues. The colonies had not all caught the cinema bug to the same extent. On arriving there from Dakar in 1936, Doctor Sultan was greatly disappointed to discover that there was no cinema in Kankan, the second largest town in Guinea, where he was sent to work as a doctor. Conakry, the capital, for its part, did not have a real cinema before 1945. Opportunities to see films thus remained rare. The same was true in Dahomey (today's Benin): other than the Bayol Hotel in Porto-Novo, the colony had only one open-air cinema, in Cotonou. Similarly, in Upper Volta (Burkina Faso), the governor disdainfully responded to a 1948 survey, describing 'the inexistence of veritable performance venues in Upper Volta, a designation that can only be applied with difficulty to Bobo-Dioulasso's open-air cinemas.'[25]

Administrators, foreign observers and guidebooks all maintained a clear hierarchy between screening venues. They lauded the covered or semi-covered cinemas, whose names demonstrated a European affiliation and reinforced the imaginary elsewhere with which entrepreneurs sought to associate this new leisure activity. Having crossed the Mediterranean, movie theatres mimicked the names of their Western predecessors. They evoked the venue's magnificence (the Palace), nostalgia for Roman imperialism (the Rex, the Vox), or exoticism (the Rialto, the Alhambra); others copied the names of major Paris or London theatres (the Bataclan and the Palladium, respectively). Local references were the exception (such as the Sandaga, the Soudan Cinéma, and the El Duniya in Kano, Nigeria). This type of name developed in the 1950s, when cinema reached further-flung districts: the El Hadj in Saint-Louis, for example, or the El Malick in Dakar. For simplicity's sake, circuits sometimes adopted the same names, as with the string of Vox and Rex COMACICO cinemas which were found from town to town and, in general, put on the same programmes. In Zanzibar, the Sultana Cinema celebrated the island's history, whereas elsewhere, various cinemas asserted their connection with the Empire.

A Hierarchy of Practices and Venues

The impacts of the first screenings on viewers are well documented; they generated an array of expectations and behavioural models depending on the audience and setting, which ranged from indoor cinemas, to outdoor cinemas protected by a canopy, to the more or less delimited open-air venues. The characteristics of the venue give an indication of the atmosphere too: outdoor screenings took place under the night skies, often in a familiar place and accompanied by other forms of entertainment, especially in the early days of cinema before movie theatres became the norm. In Freetown, film screenings were often combined with other activities. In 1913, 'A GRAND CINEMATO-GRAPH SHOW, CONCERT & DANCE' was announced, and in 1916, 'A GRAND SOCIAL' with 'Highly interesting war and other pictures ...; Instrumental and Vocal Solos...; A variety of indoor games; ... a Military Magician and Ventriloquist with an Orchestra.'[26] Cinema was first introduced in combination with existing forms of performance and entertainment and therefore elicited similar audience responses, such as running commentaries, exclamations, gesticulation, and laughter—or, alternatively, prim responses. In Ghana, tales of the trickster Ananse the Spider were told in communal story-telling sessions to loud, demonstrative responses, and audiences brought these practices to the cinema. Such behaviours reflected spectators' cultures and identities, and they adapted to this new media according to their social status, leisure habits, and gender, forging their own relationship to cinema. In the colonial context, the question of different groups sharing leisure time and spaces was nonetheless crucial.

While reception halls, such as the Cercle de l'Union in Lomé, and most hotels were places where an exclusively European clientele socialized—places that became all the more exclusive as the colonizers increasingly closed ranks in the 1920s—other venues were frequented by a more mixed group of specta-tors. Over the years, however, the divide was accentuated. The differences in judicial status (subject/citizen), nationality, and above all socio-economic position were fundamental. Sources consistently specify the identities of spec-tators, and nothing was left to chance in this respect. In the colonies studied, however, discourses expressing a real fear of mixed audiences were rare, in contrast to the prevailing ideology in South Africa, or India in the 1920s. An array of parameters needs to be taken into account to grasp the complexity of specific cases: the regulatory apparatus; societies' characteristics; the size of towns and thus their offer of cinemas; and the cinemas' political economy.

Hierarchy was a characteristic of screening venues all around the world. To ensure its own development, the film industry attracted the least well-off ele-ments of society while at the same time seeking to give cinemas—the turn-of-the-century 'Palaces'—the trappings of bourgeois theatre, and thus an enhanced status. Not only were separate venues constructed, but also different spaces within the same venue. In France, ticket prices could vary from one franc (standing in the gallery) to ten (seated in a box), but the most expensive tickets were usually only double the price of the cheapest (Bosséno 1996). In Lyon, however, prices ranged from one to five francs in the same cinema, and could be twice as much in the city centre as they were in poorer neighbour-hoods (Chaplain 2007). How did this differentiation work in the colonies? For some investors, providing different types of venue or seating for Europeans and Africans was self-evident, so rooted was racial ideology. Bartholomew indeed organized several European-only film showings in Accra, which were criticized (McFeely 2015: 142). H. V. Harrison, director of the Overseas Film Service Ltd, which began importing films to Nigeria in 1912, specified, in his 1931 project to create a chain of cinemas, that his Picture Theatres would provide 130 places for Europeans, equipped with the best seats, and 960 for the 'natives'.[27] Likewise, the Lebanese businessman who built the Rex in Kano planned to hold specific nights for Europeans and Lebanese, and others for Africans (Larkin 2008). These projects did not materialize, however, as the situation on the ground was far too complex, in both ideological and financial terms. The implementation of discriminatory, or even strictly segregationist practices considerably varied in reality, depending on the mode of coloniza-tion and on local societal characteristics.

Sharing the same space was out of the question for colonizers and the colo-nized in colonies where segregation determined all social practices, and thus necessarily the frequentation of leisure venues: this was the case in Southern Africa, Kenya, and, to a lesser degree, the Belgian Congo (Ambler 2001; Burns 2002b; Ramirez and Rolot 1985). While audiences in Tanganyika were mixed, in the settler colony of Northern Rhodesia segregation was the rule. Nine of the country's eleven cinemas were reserved for 'Europeans only'.[28] The question of sharing a movie theatre thus did not even apply. Elsewhere—that is, in the majority of colonies, where Europeans were limited to the adminis-trative and economic spheres—the situation was more subtle. There was an adroit balance between legislative frameworks (what the law said) and prac-tices (what was actually possible)—between official interdicts and colonial taboos. While the law may not have distinguished between audiences, indirect forms of separation were indeed established. These translated to seating arrangements inside the cinema, with different categories of ticket prices, and ultimately to an internalization of hierarchies, which was reinforced by the cinemas' actual locations in the towns. Diverse factors thus came into play: ticket prices; the range and variety of cinemas; local history, and so forth. The question, then, is not only whether regulations created a colonial subject cat-egory in the cinemas; it is also one of filmgoing practices.

There were often two, and sometimes even three or four categories of ticket prices depending on the comfort of the seats (ranging from armchairs, to benches, to standing room) and their distance from the screen. In Freetown, the distinctions were explicit. The back seats (two shillings in 1914) were distinguished from the front seats (one shilling), while children paid half price (six pence). Reserving a seat cost more, whereas coming as a couple was advantageous. A 'double reserved' cost three shillings, a 'single reserved' two shillings, and a 'front seat' one shilling (1915). In 1922, the Lisk-Carews proposed three prices, of one, two, or three shillings, and six pence for children; dances, by comparison, cost five shillings. The cinema was an accessible leisure activity, then, or, as the press put it, 'within the pocket-depth of all'.[29]

The varying prices reflected the usual differences in urban living standards. In the colonial context, there was nonetheless a certain ambiguity around this distinction, which was apparently social rather than racial or statutory. Well-off colonial subjects were able to access the most expensive seats, as Amadou Hampâté Bâ describes: 'Depending on how much you paid, you were given a 1st-, 2nd- or 3rd-class ticket. The 1st-class was reserved for the Europeans. But there were a few rare exceptions, a few privileged Africans (1967: 18)'. As a colonial clerk and a 'white-black', as he put it himself, he clearly fit this category.

The size of the town also played a role, as a cinema's existence depended on a regular clientele in order to cover its costs. Only the most populated cities, such as Accra, Lagos, Dakar, or Abidjan, rapidly developed a range of screening venues accommodating different categories of audience. Europeans and elite Africans mingled, therefore, but independently from the majority of film-goers, who would congregate either right at the front of the movie theatre, or in separate venues in the outlying districts. In smaller towns where there was only one cinema, the only choice audiences had was of different screening times, if that. Audiences thus necessarily shared the same venue, but on what terms?

The history of a town and its population was also a determining factor. Situations varied according to local cultural policy, the role of the trader bourgeoisie, the proportions of new urban categories—employees, skilled craftsmen, school-goers, 'educated natives'—and finally the impact of existing leisure practices.[30] Moreover, the size and composition of the population strongly influenced demand and practices. Certain cosmopolitan groups—both foreign and local—played a leading role in the development of cinema, for example the Ghanaian trader class, or Zanzibar's Indian population.

Finally, factors pertaining to the political economy of a cinema also help us to understand screening conditions and the viability of a venue: notably the management or hiring of the venue, the purchase or, later, rental of films, usually as part of a circuit, the hiring of staff, import hazards, and so forth. For cinemas to last, their activity had to be cost-effective. Screenings thus ceased in Kayes (French Sudan) during the 1930s, as the operator was unable to cover costs.[31]

The combination of these elements reflects the diversity of experiences from town to town, or cinema to cinema. Colonial dynamics were incorporated into a socio-demographic environment from which they cannot be dissociated. Towns of a similar size, such as Conakry, Bamako or Lomé, did not offer the same cinematographic landscape, marked as they were by their respective histories.

'The Negros say: screw you!'

What follows is a fine, but rare, example of a film screening becoming a political statement within a context of limited agency:

> At the Buffet de la Gare was the ever-welcoming and maternal Mama Bousquet, replete with her Limoux accent and her straight-talking.

> That 13 December, I had overrun my leave, when Cissé asked me to go to the Buffet de la Gare cinema with him. The film was *Life Dances On* [Duvivier 1937], which I had already seen in France at least three times.

* * *

> We arrived a little late. Mama Bousquet showed us to two armchair seats in the back row. To the right and to the front were the benches for the 'natives'.

> As I sat there, I saw my department head and his deputies pass by on their way to the middle row ... when I heard behind me:

> – Too bad the *chicotte* [whip] is no longer in use. What a disgrace to see whites having to stand while Negros sprawl out in the armchairs.
> I turned to see a man built like a brick house towering over me.
> And I struck up an exchange:
> – The Negros say: screw you!
> – What?
> – I said, the Negros say: screw you!
> – Step outside and say that again.

> Outside was the courtyard, the dance floor, and the restaurant, all of which were open-air like the cinema.
> – Apologise.
> – Apologise? Apologise for what?

– For what you said.

– For what I said? That the Negros say screw you? Of course, they say screw you!

On which, I saw my interlocutor's fist come flying. I turned my head, throwing my glasses as far as possible onto the sand around the dance floor and I received a heavy blow to the left cheek (Diop 1978: 160).

This autobiographical account is precisely dated 13 December 1938, which shows how emphatically the episode marked Birago Diop's memory. This young Senegalese man, a member of the elite posted in Bamako, hereby testifies to the hierarchy that existed inside the movie theatres. It was the reference to the *chicotte*, a type of whip that symbolized colonial violence, that triggered his strong reaction, provoking the confrontation between the two men. Diop challenged the European spectator and his attempt to assert his ostensibly superior colonial status in order to exclude Diop from a privileged zone of the movie theatre. Diop thus contested the idea that he, a *Blanc-Noir* as Bâ would have characterized him, or a 'white-black' member of the African elite, should have less right to a decent seat. In the cinema, however, both the Africans and the Europeans took Diop's side. After the scuffle, the manageress seated him in the gallery. He was fully aware of the symbolic significance of his act: 'I had "cured" Bamako's youth of its longstanding reverent fear of the *toubabou*, the white' (Diop 1978: 164).

A citizen of the Four Communes who studied to become a veterinary in Toulouse, married to a French woman, Diop opened doors to others who were more directly subjected to domination and more susceptible to the sense of inferiority conveyed by colonial ideology. This anecdote quickly circulated throughout the whole of Bamako, which proves its importance. It earned Diop the congratulations of Galandou Diouf, the parliamentary deputy of Senegal, and his wife earned the nickname of 'the boxer's wife'. An invisible barrier had been transgressed thanks to Diop's wilful personality and his social position in colonial society. The memory of this episode was passed on and kept alive: twenty years later, at the Mali Federation's 1959 independence ceremony, he still had a clear reputation among the politicians of the French Sudan.

Members of the general public could clearly not have acted in this way, and it is easy to detect the hierarchy of status and rank implicitly at play: 'While cinemas were mixed, Africans were only allowed in the ten front rows. They had to form a separate queue. There was no regulation stipulating this. It was simply behavioural conditioning' (Méker 1980: 36). This account, written by

Maurice Méker, who lived in Abidjan in the 1930s, testifies to the rigidity of mental boundaries. In this town, which at the time had recently become the capital of Ivory Coast, practices were shaped by the colonial hierarchy, which was all the more rarely questioned as the local population did not have the same long history of international encounter as the Senegalese, Gold Coast or Togolese bourgeoisie. Similarly, the 'educated natives' of Equatorial Africa— be they in the French or the Belgian Congo—suffered from the proximity of the South African model of apartheid. 'The only cinemas in operation in AEF [French Equatorial Africa] were in Brazzaville and Pointe-Noire and they were in principal reserved for European spectators.'[32]

The words 'in principal' indicate that these were conventions, not laws. Might it be imagined that there were exceptions for a select African public? A slightly later account suggests not. Jean Hilaire Aubame, an 'educated dignitary' who later went on to have a political career in Gabon and at the time had been appointed President of the Brazzaville Poto-Poto town council by Félix Éboué, had difficulty getting into a cinema in the European quarter in the mid-1940s. Social mobility was, in general, more limited in Central Africa. Can it be deduced from this, however, that the limited number of Europeans was sufficient to guarantee the profitability of the region's cinemas? In the majority of cases, cinema venues were shared for pragmatic reasons, but audiences were still differentiated by social factors. The 1932 survey, carried out during the economic crisis, described two venues in Bamako in terms of their clientele:

> The cinema at the Buffet de la Gare is above all frequented by Europeans, due to the nature of the films shown, which are quite interesting. But the high ticket prices prevent them from going regularly. For a population of 500 Europeans, there are barely fifty spectators maximum per show. The indigenous element ... constitutes only approximately one fifth of the spectators.[33]

Only a handful of Africans could attend the Buffet de la Gare, and during this period of economic crisis, not all Europeans were able to afford a movie show either. Conversely, while 'little attended by Europeans', the cinema run by Madame Mähl was 'frequented by the lower-class indigenous element. The main reasons for this are the cheap ticket prices and the nature of films shown, whose action they follow better'.[34]

This precise description illustrates both the notion of a space shared by Africans and Europeans without overt discrimination, and the reality of spectators' apparent preferences in terms of price and film type. A 1937 report confirms the situation, reporting seats 'reserved' for Africans in Bamako's two cinemas. The information available for Lomé also confirms this practice. Likewise, in Kayes, where Europeans and 'natives' attended the same screenings in the courtyard of the Hôtel Ferrari, one may assume that an implicit separation of spaces was in force, mentally and concretely marking a frontier between different audiences that few dared to cross. The status of African administrative or business employees, and the local history of elitism, played a fundamental role in this. A partition wall sometimes materially enforced the distance desired by Europeans, for example at the Florida in Bobo-Dioulasso in the 1930s. The administration nonetheless disapproved of this practice, as a 1948 report demonstrates: 'I hereby inform you that the partition wall at the Florida Cinema between the seats reserved for Europeans and those reserved for Africans has no justification ... You are thus requested to ask the director of the said cinema to remove the barrier.'[35]

In 1918, a municipal by-law authorized 'on the pavement by the Grand Hotel in Conakry, for the purpose of running its cinema, the installation of benches and seats destined for native spectators.'[36] How should one interpret this by-law given that, since the adoption of strict zoning in 1901, the hotel was located in the European quarter? The reference to 'native spectators' points to the presence of colonial subjects in the white district, a presence that, for many, was justified in the daytime by their professions (administrative clerks, dockers, handlers on the Decauville railway), but not after nightfall when the screenings took place. Was it a separation between the indoors, reserved for Europeans, and the outdoors, accessible to colonial subjects? The ambiguity persists, as the by-law mentions two types of seating, benches and seats, implying a further hierarchy among colonial subjects. Did the hotel owner want to introduce more inhabitants of Conakry to this novelty now that the electric power plant, completed in 1910, supplied electricity? Was he targeting Sierra Leonean migrants, who boasted a higher level of education and revenues? Or the Lebanese and Syrian traders who lived nearby? Or was it an attempt to guarantee the film equipment's cost-effectiveness at a time when the Europeans had deserted the city because of the war?

It is impossible to be sure whether the by-law implies separate shows or separate spaces. A later indication suggests a separation of audiences, even if the 1918 war context could have favoured the contrary option; the possible change of atmosphere in the space of a few years cannot be overlooked. Lucie Cousturier, who stayed at the Grand Hôtel in 1921, makes mention of the contempt in which Africans were held. Her 'boy' and travelling companion, who came with her from Dakar, was not able to meet her at the hotel without authorization. She rapidly left the hotel to rent a room in the African quarter of Sandervalia (Cousturier 1925 [republished 1980]: 54–56). At any rate, the Grand Hôtel's cinematic activities did not last, either indoors or out. A 1934 convention signed by the company Besse—owner of the Grand Hôtel, the Hôtel du Niger and the ice plant—and the Conakry municipal authorities stipulated that the annual electricity flat fee did not include any electricity used in the event of a film show.[37]

Similarly, what can be made of the different ticket prices proposed by the Bataclan, in the centre of Dakar, in 1936? There were three different prices for the evening shows: ten francs standard; six for petty officers; and four for a medley of 'children, soldiers, natives'.[38] What was the purpose of this heterogeneous group, considering that the 'citizens of the Four Communes' made up the majority of Dakar's population? It is hard to imagine the person at the box office asking clients to prove their status in order to distinguish 'native subjects' from citizens, especially in a town full of (non-citizen) migrants; it would have been considered an affront by these long-time colonial subjects and city-dwellers.[39] The pervasiveness of the colonial hierarchy nonetheless characterized the colonizers' vision, as can be seen in the first *Guide de l'AOF* (*French West Africa Guide*), published in 1939, which distinguished between three groups of residents in Dakar: 4,941 'European French', 1,567 European foreigners, and, lastly, 86,126 'indigenous French subjects'. This index fails to recognize the city's specific political status; Dakar was one of the 'Four Communes' of Senegal, granted special citizenship rights in the nineteenth century.

Social mix, racial mix?

Choosing a cinema was no easy thing in the colonial period: personal status, or rather colonial subjects' lack of rights, were generally more important than social standing and determined the geographical dimensions of cultural practices. Marginal freedoms did exist, however, as Amadou Hampâté Bâ and Birago Diop's respective 1967 and 1978 accounts demonstrate. What margin of manoeuvre did individuals have with regard to the law, representation, and interiorized discrimination? Accounts describe cinemas as sites of social mixing, although considerably hierarchized by the ticket prices. Without needing to resort to discriminatory laws, the variation in prices clearly made it possible to select the audience, or to restrict it to specific spots. In the mid-1930s in Dakar, Doctor Sultan, who often frequented the Rialto, described the existence of two classes determined not by race, but by price. Amadou Hampâté Bâ (1967) confirmed that this was also the case in Bamako: 'There is a strict control of tickets and policemen check that everyone goes to the place indicated.'

Like other venues, cinemas spatialized these social hierarchies by differentiating entrances, through the arrangement of benches and seats—the latter symbolically raised and situated at the back of the cinema in an area protected by an awning—and the layout of the bar and outdoor spaces. At the Empire Cinema in Freetown in 1939, the balcony (two shillings and six pence) was thus separated from the stalls (one shilling for the front rows, and one shilling and six pence for the back), with the sharp contrast in prices upholding class difference, but also ensuring that access to the cinema was available for all (Anthony 1980: 138). In Accra, competition from the Ocansey cinemas forced Bart's to lower its prices to six or even three pence, which attracted an increasingly low-income clientele who were shown mediocre old films, compared with prices of two shillings, one shilling and six pence, and finally six pence for the cinemas frequented by Ghana's business class. This was nothing compared to the shows put on for a select public at the Sea View Hotel in 1937, however: prices were fourteen times higher than at Bart's and two to seven times higher than elsewhere (McFeely 2015: 142, 153). In Dakar, the high prices of the Plateau cinemas were off-putting for the majority of African city-dwellers. At the Palace in 1936, the matinee cost ten, seven, and five francs for the box, reserved, and front seats respectively, and the evening screening twelve, ten, and eight francs. On the other side of town at the Médina, seats costs three to five francs. At the time, a 100-kilogram sack of rice cost the equivalent of fifteen tickets to a cheap cinema, while a civil servant earning a modest salary of 450 francs a month would spend approximately 10 per cent of his salary on going to the cinema twice a week (Seck 2008: 70).

Each therefore went to the cinema according to their means, regularly or rarely, sitting at the front or the back. For all that, did this tolerated sharing make the cinema a place where colonizers and colonized met? It is unlikely. Co-existence in front of the screen may have created a fleeting sentiment of camaraderie, but one can more easily imagine discreet avoidance strategies on departure, with each heading back to their own district. We might also ask whether Europeans went to watch films in working-class cinemas. This practice became manifestly rarer when the choice of cinemas was greater. Nonetheless, it did occur in towns with just one cinema, and where isolated

Europeans had few leisure activities. The demographic make-up of a town played a role too. In the Gold Coast in 1931, the mixed cinemas of Kumasi, Sekondi, and Tarkwa contrasted with those that catered to an exclusively African audience in modest towns such as Koforidua, Nsawam, Keta, and Prestea. The situation was the same in 1932 in Nigeria, where Lagos's five cinemas were open to mixed African and European audiences, whereas those in Benin City, Port Harcourt, or Jos, a mining town in Plateau State, were essentially frequented by Africans, a few Syrians and, rarely, some Europeans.

When they had no choice, African and European spectators thus shared the same spaces, but in highly variable proportions. For the predominantly single male Europeans who were already familiar with cinema back home, this leisure activity was a way of filling their long, lonely nights. In Kayes in 1932, they thus regularly attended the cinema 'far more out of boredom, due to the lack of other distractions, than out of interest for a given programme.'[40] The cinema broke up the monotony of the night for those just passing through. Michel Leiris, part of the Dakar-Djibouti expedition, noted in his diary on 9 June 1931: 'In the evening, Griaule and I go to the cinema, the B—s. We are bored' (Leiris 1934 [republished 1981]: 35). In the provincial capitals, the range of activities and meeting places was wider, but cinema was a popular means for Europeans to socialize with one another, whether in the familiar settings of hotels or in the town-centre cinemas.

In Elisabethville in the Belgian Congo, a mining town that sprung up in 1910 around the copper mines, all of the Europeans frequented 'the Grand Cinema, a brand-new movie theatre [where] work overalls and dinner jackets are found side-by-side': a sign of social, but not racial, mixing (Weulersse 1931 [republished 1994]: 162). In the Gold Coast, on the other hand, a country where cinema was popular, handbooks designed for British colonialists and civil servants did not mention this leisure activity; on the contrary, in the interwar period, they promoted a vast range of activities focusing on a hygien-ist conception of the body and leisure: tennis, golf, polo, cricket, shooting, cycling, football, hockey, and squash, but also bridge and billiards.[41] Cinema's absence from this list shows that it was not part of the colonizers' mental universe, even though Accra had many movie theatres. Individually, some Europeans did, of course, go to the cinema. Nevertheless, these exclusive lei-sure activities reinforced the Europeans' inclination to keep themselves to themselves, which was accentuated by residential segregation, societal disap-proval of relationships between European men and African women, and the concomitant arrival of European women in the colonies. Depending on the town, then, the colonisers represented a more or less significant proportion of viewers. But what about the first African cinephiles?

Profile of the typical early film spectator

> The huge Rialto cinema was unmatched in Dakar. It was open-air, flooded with light. It was a magnificent film facility for the colonies. From its comfy seats to its wooden chairs with rickety backs, all walks of society were found there, from the most distinguished Europeans to little local kids (Sadji 1958: 100).[42]

In his novel *Maïmouna*, set in the 1930s, Abdoulaye Sadji describes the whole range of seats and spectators, and, accordingly, the various atmospheres within the movie theatre, with each group experiencing the show in a different way.

The increasing number of film shows in the 1930s went hand in hand with a progressive rise in the number and diversity of spectators. However, there was no comparison between the clubs and concessions of Lomé, to which some thirty African spectators flocked, the Buffet de la Gare in Bamako, with its limited and heterogeneous crowd of about fifty people, and the vast cinemas of Accra or Dakar. Even if the big cinemas were rarely sold out, audiences there had a variety of motivations and experiences; cinema-going could be a convivial activity between people who had already met at work or in the shops, or be motivated by the love of film alone. Screenings were thus both a social space and a site of fleeting coexistence between anonymous cinephiles. The capacity of the first cinemas varied enormously. In the British colonies, the average capacity was around 150 to 200 seats, according to a survey carried out in 1931. In Ghana, this ranged from sixty-four seats in Keta, to 800 in an Accra movie theatre. In Lagos, audiences were estimated at almost 4,000 people a week, spread across five cinemas, for a population evaluated at 126,000 inhabitants, whereas in Kumasi and Accra, which both had populations of about 50,000 people, the cinema drew only 900 and 1,370 spectators a week, respectively. In Bamako, the population's enthusiasm was confirmed as, at the end of the 1930s, both the frequency of screenings and their seating capacity grew. Across three nights, Madame Mähl offered 600 weekly places, whereas the Buffet de la Gare offered 650, spread over four nights. This indicates that cinema was a big hit: 'It is true that all the places are taken at least every other show, and that the average native attendance at screenings is of approximately 500 people for each of the two movie theatres.'[43]

Spectators' regularity was all the more remarkable considering that access to the cinemas was expensive in relation to people's limited resources:

> Attendance at each showing stands at around 15 per cent for the European population and 2.5 per cent for the native population. This latter figure is considerable and reflects the natives' pronounced taste for cinema. Indeed, given their average revenue, this assiduity represents a major sacrifice for them, despite the low cost (two to five francs) of the seats reserved for them.[44]

A regular audience of 1,000 spectators at the three to four weekly showings was remarkable for a town of approximately 25,000 inhabitants. Were they devoted film-lovers coming to see new releases or to enjoy rewatching a famous film, or, on the contrary, was there a constant turnover of spectators? Demographic and sociological data suggests that the first hypothesis is more likely, as the pool of potential spectators was limited. In Dakar, where the biggest cinemas such as the Rialto held over 1,000 spectators, thousands of film-lovers gradually developed a film culture and integrated this leisure pursuit into their free time. To those living in Dakar, Kumasi, or working-class neighbourhoods of Accra, certain cinemas offered films as a daily activity. For those in Lomé, Bamako, or even Lagos, this pastime was on offer only thrice weekly. In other cases, it was even more infrequent: in Freetown in 1931, screenings were only held on the first day of the month, but the situation did improve over the course of the decade.

On the whole, the cinema remained an occasional leisure activity. It slotted into the rhythm of the week, and the clockwork alternation between work and free time that developed alongside the rise of the salaried workforce and the colonial conception of time, which was regulated by office hours. Shows were generally held two to three nights a week, or on just one night at the end of the week. Sundays off became the norm in the weekly schedule of the workers, administrative employees, and trading house staff who represented the majority of the audience. Was this rhythm the norm for other groups, such as artisans and traders? Or was it for them that certain cinemas screened films almost every night, notably in the most highly populated neighbourhoods? That was the case at a cinema in Accra and another in Kumasi, but their screenings were manifestly not full: in Accra, where the cinema could seat 500, there were only 750 spectators a week. One can imagine that there, like everywhere, the audience was biggest at the weekend.

How do we reconstitute the atmosphere of these venues and the viewers' behaviour given the diversity of experiences depending on age, social category, gender, and status? A survey carried out in the French colonies in 1932 attempted to get a picture of the viewers as a necessary condition to instigating a film policy. It sought to 'distinguish between categories of spectators: Europeans and populations from the colony, or the territory (separately indicate *assimilés* and those of native status there where the two groups co-exist, and if possible, their social rank).'[45]

Other distinguishing traits were status, nationality, and the degree of education or cultural belonging. Understanding the channels of film distribution also gives a better picture of early spectators, revealing how people were introduced to cinema. In the mining camps of Southern and Central Africa, the answer is simple: film screenings were part of the strategy to manage the workforce. They were destined to keep the single, male workers—often temporary migrants, non-literate, not always sharing a common language—occupied, and to maintain control of their activities during their leisure time (Burns 2002b). In other South African towns, cinema concerned all social categories, both European and African.

In West Africa (and partially in Central Africa), the question of the first spectators' identity is complex. Going to the cinema was both an individual undertaking (a choice among other leisure activities), a form of curiosity, and a question of means—both time and money—which disadvantaged women and young people. Nevertheless, the initial core of spectators was the same everywhere. In Bamako in 1932, at the Buffet de la Gare, 'the native element [was] only represented by a small number of literate, more evolved individuals, civil servants or commercial employees.'[46] In Lomé, the Africans who frequented Luna-Park were 'sales agents, civil servants, workers and domestic staff'—in other words, hardly different from those who attended Albert John Mensah's, who were 'commercial employees, civil servants, and school pupils.'[47] This busy little cosmopolitan town comprised a sufficient clientele of film-lovers and curious participants, who were thirsty for entertainment.

From Bamako to Kayes, Dakar, Lomé, Freetown, Accra, and Lagos, it is possible to establish a profile of the typical first spectators, most of them men: civil servants, workers in the trading houses, and domestic staff employed by Europeans—in other words, salaried employees—who had often attended the colonial schools. They constituted a modern elite that was itself hierarchical. This portrait needs to be nuanced, however, as the cinema was also appreciated by other lower-class and often non-literate groups. The two surveys carried out in the French Sudan in 1932 and 1937 specify the nature of these groups. In Kayes in 1932, it was reported that: 'The native element is, for the main part, represented only by young, mostly non-literate people. Dignitaries and women rarely go to the cinema. None, for that matter, grasp much of these representations that they follow very irregularly.'[48] And in Bamako, in 1937:

> The clientele indeed comprises not so much the wealthier classes of the population (civil servants, commercial employees) as workers, drivers and domestic staff. It would seem, therefore, that the most fervent film-lovers are natives who live in close contact with the Whites and who seek to imitate them. The elite, on the other hand, steers clear of this kind of spectacle. It must be noted that the audience comprises a significant number of women.[49]

The cinema also found many a fan among new city dwellers and the intermediary social groups of this world in flux, who actively participated in change and modernization. As was the case for migrants in the United States, or young people in European suburbs, cinema served as an interface with a new world, a 'toolbox' that staged certain forms of modernity: the sense of an elsewhere, of alternative cultures abroad. The development of cinema was contemporaneous with a rural exodus, itself accentuated by economic crisis. Migration, of course, created a rupture, freeing people from certain social constraints and enabling the invention of new forms of entertainment that incorporated—or conspicuously did not—the sociocultural practices of the village and codified gender relationships. Does that explain why in 1937 more women went to the cinema in Bamako, the district capital and a migratory hub, than in the sleepy, medium-sized town of Kayes in 1932?

Even though cinema, unlike other ways of occupying free time, cost money, the range of prices excluded almost no one. Cinema had a popular appeal and was accessible to the majority, if one includes the cheapest seats in the bottom-of-the-range cinemas. In Freetown, kids would scrape together their pennies to go to the cinema, although they sometimes resorted to an array of crafty strategies to get in for free: slipping up the stairs amidst the bustle to dodge the ticket controls; passing their ticket stubs from row to row; unlocking the security exits; and so forth (Anthony 1980: 138–39). Cinema-going as a leisure activity soon became habitual in the 1930s, as Amadou Hampâté Bâ noted: 'In the major *tubabudugu* [towns inhabited by a white majority], the cinema is a spectacle that attracts a lot of people' (Bâ 1967: 18).

However, access to the best seats—a sign of viewers' status—was often inaccessible to the majority of African civil servants. In 1936, ticket prices at the Palace ranged from five to ten francs for a matinee, and eight to twelve in the evening, whereas tickets at the Médina ranged from three to five francs, a precious, if not prestigious, alternative (Seck 2008: 70). The question of the elites' relationship to cinema is at times opaque, for reasons that were largely based on morals rather than preference. Once the initial curiosity passed, the local bourgeoisie in Freetown and Accra turned away from the medium, which was accused of perverting the lower classes (cf. Chapter 2). Elsewhere, as in Dakar, Abidjan, and Zanzibar, elitist forms of film-going emerged. Whether audiences were predominantly literate or working-class, and women present or absent, typologies were thus complex and variable.

Spectatorship and moral, gender-based and religious considerations

All available interviews and accounts unreservedly, and even enthusiastically, evoke the presence of women in cinema audiences, but also mention the restrictions weighing on them. These were most notably of an educational and moral order, or were related to women's more limited leisure time and access to money. Age was also a factor in societies where women very often transitioned directly from childhood to adulthood through marriage, usually shortly after puberty. Adolescence was short-lived for them. On the whole, women were underrepresented in the new categories of urban cinephiles. In the interwar years, schoolgirls and salaried women (often midwives and teachers) were scarce. Those who, like the Gulf of Guinea merchant women, acquired sufficient financial and social autonomy through their trade to go to the cinema were even rarer. Unaccompanied film-going was generally taken as a form of solicitation. The cinema was not for respectable women, it was often said. But cinema did not always have this reputation for immorality, which, for that matter, stemmed less from the films themselves than from the venues where they were screened.

Women and girls were just as swayed by cinema's power of attraction as men. While boys frequented cinemas in groups, girls went escorted by adults or within an institutional framework, for example with their schools. Frida Lawson, a student at the École normale de Rusfique (a teacher-training college) in 1941, had fond memories of a stop-over in Bamako during the long homeward journey from Senegal to Lomé: 'To keep us occupied, the headmistress once paid for us to go to the cinema.'[50] As stated above, it was not the films themselves that were considered immoral. Thanks to the texts they studied, the songs they listened to, and their peer discussions, students' tastes conformed to a romantic and monogamous conception of relationships, albeit not a prudish one: 'The film was wonderful, a romance naturally. It did not, I hasten to add, shock us at all.'[51]

Cinema-going was therefore not subject to opprobrium as such, but girls were to be accompanied and kept under strict surveillance, as shown in the account of a teen from Mamou who dared to disobey her grandfather, a political and religious figure in the Fouta Djallon region of Guinea. Giving her some money, her grandfather made her promise not to go to the cinema, but she went anyway. She was discovered and denounced, and long feared that a punishment would ensue.[52] This tale of transgression illustrates the attraction of the cinema, but also shows that, in a medium town such as Mamou, girls' presence in a cinema was not socially interdicted. The nature of their education and modes of socialization did limit girls' margins of manoeuvre, however. In general, in addition to being accompanied, they were only allowed to go to matinees, partly because it was hardly acceptable for them to go out at night, but also due to the rowdy, or even violent, atmosphere that frequently characterized the later screenings.

Once married, women rarely went to the cinema. They could go with their husbands, but this practice was only adopted by a minority of couples: those who shared leisure activities, such as Amadou Hampâté Bâ, who regularly went to the cinema in Bamako with his wife. Similarly, the dignitary mentioned above, who wanted to preserve his granddaughter from the dangers of the cinema, used to go himself with his wives. Religious values were not the main reason for forbidding this activity, then, but rather social conditions and strict educational criteria—within an aristocratic Fulani context in this case, but found in other cultures too.

Practices overtly regulating the presence of women, in force elsewhere, were very rare in West Africa: these included separate entrances, found in some cinemas in India; specific showings, such as matinees in Damas, Egypt, or ladies' nights in Lamu, Kenya; and reserved seating, which travelling film shows in Kenya marked off at the front for women and children, another demographic deemed vulnerable. Similarly, in Zanzibar and Dar es Salaam, Ladies' Shows were held during the day in the name of respectability (Fair 2018: 12, 155, 209–10 and 214–20). These regulations asserted moral norms that were aimed at keeping women—perceived as moral guardians—distant from potentially dangerous places or images reputed to be evil. But here too, the degree of social condemnation depended on the cultural context. And, questions of regulation notwithstanding, the cinema had a manifest impact on ideas of gender. Even if men, particularly older men, were clearly predominant, this new public space, lying out of sight of the usual moral authorities, was a space of renegotiation of gender relations: a negotiation incarnated in behaviours adopted inside the movie theatre, but also, and above all, on the screen.

Films proposed alternative models of amorous conduct, male–female relationships, and conjugal behaviour, but also new figures of femininity and masculinity. A nuanced analysis is necessary here, taking film genres into account. It is not always easy, when exploring a social and cultural practice, to determine the part played by moral values, religious precepts (be they ancient or acquired), and elite codes. The Fouta Djallon anecdote is symptomatic of this: it is less a reflection of Islam, and more illustrates the weight of the dominant classes' strict education. The cinema was often pejoratively associated with the notion of *woulah*, which, in Fulani, means 'a waste of time'. The desire to preserve children from certain novelties, and parents' resulting reticence to allow them to go to the cinema, clashed naturally with children's burning desire to see films. They often did so by going without permission and then presenting this to their parents as a fait accompli, a practice that was more accepted in boys than in girls.

Signs of a total prohibition of moving images in the name of Islam are extremely rare. According to Amadou Hampâté Bâ's account, in Bandiagara in 1908 dignitaries ordered the canton, the district chiefs, and a dozen officials, who were obliged by the district officer to attend this 'devilry', to shut their eyes during a film screening. These Muslim dignitaries, who were members of the highly rigorous Tijaniyyah order, condemned the screening from the outset: 'The attraction proposed is obviously a satanic one. If it weren't, they would not have chosen the dark of night to present it.' The word thus went around to boycott this 'moving shadow' event: 'The instruction that each brother must give the next is that it is absolutely forbidden to go to see the white wizard's infernal spectacle.' Bâ found himself among the small group of spectators, his young age—approximately eight years old—apparently absolving him of the ban. 'The screening took place, but no one apart from Alfa Maki, a man very open to progress, agreed to watch these diabolical images. Everyone took advantage of the dark to close their eyes' (Bâ 1967: 10–11).

The Bandiagara ulemas thus condemned the cinema. The same ban existed for a while in Dinguiraye—the former residence of scholar and reformer Al-Hajj Umar Tall—in Upper Guinea, a region which was marked by a similar religious rigour and condemned both cinemas and dance halls.[53] Some years later, in the 1930s, Bâ managed to convince his religious master, the famous Tierno Bokar, to accompany him to the cinema in Bamako. Bokar produced a theological analysis of the event, viewing the screening as a parable of heaven and putting forward a religious reading adapted to this most contemporary of human creations. Similarly, Bâ's mother Kadiata Paté, a pious, strong-willed character who reluctantly agreed to go to the cinema with her son at his insistence in 1934, drew the following lesson from it: 'Just as the big cloth [the screen] is necessary for a clear vision of the image and to discern the origin of the sound, an intermediary is needed between us and God to understand the holy message' (Bâ 1967: 16).

The curiosity that the 'moving shadows' aroused gradually won over spiritual fears and condemnation, which were transformed into warnings to be careful and moral alerts. In Senegal, too, religious authorities, although initially hostile to the cinema, adopted a more flexible attitude. Islam was thus not in itself an obstacle to the spread of cinema, in the south or the north, but it may have delayed or slowed its dissemination. Cinema was ultimately incorporated into a discourse of modernity, and perceptions of it varied depending on the theological current or individual personality, as can be seen in the example of Kano in northern Nigeria. There, in 1937, the doctor William Sellers, first director of the British Colonial Film Unit, persuaded the Emir, despite the reluctance of some of his advisors, to screen medical documentaries in the vast courtyard of his palace, in parallel with screenings organized for Nigerian and British dignitaries (Larkin 2008: 84). In the same year, the Rex, built outside of the old city and targeting a mostly Christian audience originating from the south of the colony, attracted many young local Muslims despite the conservative religious authorities' negative vision of the cinema and their tendency to perceive film-goers as thugs. Tensions between certain conservative segments of society were strong, but young people were fascinated by the moving image, whatever their religion. A few years later, in 1951, the death of 300 people in a huge fire at the El Duniya Cinema reinforced this condemnation: the tragedy was interpreted as a punishment from God. However, this did not prevent the opening of a new cinema in the old part of the city, so popular was the medium by then.

From Dakar to Brazzaville, Bamako to Lagos, audiences progressively grew, even if not all social or generational groups shared this passion to the same degree or for the same reasons. But as films circulated throughout the world from the 1920s onwards, which films were screened? And how did the authorities react to this flow of images that might destabilize their power?

2

REGULATION, CONTROL AND CENSORSHIP
IN THE INTERWAR YEARS

As long as cinema operated out of courtyards and hotels, drawing just a few spectators, it was of little interest to the colonial authorities. It did, however, become the object of intense scrutiny at the turn of the 1930s, but for financial and political reasons this concern led only to censorship and fell far short of any ambition for a real film policy. In 1946, then, Albert Lacolley, a trainee administrator at the ENFOM (École nationale de la France d'Outre-Mer, or National School of Overseas France), declared: 'A cinema policy is needed, yet none exists in the French or other foreign colonies' (Lacolley 1946: 12). This categorical statement reflected the general sentiment that cinema was not the priority, even in the British colonies, where governmental action took place earlier. Nevertheless, by the 1920s an entire discourse had emerged concerning this new media, which had a profound impact on modes of representation. The cinema provided colonial subjects with images that contradicted colonial ideology and opened a window to other worlds. These images were considered all the more dangerous as, due to colonial stereotypes, colonized peoples were considered intellectually limited.

At its outset, cinema developed beyond the control of the authorities, through the initiative of dynamic entrepreneurs. Long limited to confined spaces and small audiences, this new leisure activity was not considered a cause for concern. As cinema took root and spread, however, the administration woke up to its potentially subversive power. The colonial authorities thus sought to regulate and keep an eye on cinema entrepreneurs. This did not immediately result in the strict regulation of film activity. However, even though regulations were slow in coming, their chronology is a significant indication both of cinema's governance according to country, and of the stages of control: on the whole, laws did not anticipate developments, but instead regulated specific practices or responded to unforeseen conflicts. The albeit rather marginal impact of the early measures has left little trace in the archives and testimonies, but a process was instigated from which postcolonial policies took inspiration, so little did the logistics and tools of repression change after Independence. Debates were nonetheless intense, focusing on the power of the cinematic image, but also on the role of the state and on the political and social vision of Empire. Convinced that, as in the West, film was an effective propaganda tool but also a threat—especially when the industry progressed from silent films to talkies—many politicians, administrators, educators, moralists, and entrepreneurs encouraged the colonial authorities to instigate a 'film policy'.

Protecting 'child-like' audiences: from spectator 'naivety' to the impact of schooling

Both in theory and in practice, each of the colonial powers dealt with the question of cinema differently, according to their own cultural traditions and national policies. With the precedent of its India Office and the example of its other dominions, Britain was quicker than others to address these issues. The question of cinema was broached relatively early in the Imperial Conferences, but to differing degrees depending on the territory. Proportional to its strategic interest and demographic weight, the attention given to tropical Africa—a designation that did not include Southern Africa—was minor. Awareness of the issue came later in France, and there, too, sub-Saharan Africa was not a priority. As for the Belgian Congo, the missionaries' predominance influenced the consideration of film in the area. Reflections on cinema were also conditioned by a hierarchical conception of races and cultures, in which Africa epitomised the archaic.[1]

This conception generated on the one hand a theoretical discourse on Africans' supposed intellectual capacities, and on the other the idea that they needed to be protected from the transgressions of cinema. Considered incapable of reading film images and understanding their complexity, African spectators, it was thought, had to be shielded from cinema's potential evils.

The archetype of the 'noble savage' went hand in hand with, and reinforced, the notion of 'childlike' viewers. These prejudices shaped the attitude of the authorities towards cinema, justifying the exclusion of certain films deemed dangerous for a supposedly unenlightened public, or incompatible with local cultures that were readily instrumentalized. In zones where cinemas were segregated (the settler colonies and Belgian Congo), they also led to the production of films exclusively designed for an African audience, assuming—without any real knowledge of these potential audiences—a specific relationship to the image.

To understand the reasoning behind this, it is worth considering certain analyses of cinema in the West from this time. According to the 'cause and effect' theory prevalent in the 1910s, the glorification of certain characters' crimes and immorality was thought to encourage similar behaviour on the part of spectators. Defenders of the moral order held the cinema responsible for social problems. Such anxieties particularly centred groups considered vulnerable due to their age, level of education, or living conditions. Colonized peoples, like the working classes or children, were stigmatized as impressionable. This line of reasoning legitimized the perceived need to protect them from the nefarious influences of film. Film controls, which made no attempt to investigate actual similarities and differences in codes of reading across cultures, were introduced to this end.

In Southern Africa, the spread of cinema went hand in hand with fundamental changes in political theory and the representation of colonial subjects (Burns 2002b). A discourse which depicted Africans as essentially different pervaded society. These prejudices played a key role in the colonial construction of race, which sought to characterize ethnic groups while also dividing them up into categories such as the 'educated natives', Creoles, and 'evolving and evolved primitives' of the Belgian colonial system. Accordingly, only a minority of Western-educated individuals were considered worthy of accessing the same films as Europeans. In practice, however, an instruction or regulation could be interpreted differently according to the character of the administrator in question and to the local context.

In the British Empire and the Belgian Congo, where the missionaries were pioneers in this respect, the idea that films needed to be simplified through censorship, or produced specifically for colonial audiences, firmly took hold by the 1920s and was the object of extensive discourse. Some colonizers suggested teaching Africans to watch films, considering them incapable of decrypting the images, whereas others insisted that these viewers' lack of knowledge of Western societies would prevent them from grasping the films' messages. With regard to the former argument, the authorities asserted the difficulty that 'native audiences' had in understanding non-sequential sequences, flashbacks, or the changing scale of objects or characters on the screen.[2] This was illustrated by an anecdote concerning a screening in which a giant mosquito that took up the entire screen was said to have both terrified spectators in Central Africa, and reassured them given the lack of such creatures where they lived (cited in Burns 2002b; Kerr 1993). The tale was often repeated by those who proclaimed the inability of uneducated audiences to distinguish between an object and its representation. Any divergence from such racist theories was unthinkable, even if empirical observations contradicted these clichés: the unmitigated success of films shown at the time clearly indicates that audiences understood them without any difficulty.

In the 1920s, the British set up a system to produce films specifically destined for the colonies. In the late 1930s, they progressed to actually making films in the colonies (see Chapter 3). In addition to the instructions issued from the metropolis, certain governors took their own initiatives. In the Gold Coast, where cinema was vibrant, Governor Gordon Guggisberg (1919–27) held that the ability to understand films' meanings depended on educational background. He thus believed that film could be used for educational purposes among the school-going elite, but was concerned about the impact of certain films on 'half-educated and illiterate groups'.[3] Envisaging the differentiation of audiences according to conceptions of evolutionary anthropology, this position foreshadowed a future development: the collusion between modern elites and colonial powers in trying to control which films were shown to the masses. In the meantime, it led to the participation of the Ghanaian elite in censorship boards.

In the French colonial context race was theorized less, but a racist vision prevailed in and underscored both the rare films produced by colonial agencies and missionaries, and attitudes to African audiences. In 1932, the governor of Togo described spectators who 'could only follow the unfolding plot with difficulty', and requested 'simple films, perfectly adapted to the mentality of the natives targeted', while at the same time acknowledging that it was too soon to make a definitive judgement on the sophistication of audience responses.[4] The governor of French Sudan (Mali) described 'our natives' incomprehension before the screen.'[5] At the same time, these reports of spectators' naivety regarding cinematic images did not prevent the application of an assimilationist logic, which envisaged the evolution, albeit limited, of audiences. In the 1932 survey, school screenings in the French Sudan were taken as an example of how 'our black pupils' reacted to film; the survey concluded by stating 'the difficulty that Blacks have in reading images, even when they are still images'.[6] Pupils were unable, it was reported, to grasp the meaning of a rapid succession of shots or to understand the effects of perspective: assertions that readily combined biology, essentialism and culturalism.

Even before the advent of moving images, static images had already caught the attention of the governors of French West Africa (FWA), who were concerned about their influence on the 'unsophisticated mentalities of the natives' (Thioub 2005: 82). The authorities particularly feared the circulation of religious prints from the Ottoman Empire on the eve of the First World War: 'One cannot deny what a wonderful instrument of propaganda the propagation of thousands of copies of these vulgar, garish prints constitutes here, presenting the defenders of true religion [Islam] in a favourable light' (William Ponty's 1910 circular, cited by Thioub 2005: 82).

The same line of reasoning lay behind the control of cinemas. In 1932, the Minister of Colonies summed up the complexity of the phenomenon: 'The impression produced varies ... depending on the degree of receptivity of the audience. Indeed, spectators' mental dispositions differ according to their personal convictions, their intellectual education, concepts specific to their race, and the preconceptions of the social group to which they belong.'[7] He went on: 'Even more than in the metropolis, the psychology of the spectator must be established in our distant territories. In each of our establishments, and in addition to considerations of race and milieu, the level that the evolution of people's intelligence has reached must be taken into account.'[8]

The question of spectators' literacy, or their familiarity with written culture, was pertinent, but the conclusions drawn more often than not reflected enduring prejudices. In 1951, the head of the Belgian colonies' film services thus asserted: 'The film must contain a single event likely to solicit an emotion, which ought to trigger an idea.'[9] His judgement reflects the stereotypical idea, dating back to the 1920s and '30s, that African audiences could only process one thing at a time, be it an event, emotion, or idea (a notion clearly refuted by the great success of Hollywood movies in Africa at the time).

The Empire, a market; the cinema, a stake

During the First World War, the warring parties became aware of the impact of visual propaganda. It was in this context that film policies emerged in the metropolises and in certain colonies.[10] Meanwhile, the United States asserted its cinematic dominance, with its film industry developing far from the battlefields. In 1916, the Governor-General of French Indochina, Albert Sarraut, set up the General Government of Indochina Film Mission, although he encountered many hurdles in its creation: the difficulties of organizing screenings; the poor state of the roads, which hindered the circulation of mobile cinema vans; and so forth (Lacolley 1946: 6). The war justified the stated urgency of instigating an official film policy:

> The importance that propaganda, disseminated by means of appropriate films, took during the war in both the Allied countries and the central Empires, has drawn governments' attention throughout the entire civilized world to the resources that the cinematograph offers in the circulation of ideas, the propagation of teachings, and the vulgarization of concepts.[11]

Henceforth, the authorities turned their attention to this medium, as testified by a survey carried out in the British colonies in preparation for the 1926 Colonial Office Conference; reports compiled by the British Colonial Films Committee in 1927 and 1930; and a French ministerial report and circular in 1932 on the 'need to adopt a "film policy" in the Colonies', excerpted above. In the British Empire, this attention to modern technology—both radio and cinema—started in the dominions and white settler colonies, such as Kenya and Rhodesia, where the effects of cinema were keenly questioned: could members of populations who were statutorily, socially and culturally differentiated watch the same films without challenging colonial domination? In the colonial metropolises, intense debates took place at the turn of the 1930s in the context of American domination of the market, the advent of talkies, and the expansion of cinema in Africa.

The sharp increase in American production, marked by the rise of Hollywood, worried the 'old continent' for both economic and ideological reasons. Pathé, the market leader, saw its dominance drastically decline. The transition to the talkies accentuated this rupture. Mastered in 1927, sound technology started to spread in the USA in 1928–29 and in other countries a little later (1929–30 in the United Kingdom and France; 1930 in Germany), while India produced its first talking movie in 1931, and Egypt the following year. In the colonies, the changeover of technical equipment was more laborious and silent films remained the norm for a few more years.[12]

Contemporary discussions on the cinema focused on two points: the use of film for educational and propaganda purposes, and the impact of nonnational films on audiences. The declining proportion of national productions among the films screened in the metropolises, which was even more pronounced in the colonies, was a cause for concern. In 1925, the percentage of British films screened in Britain was estimated at 2 per cent, compared to 25 per cent in 1914. This state of affairs alarmed the government and the British film industry, and led to the creation of an ad hoc board in 1925. In addition to the economic implications, a key concern was the national ideologies conveyed in non-British films. This aspect was particularly important in the Empire, where the proportion of non-British films was even greater, reaching 99 per cent in the dominions. Their shared use of the English language favoured the distribution of American films, which did not carry the same values or favour the same representations. This concern was voiced at the Imperial Conference in 1926. Debates focused on the adoption of national film quotas, a solution advocated by some and contested by others. It led to the adoption of quotas in the 1927 Cinematograph Films Act. It was felt that the problems of the British film industry could be resolved via distribution in the Empire, which constituted a vast, and expanding, market.

In preparation for the 1926 Colonial Office Conference, the Minister of Colonies, Leopold S. Amery, launched an enquiry into 'the undesirable effects produced by the projection of certain types of films in the colonies'.[13] Some countries paid little attention to the question, such as Sierra Leone, whose report was even destroyed, whereas in others, such as Mauritius or the Gold Coast, the questionnaire garnered acute interest. Governor Guggisberg returned a detailed report indicating that he had already taken legislative measures in 1925. In response to these discussions, London created the abovementioned Colonial Films Committee. It presented its report to Parliament in August 1930.[14] Its objectives were to encourage cinema as a means of education and to promote British films. The British were concerned that spectators should clearly distinguish between national films and American productions, a distinction that appears not to have previously been all that obvious.[15] This concern accentuated the desire to create films for African audiences, in which any possible confusion would be eliminated. The Committee also discussed the principle of censorship. However, the resolutions adopted remained very broad, with the financial crisis of the 1930s undermining the possibilities of funding.

In France, 1932 also marked the beginnings of a concerted film policy, prepared by a senior civil servant, Gaston Joseph. He wrote his report in the context of both growing awareness of the role of cinema in the colonial empire, and economic competition exacerbated by the Great Depression. The desire to preserve the image of the French colonies before a metropolitan public, and to assert France's prestige as a so-called benevolent power in the colonies, was manifest. Joseph believed that the very basis of this equilibrium would be threatened by the distribution of certain films in the colonies, but also in France. At stake was control of the representations circulating in both Europe and Africa: 'Making films about colonial subjects and the massive import of foreign films to the colonies risk undermining the entire colonial policy of a great nation.'[16] On the subject of the metropolis, he continued:

> Documentary-type films shot in distant African or Oceanian countries have an even greater impact on the opinion that the civilized world forms of life in these countries because they flatter sedentary spectators' particularly pronounced love of travel. Yet it suffices that such a film linger on the natives' moral decadence, their social poverty, their arduous work conditions, and the flawed organization of hygiene, for doubt to be planted among the general public concerning the colonizing qualities of the State possessing these colonies.[17]

Highly impressionable and susceptible to exoticism, the French might, the author feared, end up questioning the legitimacy of the colonial enterprise, as films often highlighted archaism in the colonies. The danger was considered even greater in the colonies themselves, as the lack of information available rendered the colonized populations particularly 'vulnerable' to images:

> Perhaps even more serious still is the influence of films on native opinion with regard to their tutor. Thanks to contact with us alone, the inhabitants of our colonies have become aware of all the discoveries of modern technology. They confuse world civilization with French civilization. ... The films we show them only make our influence greater in this respect. Unfortunately, our film production is far from satisfying the demand of the directors of entertainment venues in our possessions. The increasingly numerous foreign films shown in these theatres are making colonial spectators accustomed to admiring the industrial organization, the wealth, and the well-being of other people ... and, thus, to drawing unfavourable comparisons with their protector nations.[18]

If they did not control the dissemination of cinematic images, the colonial powers stood to open Pandora's box. By screening foreign films that celebrated the achievements of other Western countries, France risked being unfavourably compared to them by colonized spectators. If nothing were done, the danger of losing all legitimacy in the eyes of the dominated populations was thus considered a major risk; these concerns demanded the adoption of a more offensive attitude. The array of perceived threats was considerable, ranging from 'footage thought to be currently edited in Moscow to display admiration for the Soviet paradise', to the Americans' intention to 'shoot films denouncing so-called atrocities in our penal colonies'.[19] Moreover, Africa was directly associated with the activity of American missionaries, who demonstrated 'particular concern for our French Africa' and were thought to have other motives: 'There is every reason to believe that films will follow next after their Bibles.'[20]

These completely excessive speculations reveal the tense state of international relations and the stakes of cinema. The French felt the need to defend themselves from the foreign films that dominated the colonial market, and threatened France's reputation. In order to decide on a course of action, Joseph recommended the organization of a vast survey, whose responses would 'make it possible, without delay, to precisely determine a "film policy", whose adoption the needs of the moment ... appear to impose for the safeguard of our Empire.'[21] A March 1932 circular specified the conditions of this survey.[22] Its premise was straightforward: fiction films or documentaries could serve the interests of colonization or, on the contrary, damage them. The aim of the survey was to obtain as much information as possible to gain a better idea of who spectators were, and to prepare programmes. An enquiry placing its emphasis on films, rather than audiences, had been launched in 1929 at the behest of the League of Nations' International Educational Cinematograph Institute. It had met with a lukewarm response: of the French colonies in Africa, only Togo, Cameroon—both of which were territories under mandate and thus directly connected to the League of Nations—Madagascar, and French Somaliland responded. This lack of interest resulted from the still limited development of cinema. By 1932, it was necessary to update and complete data.

All the colonies were called upon, and their reports were expected back within an incredibly short three-month period. The survey aimed to determine 'the ground gained by foreign influences that, along with other mediums, may be using the cinema to consolidate their offensive.'[23] It also sought to identify the public's taste in order to try, where possible, to meet it with French productions. Twelve sections set out across two pages were sent to the governors, who were asked to supply any information judged useful, and to formulate suggestions. These sections covered a range of elements: an evaluation of regulatory texts (1); an inventory of cinemas, entrepreneurs, and audiences (2); the characteristics, market share, and impact of national and foreign films (3 to 7); and educational cinema (8). The ninth and tenth points raised the question of propaganda and the position of French films. Financial questions were also evoked (11). One of the objectives was to evaluate the influence of foreign films by identifying the 'possible screening of tendentious films of a nature likely to undermine French prestige'. The sixth point explicitly requested a 'distinction between openly anti-French films and films that may appear objective, but are of a nature that invites an unfavourable comparison with our country'. Emphasis was also placed on the importance of playing an active role, as demonstrated by the seventh point: 'What type of film would appear to best serve French interests? What dispositions might be susceptible to facilitating our propaganda?'[24]

Finally, a last question enquired about 'the pertinence of contacting and informing [the] secretary general of the Conseil supérieur du cinématographe of our colonial cinematographic action.' This Superior Council, set up by decree in August 1931, advised the government. The co-operation proposed between the metropolis and the colonies reflected the centralization of colonial management, which complicated the question of censorship.

This array of questions was ambitious and could have yielded great insight, but the governors appear not to have responded with the enthusiasm expected, with the exception of the governors of French Sudan and Togo; the survey thus had a limited impact. By the time responses trickled in to the Ministry of Colonies, Chappedelaine, the minister overseeing the survey, had been replaced, as the position had a rapid turnover. As in Britain, film policy was not the priority in a time of crisis, and the decision-makers were not willing to devote the necessary financial resources to it. The process initiated by the March 1932 circular thus culminated in a March 1934 decree which placed emphasis on censorship. With the exception of another survey launched in 1937, nothing more was attempted in the interwar years.[25]

The security of venues and the control of images

In the early days, entrepreneurs took advantage of the haziness surrounding film industry regulation, most notably with regard to taxation and customs policies. Given the repressive colonial context of that time, cinema was relatively free. To bring this technology under control required a series of administrative adjustments, not only in terms of regulation but also on a social level, with regard to behavioural patterns. These adjustments concerned both distributors and spectators. Different societal groups and entities—elders, religious authorities, parents, associations—were affected by the discourses and measures put in place by the colonial authorities. Increased control multiplied instances of confrontation, but in certain areas some freedom remained.

The first measures, taken in the name of safety and public order, concerned the venues themselves. It was only later that the authorities focused on screenings' actual content. Compiling a list of decrees, rulings, ordinances and other regulations does not tell us much, given that their implementation was random or piecemeal. Nonetheless, their very existence—at times simply as a Sword of Damocles—was symptomatic of the desire to control this new medium.

In France, the surveillance of cinemas and the introduction of measures to limit danger also allowed for the control of content.[26] In Britain, the first Cinematograph Act was passed in 1909. But in the colonies, screening venues—most of which were open-air—did not invite such measures. The avoidance of fires was hardly pertinent before the advent of indoor cinemas, which only affected a minority of towns before the 1950s. Rulings were nonetheless adopted, following the logic of metropolitan laws: the fear of fires was foremost, due to the highly flammable nature of film stock.[27] Equally, concerns for public order and the prevention of noise pollution were apparent—concerns which were not limited to film activity, and also reflected the desire to control urban public spaces.

The colonial administrative framework was thus progressively adapted, adding cinemas to the list of establishments subject to control in FWA. Senegal innovated with a local ruling issued in 1922, inspired by the metropolitan model and 'concerning the regulation of the policy and exploitation of theatres, cafés, concert halls, cinemas, dance halls and all public shows in general.'[28] This confirmed Senegal's position as a forerunner in terms of film distribution; the capital of FWA had a large population, attracted migrants, and had a high concentration of Europeans, all of whom were potential spectators. A technical—not censorship—board was set up to control hygiene and security conditions. The regulations that it instigated were hardly restrictive, as cinema remained an open-air activity. Similarly, a general ruling for all of FWA, dated 28 April 1927 and issued in accordance with the 20 October 1926 decree concerning 'dangerous, unhygienic, and improper establishments' and notably aiming to prevent fires, did not expressly include cinemas. Article 5 did specify that the list could be augmented as technology changed, but this did not occur within the interwar years. Equally, the 3 December 1927 ruling in Senegal 'concerning improper and unhygienic establishments' did not mention entertainment venues. This confirms that cinemas were not a central preoccupation for the authorities. The resulting administrative vagueness subsequently fuelled legal wrangles that more often concerned rivalry between entrepreneurs than genuine concern about fires or noise.

The regulations drawn up for Senegal were also applied elsewhere: in the French Sudan and Togo in 1928; Guinea in 1931; Ivory Coast in 1936; and finally Dahomey (now Benin) on 9 July 1943. The local Guinean ruling focused on buildings' conformity to security regulations. Article 13 listed the precautions that 'cinematograph directors' needed to take to prevent fire hazards. The text went further than this, however, as Article 14 also introduced the requirement to gain authorization for plays or films. This authorization was obtained by submitting the planned programme, but modalities were not really fixed; this was clearly more a legal precaution than an effective practice. No concrete trace of an authorization of this type figures in the archives.

Some colonies did not even adopt a judicial framework, as the evaluation carried out by the general government in 1948 indicates. This illustrates the limited distribution of film in certain regions and the unequal spread of cinemas, which in some locations were rudimentary in character and in others were entirely absent. Mauritania, for example, was not affected as 'no cinema exists' in the country, while the absence of regulation in Upper Volta (now Burkina Faso) was justified by the 'inexistence of any real entertainment venues ... and it being difficult to apply this designation to Bobo-Dioulasso's open-air cinemas'. The same went for Niger: 'As the film screenings, which constitute the main type of entertainment, take place outdoors, the risks of accidents are extremely limited.'[29] In the French Sudan, the head of the Public Works Service offered a very simple evaluation in 1947: 'We add that in the Sudan, spectators' safety only requires very simple measures, as the theatres are open-air.'[30]

The fact that the governor-general of French West Africa waited until 1948 to assess the situation is itself a sign of the limited place that cinema occupied in colonial policy. Nonetheless, screen content was controlled through alternative avenues to policing the cinemas. Local mechanisms, more appropriate to the small size of towns and audiences, were often favoured. In 1932, the governor of Togo stated: 'Until now, the police services have never witnessed the screening of tendentious or anti-French films.'[31] This affirmation nonetheless indicates a regular police presence, which guaranteed an ad hoc surveillance of the population and of what was on the screen. Amadou Hampâté Bâ's account of police activity in Bamako in 1937 is even more explicit: 'Police officers were posted at the entrance, others paced up and down the street. ... Tickets! cried another officer' (Bâ 1967).

In the British colonies, measures were similarly taken to control cinemas and the images they screened. In Southern Nigeria, a series of regulations concerning entertainment venues, entitled the 'Theatres and Public Performances Regulation Ordinance', was adopted in 1912, to which the 'Cinematograph Ordinance' was added for the rest of the territory in 1917. As in Britain, no film show could be organized without paying for a license. To this was added a permit, granted by a civil servant on the presentation of a description of the show. The decision to ban a show could be made without any explanation being given, and film screenings were immediately jeopardized. Initially comprehensive, in 1924 the licence was divided into six rates, ranging from £1 for under twenty different reels screened in a month, to £4 for an unlimited number.[32] The system was modified in 1933, with payments varying from a licence, whose cost depended on its duration (£1 a month, or equivalent fractions of months; five shillings a week, or equivalent fractions of weeks), to a tax based on the number of reels submitted to the censorship board. The policy was clearly empirical, with the authorities attempting to take into account a diversity of situations—from one-off funfair screenings, to school screenings, to commercial cinema.

The first regulation adopted in the Gold Coast in 1925 also took cinema's safety conditions into consideration. These were later accounted for by a highly detailed 1932 regulation, the majority of whose thirty-four articles were devoted to security, while also focusing on licences and the Board of Control. Nothing was overlooked: the number of exits, whose doors had to open outwards; the presence of responsible staff for the duration of the screening; and the functionality of fire-fighting equipment, projection booths, rewind rooms, and electrical installations. The police were responsible for verifying these requirements. In 1927, a one-shilling tax for all importations of 100-metre lengths of film was adopted: in other words, the same price as a gallon of cider or beer. This tax was in addition to the licence fee that cinema operators paid. It was not modified in the interwar years, although the equivalent tax for alcohol did double. These different taxes weighed on film activity, provoking protests and dissuading some from launching local initiatives.[33]

This early control of images—for images were indeed feared at this time—has left very few traces in archives or personal testimonies, mainly because envisaged laws only materialized as unfinished projects, or pious circulars, and their implementation was hazy, once more demonstrating a certain disinterest on the part of local authorities. It must not be forgotten, however, that by the time a film was released in Africa, it had already made it over several hurdles, independent from the local market. The first came well beforehand: producers and filmmakers often practiced self-censorship in order to access national and international markets. The second was the verdict of the metropolitan censorship boards. It was from these boards' stock that distributors importing films picked works, although some direct imports were made in the English-speaking colonies. As they were advancing funds, they had no desire to risk the proscription of the films once they reached the colonies; they, too, therefore anticipated possible bans. The authorities were well aware of this, and sought a balance between the imperatives of public order in the colonies and the interests of entrepreneurs, who were often influential in colonial society. But according to the Governor of the Gold Coast, Gordon Guggisberg, the former concern took precedence and the censors had to be severe, as any indulgence would encourage distributors to import films that were 'all the more detrimental and vulgar'.[34] Censorship in the colonies themselves was thus the final stage, and authorities in all territories had every intention of implementing it.

Modes of censorship reproduced the mechanisms that existed in the metropolis, both in their structures (the functioning and composition of their boards) and their criteria. Indeed, the original texts of metropolitan regulations were at times reproduced word for word. The immediate effects of censorship, and notably the bans imposed by the police, often escape the historian. However, it is often possible in sub-Saharan Africa to detect affiliations between the earliest regulatory texts and the more widespread censorship of the 1930s. The same colonies can even be seen to play a precursory role: in 1912—the same year that the British Board of Film Censors was created—Mauritius and certain colonies in Southern and East Africa, as well as French establishments in Oceania, adopted censorship. This underlines the continuity and circulation of regulations, and their relative chronologies. In Oceania's French colonies, all films 'including scenes of theft, burglary, and murder scenes that take place in contemporary settings and that are not directly related to a historic or mythological episode' were banned.[35] A local censorship board was created in 1917, two years after the introduction of a *visa d'exploitation* (film distribution certificate) in France. Oceania's distance and the significant number of American films screened there explain this early measure. Other territories followed suit: Madagascar in 1920, where four towns set up boards, then Cameroon (Yaoundé and Douala) and the French establishments of India in 1929, followed by French Guiana in 1930. It is interesting to note these boards' municipal character and their assertion of their autonomy, a decentralization of censorship that was found nowhere else, not even at a later date.

Along with Southern Africa, the Gold Coast, where censorship was introduced between 1925 and 1929, stood out as a model. Mention has already been made of the Gold Coast's social and cultural dynamism, its entrepreneurial spirit, the openness of its urban populations, and its governor's proactive policies. As film imports soared, Guggisberg instigated a policy in line with his educational programme, which was concretized by the creation of an ambitious teaching institution: the Prince of Wales College. The College's objective was to train a modern elite, with an eye on self-government. Quality cinema was incorporated into this educational policy. The Ghanaian intellectual elite was fully involved with this control thanks to their participation in the Board created in 1925. Over the years, legislation was modified to ensure the Board's effective functioning, but early ambitions regarding the frequency of its meetings, the number of its members, and their representation of a range of groups were soon abandoned. The Board was characterized by the prominence of its civil servant and teacher members, and by the role of African dignitaries, all of whom were formed in the same educational mould.

In 1927, the Board was composed of sixteen members, with the majority missionaries and dignitaries, around one-third civil servants, and a few teachers in addition—including a woman teacher, whose presence was explicitly requested. It was reduced to five members in 1932: three civil servants and two African dignitaries. Based in Accra, the sole place where films were authorized to enter the country, the Board of Control examined all requests, theoretically submitted by the distributors at least six working days before a screening—which implied a costly immobilization of the films—then issued a written notification, without having to justify its decision.

The Gold Coast's policy, which was singular at the time, later became routine and continued to give Africans a central role in the process. It may be noted, however, that they simply reinforced the censorship of films destined for working class viewers, the censors' concern focusing above all on 'property crime and gun violence' (McFeely 2015: 106). In 1929, before it became obligatory in 1931, film posters were added to the Board's jurisdiction. This extension of their authority to the still images that were exhibited in the streets—and thus visible to passers-by of all ages and conditions—demonstrates the power that images were seen to have.

Faced with other territories' inertia, and on the recommendation of the Colonial Films Committee, in 1931 the Colonial Office proposed a centralized censorship operated from London. It soon abandoned this idea after protest from the colonies, which gradually adopted their own censorship mechanisms—in 1933 in Nigeria, for example. Local expertise was thus defended; the importance of this was asserted in FWA, too, but overarching regulation was soon implemented there.

'Preserving national mores and traditions'

Referring to the 1934 Laval Decree, pioneering West African filmmaker Paulin Vieyra mused: 'Did the advent of the talkies give the French authorities a scare? Silent cinema enjoyed a freedom that was soon to be questioned in Africa by the change of policy in France' (Vieyra 1958a: 109). Vieyra highlights a changing era characterized by technological advances, the spread of cinema, and the realization of moving images' potential impact. The fear of losing control applied to all aspects of cinema, from the content of films to advertising, distribution circuits, screening venues, and their environments. Resituated in its original context, however, the March 1934 decree might be understood from another angle, namely as the fruit of efforts made by a colonial lobby frustrated at not having obtained real visibility in metropolitan censorship boards. Unable to assert enough influence at the centre, this lobby imposed specific regulation in France's overseas territories. The recognition of a colonial specificity was combined here with a federal logic. The Laval Decree also reflected the desire to unify an embryonic regulatory judicial framework. The standardization of measures after rulings had been issued locally, or the extension of a common decree were indeed frequent procedures in FWA.

Before 1934, regulation concerned entertainment venues and not film activity itself, which theoretically came under rulings concerning the press. The 1932 enquiry demonstrated that the Ministry of Colonies only had a vague idea of the 'acts regulating the screening and control of films and the obligations imposed on film operators'.[36] While regulation was rare, it was not difficult to control cinemas, as they were easily monitored microcosms. The governor of French Equatorial Africa thus asserted in 1934 that no film, be it from Hollywood or elsewhere, could escape the authorities, as only one cinema screened talkies (Martin 1995: 122). His remark applied to the majority of towns in the region.

The 1934 decree put an end to debates on a 'film policy in the colonies'. It was adopted when Pierre Laval, later famous for his prominent role in Pétain's Vichy Regime, was Minister of Colonies, although it was the result of ongoing reflections as well as new concerns arising from the belief that 'a film shot with no particular reason for concern in the metropolis may be damaging in our colonial possessions'.[37] As a result, instances arose where films that were authorized in the metropolis were banned overseas, provoking protest on the part of entrepreneurs who had imported them at great cost. From 1925 to 1931, various suggestions were made to include colonial civil servants in metropolitan censorship boards, which nonetheless did not satisfy the Ministry of Colonies. The only solution was thus to adopt legislation specific to the Empire, which, for French West Africa, took the concrete form of the 8 March 1934 decree, a founding act that was a constant point of reference henceforth, in similar fashion to the 1925 Gold Coast legislation in Britain's various territories in Africa.

The decree, which oversaw the control of cinema films, phonographic records, cinematographic shooting, and sound recordings in FWA, was directly inspired by the 1928 French law. It was extended to French Equatorial Africa in November 1934, and marked a break with former practices by introducing specific, locally granted visas for FWA: 'No cinema film can be screened in public in French West Africa unless the film, its title and its subtitles have obtained a distribution certificate from the lieutenant-governor of the Colony in which the screening is to take place.'[38]

Distribution certificates were granted by a board set up in the main city of each colony and in Dakar, the capital of the Federation of French West Africa, to 'examine the booklet or screenplays, posters, programmes and, where possible, the films themselves.'[39] Decisions were made immediately on inspection of the screenplay, or within three days if a film was screened. The board was required to roughly indicate the passages that it had censored in its minutes, and the colonial authorities validated the list of films authorized. This local distribution certificate was granted in addition to the metropolitan one; it was a second level of censorship, designed to take into account the considerations specific to each colony. In addition to this, district officers could always ban a film in the name of 'local police measures', as specified in Article 11.[40] In the event of an infraction, Article 12 stipulated that fines and penalties were applicable, the ultimate risk being the closure of the establishment concerned.

The woolly formulation of the decree demonstrates that the aim was above all to provide a general framework. Making a ruling on screened films within a maximum of three days was unrealistic, for example, as films were rarely programmed for more than a few days. Moreover, various key elements were not regulated, starting with the composition of the boards themselves. In reality, few were actually set up. Instead, a board was immediately created in Dakar, the films' point of entry; its rulings were authoritative, even beyond the Federation of French West Africa.

The decree was applied most concertedly in the French Sudan and Togo, colonies whose interest in cinema was made manifest by their swift response to the 1932 survey. Their boards comprised administrative officials (representatives of the governor, the police, or the security forces), and sometimes a spokesperson from the trading world. Local dignitaries did not participate, contrary to common practice in the Gold Coast. The French Sudan's reports are available for most of 1936. Its board, which met once a week, was composed of the head of the political bureau, the head of the security service, the head of customs, and a delegate from the Chamber of Commerce. The sessions soon took on a routine format, without any real debates taking place. From July to November 1936, the conclusions of the board's succinct reports repeat the same formula, only altering the names of the films and cinemas concerned: 'The said posters and programmes do not display a tendentious or subversive character that would make it necessary to ban or censor the films to which they refer.'[41]

No bans were imposed, therefore, and the head of the colony simply approved the list submitted to him. The reports reveal more about the films screened, their turnover, their screening venues, and the administrative practices resulting from the decree than about censorship itself. The board gave its verdict after 'examining the posters and schedules', without screening equipment and certainly without the facilities to cut scenes.[42] The only solution—rarely adopted—if suspicions were universally shared was an outright ban. It often happened that the board met on the very day of the screening or on the day after the first showing, when certain spectators had already seen the offending film. Naturally, the decision to ban a film could still be taken if unruly reactions were reported in cinemas; in such an event, the censorship became overt. In some cases, the documentation necessary to review the films was unavailable. In this event, the board would turn to the federal authorities, as in the following instance: 'The film *Les Deux Mondes*, which was approved for screening in Dakar, but whose poster has not reached Bamako, can be screened by Mr Petit with no problem.'[43]

Indeed, films came with the Dakar censorship board's ruling attached, which colonies with no board of their own followed. The competence of this board's members—overworked civil servants and voluntary traders—and their knowledge of film, isolated as they were in Africa, may of course be questioned. Their qualifications did not make them moral authorities or cultural experts, but were more a reflection of the association of censorship with public order, and of stereotypes about these professions. The situation was the same elsewhere—for example in Zanzibar, where police officers, disinterested in controlling films, were replaced in 1924 by a board comprising civil servants, two Indians, and an Arab, but no representatives of the African population (Reinwald 2006: 97).

Despite the lack of sources, analysing the ways in which early censorship measures were applied highlights certain qualities that were to endure: improvisation, tight deadlines, and a shortage of equipment, but also arbitrary decisions that resulted from vague criteria or incompetence due to lack of expertise. The main goal of these censorship boards was to stop cinemas from screening films that might compromise the colonial project. But what guidelines or models did they employ to achieve this? How did they operate at a time when moving images were transitioning from silent films to talkies, radically modifying the relationship between words and gestures? While it is possible to imagine the board meetings held in offices of the secretariat general by studying their materials and the minutes of certain sessions, it is hard to penetrate the minds of the censors to grasp their motivations and decisions, and all the more difficult to get a sense of how audiences received films.

In Europe, censorship boards were suggested, or even organized, by the film industry itself—in Britain in 1912 and in France in 1919, for example—in order to avoid arbitrary local bans. The establishment of their criteria was laborious, however. The board in London only received two instructions at the time of its creation: 'no representations of Christ, no nudity'. However, more and more stipulations were added: there were twenty-two in 1914, forty-three in 1917, and more again in 1926. These covered the areas of religion, politics, the army, society, sexuality, crime, and cruelty. Preventing violence and preserving morality were at the heart of the apparatus (Low 1997; Phelps 1975; Robertson 1985, 1993). In France, very vague instructions were drawn up in 1928, a decade after the adoption of film distribution certificates: 'The board takes into consideration the ensemble of national interests at stake, particularly in the interest of preserving national mores and traditions.'[44] This formulation was repeated word for word in the 1934 Laval Decree, which simply added the term 'local'. According to its Article 4, then, the board 'takes into consideration the ensemble of national and local interests at stake, particularly in the interest of preserving national and local mores and traditions.' The mimicry is telling.

From one country to the next, similar fears prompted similar reactions on the part of those who positioned themselves as the defenders of each nation's values. Grounds for censorship in France echoed those in Britain and elsewhere: 'The scenes that are most readily cut in France are love scenes border-ing on licentiousness, scenes of drunkenness or fights, and those that display human vices, such as a penchant for drugs' (Villers 1930: 77).

These measures were reinforced by the film industry itself under the pres-sure of interest groups, the best example being the 1930 Hays Code in the United States. This extremely fastidious code designated contentious areas under twelve headings: sex, violence and crime, attacks on religion, repre-sentations of foreign countries, and so forth. Parallel to this, Christian authorities organized the Catholic Cinematographic Committee (CCC) in France in 1927, and the International Catholic Organization for Cinema (OCIC) in 1928, while the Vatican warned believers of the evils of film in the 1929 encyclical *Divini illius magistri*, and particularly emphatically in the 1936 encyclical *Vigilanti cura*. The latter recognized the ambivalent nature of cinema, deeming it capable of 'promoting good and insinuating evil', but insisted on its negative influence upon the weak especially, adopt-ing alarmist terms to hammer home the message that cinema's mission must be absolutely moral:

> We are increasingly anxious, as every day we witness the regrettable progression ... of representations of sin and vice ...; running a grave danger to populations' prestige and power ...; the destruction of the moral fibre of a nation ...; an instru-ment of depravation and demoralization ...; a terrible massacring of young people and children's minds (quoted in Lagrée 1996: 848).

In the colonial context, the fight against criminality and immorality was clearly echoed. Many theories had developed in Europe, backed up by studies carried out in metropolitan prisons, which proposed a direct link between films and delinquency, the decline of traditional values, and sexual violence. The same ideas took hold overseas. In the Gold Coast, consequently, it was stated that: 'consideration has to be given to the impression likely to be made on an average audience which includes a not inconsiderable proportion of people of immature judgement'.[45] Within the populations concerned, a divide often emerged between elites quick to adopt the authorities' paternalistic and moralizing discourse, and the viewers whom they sought to control.

It was not so much a case of censorship per se, then, but more often of censors who were informed as much by their own prejudices as by directives issued by the administrative or religious authorities. In such conditions, was censorship truly a matter of common sense, as Governor Guggisberg sug-gested? Most likely not, considering his request that 'the members of the vari-ous boards ... bear in mind that what may not be harmful, but merely disgusting or silly to a European, may be quite the contrary to the half-educated and to the illiterate communities of the African race'.[46]

Although colonizers developed discourses concerning Africans' intellectual ability to watch images, they rarely sought to understand audiences' reactions to films. The things that spectators laugh at, for example, as well as the emotion, discomfort, or surprise that this laughter can hide, can only be understood by taking specific cultural and individual factors into account. The following statement, made much later by a colonial administrator in Bangui in 1953, is enlightening in this respect:

> Once a year, a cigarette brand arranged an advertising campaign by putting on a film screening that we, all populations together, attended with pleasure. The films screened all dated to before the war and reflected the mores of that era. I remember one film, which I believe was called *Émilienne*, whose title song was on everybody's lips at the time. One of the main scenes was set in a chic cabaret, where men with brilliantined hair, dinner jackets and top hats courted dreamlike women. On stage, dancers dressed scantily in just white feather tutus danced energetically. At that point, thunderous laughter shook the whole theatre. People slapped their thighs; some even fell about on the floor laughing. I didn't understand the cause of this excessive hilarity. I called over to the interpreter: 'What's the meaning of this?' 'The villagers are laughing because they've seen that women in your country also wear feathers up their arses. You never told us!' (Bourgeois 1997).

The administrator's astonishment at people laughing was only surpassed by that of the audience, who thought the dancers' feather costumes were everyday clothing. The signification of this outfit, perceived by the audience as akin to the leaves that women in Central Africa sometimes wore, was manifestly not the same for everyone. What was true of laughter was also true of other culturally rooted expressions, of course: gestures, cries, protests, or even commotion in the cinema.

Examples of censorship include the 1927 screening in Mauritius of *Le Costaud des Épinettes*, a 1923 French film set in Paris, which, according to the censorship board, was 'nothing but a succession of thefts, knife fights, immoral dances, drunkenness and vice'; it was therefore banned.[47] Apparently harmless comedies did not escape this vigilance. In the Belgian Congo, the authorities were concerned about the impact of a scene in which Charlie Chaplin thrashes a policeman, undermining a figure of European authority (Ramirez and Rolot 1985: 273).[48] A 1931 British report requested the censoring of films in which white people appeared abject in the eyes of the 'natives or coloured races', and those in which they brutalized indigenous peoples.[49] The report cited two films which illustrated this: *Atlantis*, in which a ship captain shoots at a fleeing sailor, and Walter Futter's *Africa Speaks!*, a famous 1930 safari film set in Central Africa and dramatizing the story of the explorer Paul L. Hoefler, in which a native assistant's death is filmed as he is eaten by a lion.

In not conveying an idealized image of western societies, films necessarily offered alternative visions of white people even after they had been cut, and it was in this that they were considered a threat to colonial domination. They modified representations of the colonizers, hitherto limited to a few live specimens: administrators, doctors, traders, wives, or missionaries. The power of images therefore undermined colonial discourse. The fear that deviant western behaviour would be imitated also took on a specific dimension in the colonial context. Vices such as drunkenness, pornography, or fighting, which were considered morally unacceptable in the metropolis, were even more feared in the colonies, where they exposed the hidden realities of the colonizers and risked provoking uncontrollable outbursts that could lead to the contestation of colonial domination itself. Scenes of debauchery or criminal acts challenged the foundations of colonial ideology and destroyed its principles: they were the very antithesis of the civilizing mission. The title of an article by Henry Hesketh Bell, a leading member of the Board of Control—'Danger to White Prestige'—reflects this sense of threat. Colonial society attempted both to eliminate elements that did not conform to the ideals it preached, including tramps, alcoholics, adventurers, or prostitutes—individuals who were the living negation of white superiority—and to eliminate any white person incarnating negative values on cinema screens.[50]

In practice, however, the authorities contented themselves with reacting to individual cases when problems transpired, as the rare police sources confirm. It was not until after the Second World War that censorship really became active, in a context of political upheaval. By then, the more numerous and socially diverse spectators did not hesitate to express their shock at certain cinemetic images, which were not necessarily those that the authorities anticipated. The situation had profoundly changed.

Finally, it must be pointed out that two very different contexts for censorship can be distinguished. On the one hand, there were colonies that separated screening venues according to the population and thus the range of films screened, namely the so-called 'settler colonies', where a number of Europeans and their descendants lived, and the towns of the Belgian Congo, where cinemas were reserved for Europeans and the presence of a few 'educated natives' was tolerated. On the other hand—as was the case in FWA—there were those where there was no discrimination in accessing cinemas and the same censorship applied to everyone, whatever their status (citizen or colonial subject), their living standard, or their level of education.[51] Here, the programmes were the same for all, whether spectators were seated on wooden benches or seats, in a courtyard or a cinema, and whatever the ticket price. In this context, it is thus difficult to determine which groups were specifically targeted by censorship: the literate minority or the general mass of spectators.

3

MOBILE CINEMA AND TRAVELLING
ENTREPRENEURS

CINEMA IN THE VILLAGE (THE EARLY 1900s TO THE 1950s)

Twenty years ago, film was regarded primarily as an entertainment medium. Desirous of using every available opportunity to assist their audiences to develop, film workers amongst backward peoples began to appreciate that film could play a more positive role than that of amusement.

(UNESCO, *The Use of Mobile Cinema and Radio Vans in
Fundamental Education*, 1949).

When UNESCO published *The Use of Mobile Cinema and Radio Vans in Fundamental Education* in 1949, a veritable instruction manual for mobile cinema, this practice was already well-established. Based on the illiteracy of over half the world's population, UNESCO advocated the extensive use of mobile cinema as a means of visually broadcasting information. The onus was placed on film's potential as a source of education—and, in the colonial situation, of propaganda—although the boundaries between governmental or missionary initiatives and commercial circuits were hazy. A cartoon might well be screened before a documentary on hygiene, or a film promoting the Empire might open a western night. At an educational screening in the Gold Coast, for example, the film was followed by a programme of songs and drama, a lecture, and the distribution of literature—all of which lasted from an hour to an hour and a half (UNESCO 1949: 78). Moreover, the processes and constraints of organizing screenings were the same, whether they were commercial or governmental enterprises. The advice given was thus relevant to private entrepreneurs, too: to use an equipped truck, which was less expensive, lighter, and more flexible than a purpose-built van; to plan for journeys of several thousand kilometres; to anticipate several months of self-sufficiency; and to hire staff who were capable of handling the inevitable mechanical failures along the way.

The 1950s saw a rise in the popularity of mobile cinema for both pedagogical and recreational purposes, yet mobile cinema had a much longer history, going back to the war years. It is worth looking more closely at its development and transformations over time. While commercial circuits were numerous in the French colonies, they were not particularly active in the Belgian or British territories (McFeely 2015). There, public intervention was favoured, while the use of cinema for propaganda or for educational purposes came later in French West Africa (FWA).

Early mobile cinema (the early 1900s to the 1930s)

Travelling film shows were contemporary to the spread of cinema, and could even be viewed as inherent to this new leisure activity at its outset. Before permanent installations or regular screenings were introduced, improvisation was the norm, and depended on the passing through of someone with a projector and films. Without giving further details, Jean Rouch mentions screenings 'as early as 1905, during which mobile cinemas screened moving images in Dakar and its vicinity' (Rouch 1962b: 10).

Amadou Hampâté Bâ clearly recalls his first experience of cinema, which took place in 1908 when 'a European came to Bandiagara to screen a film'. His account recalls an event that had taken place fifty years earlier, but the 'shadow spitting' machine clearly made an impression on the Malian child: 'I can't really remember the first film I saw, but I do perfectly remember the first screening that took place in my village' (Bâ 1967: 9). The show was imposed by the district officer, a '"White man" [who] not only wanted to show believers ungodly images, but also wanted to make them pay'. This travelling entrepreneur appears to have been a trailblazer in this remote spot at the turn of the twentieth century, but other sources testify to the rapid commercial circulation of the new media: 'Black folks adore distractions; the cinematograph, taken around the colony [Senegal] by an ingenious industrialist, draws crowds in the bush and towns alike' (D'Anfreville de la Salle 1912: 32).

These early ad hoc screenings were soon replaced by more systematic or organized tours. Many spectators had their first experience of cinema thanks to the visit of a travelling projectionist, known as a *tourneur* ('tourer') in reference to their tour circuits. Doctor Gabriel Sultan, a Guinean born in 1917, nostalgically described an episode from the mid-1920s; he recalled the projectionist arriving, like a travelling salesman, by train in the small town of Mamou, a station on the Conakry–Kankan line, with his 'machine', reels of film, generator, and folding chairs (interview, Conakry 2005). All this equipment necessitated the hire of an entire train carriage. The entrepreneur set up in a depot in the market. Sheeting fixed along the sides made it dark enough, while also shutting out fraudsters. The show, whose ticket prices were low, above all targeted schoolchildren. Local musicians were enlisted to play: drummers and balafon players attracted clients, and provided entertainment while they waited for the screening and during the inevitable changing and rewinding of reels. A film of about an hour comprised more than a dozen reels. Can we deduce that silent films were screened to the accompaniment of Malinke music? That a commentator explained the action? While Doctor Sultan managed to recreate the atmosphere in a lively way, he, just like Bâ, could not remember the first images he saw. Kamian Bakary, born in a Malian village in 1926, did for his part recall the passing through of a mobile cinema when he was about ten years old and the names of Fernandel and Josephine Baker, which is completely plausible (interview, Ouagadougou 2008).

While screenings made use of existing infrastructures, such as markets and public buildings, or took place outdoors using screens hung in café courtyards and squares or on beaches, one must imagine the perilous conditions in which journeying took place: break-downs occurred while transporting the equipment; climatic hazards affected the film stock; and electricity was scarce. Little is known about the first projectionists, who worked at a time when the cinema industry was less controlled and the trade was very new. In the 1920s, a certain Bertrand is reported to have been the first to travel around Ivory Coast, with a highly rudimentary set-up. He and another travelling projectionist named Rappet are reported to have had quite some success in 1931–32. Screenings took off not only in the two successive capitals—Grand-Bassam and Abidjan—but also inland in Guiglo, Daloa, Dabou, Tiassalé, Agboville, Grand-Lahou, Dimbokro, Korhogo, and Abengourou (Retord 1986: 15; Kipré 1985: 183).

These one-off screenings left little trace. Bernard Dadié (1916–2019) evoked them in his autobiographical novel *Climbié*, set in Grand-Bassam in the early 1930s:

One morning, the 'cinema' came to town on a truck. The news spread immediately through the living quarters and the shopping area. The nights the movies were shown were indeed like holidays. To draw the crowd, musicians were hired, and since they were entitled to free seats for the performance, they played the role of beater with gusto. The performances took place either in the public market place, or on the sand in the French quarter at the intersection of Commandant Pineau Street and Bouvet Street. ... Everywhere round about, sly fellows perched in trees or stood on barrels to see the film (Dadié 1971: 38–39).

The arrival of the mobile cinema brought much excitement and an atmosphere of festivity to the city, with musicians roaming the streets to advertise the shows and the public space occupied by this night-time activity.

The economic crisis nonetheless affected the screenings, as the audience, made up predominantly of domestic staff and small traders who liked comedies and westerns, had limited financial means. In Sierra Leone, for example, the tours organized by the Freetown-based Lisk-Carew Brothers (see Chapter 1) were compromised by the economic downturn:

Business was so bad that when Lisk-Carew, who used to tour the Protectorate holding film-shows, held his first film-show in Bonthe in 1930, he was forced to reduce his charges from five shillings for gents and two shillings and sixpence for ladies, to three shillings and one shilling respectively, and even though this included entrance to a dance to be held after the show, hardly anyone turned up (Anthony 1980: 50).

Lisk-Carew struggled to attract clients in what was one of the country's biggest port towns, even by dropping prices and putting on a dance.

Despite these difficulties, cinema, by now culturally entrenched, continued to grow. Still exceptional and highly popular, a mobile cinema's arrival in town was a celebratory moment. The entire population's participation, the role of the musicians, and the centrality of the venues chosen all made it a major event in local life. This enthusiasm, albeit ephemeral, did not escape the authorities' attention. Suspicious of these cinematic circulations, they increasingly sought to control the travelling projectionists and their activity as the practice took root and requests for authorization rose. Nonetheless, contrary to the misguided preconceptions of entrepreneurs who saw Africa as an easy terrain to invest in, travel difficulties were real, as were multiple administrative hurdles. Little is known about these interwar adventurers, whom the archives mention only sporadically. One example was the Swiss citizen Eric Rehsteiner, who, with a Belgian associate in 1934, submitted an ambitious project to the colonial authorities concerning both the English and the French colonies in a large part of West Africa:

An itinerant cinematographic tour starting in Dakar and travelling through the colonies of French West Africa, the Gold Coast and Nigeria. We shall stop for two to three days in each town or large village, putting on a show for the Europeans and the natives. It goes without saying that the programme will be of general interest and morally correct (news, comedies, popular entertainment), and which we shall willingly submit to the censors if need be.[1]

To prove his seriousness, the entrepreneur mentioned having been in Africa for seven years; his expertise did not reside in his cinematographic or technical proficiency, then, but in his knowledge of the African milieu. He voiced concern at the conditions of organizing tours in FWA, whose red tape had probably discouraged many. This project, like many others, did not materialize, but some entrepreneurs who were more realistic or already locally established managed to develop mobile cinema shows.

One man in particular did make a name for himself in FWA: Raymond Borremans (1906–88), who started to operate in 1937. Having left Europe in 1929, this self-educated roamer and musician settled in Ivory Coast in about 1934. His 1936 encounter with one Mr Eraud, an electrical equipment entrepreneur, resulted in a collaboration: Eraud provided the equipment, including a Peugeot van with a generator, a 16mm projector and a stock of films; Borremans provided his know-how and labour. This initiative was the start of a long career that ended in 1974. However, Borremans only left a limited trace of his activity.[2] His passion lay elsewhere: in gathering the necessary information to write an encyclopaedia based on his journeys through Ivory Coast, Mali, Senegal, and Guinea. A few archives, photographs, and surveys, and above all an account recorded in 1985, tell us about his work. This rare source is worth citing. Borremans appears, in an already competitive field, to have found his initial success due to his technical skills: 'I wasn't the only mobile cinema touring, but my film shows were very successful because I never broke down. I only held one intermission for changing the reels; I worked with two 1500m reels, each of which represented about three hours screening in total.'[3]

That meant viewing and scrupulously splicing together the films before each show, because the copies were often in very poor condition. Borremans also gives us an idea of the behaviour of audiences new to cinema:

The reaction of village audiences in 1937–38 was always the same: the simple slamming of a door always triggered the same reaction, wherever. At the start of the show, folks, who were often watching a screening for the first time, sat facing the projector. In the intermission, they would go to look behind the screen to try to understand how this mystery worked …

73

This reaction was hardly surprising, given how rarely film shows were held in villages. Everything was new, from the machinery and the technology to the images. Nonetheless, Borremans points out that spectators were demanding, requesting in-focus images and audible sound:

> I began cutting the darkest moments of the film and those where the sound was too low; the audience did not like the screen to be dark, nor whispering in the dialogues. Too bad if the comprehension of the film was affected ... It seemed that the audience wanted the intensity of the light and sound to be maintained—that is, constant action, and thus solicitation—for the duration of the show.

Borremans thus adapted the reels with the means available to him, according to his perception of the audience's reaction. Audiences thus contributed to the screening conditions, which were created in accordance with their criteria. They did not, however, have a say in the film screened. Borremans, as he recounts it, took on the role of censor:

> For a long time, I refused to show westerns, because I thought that they were a bad way to educate the audience, showing too much violence. But my competitors did not share this same scruple and I was losing clients. So, in 1946, after the war when I started touring again, I decided to give in to the fad.

Due to a petrol shortage, Borremans interrupted his tours in 1940, but he remained in the business from 1943 to 1946 as the manager of two cinemas in Abidjan—the Super Vox and the Club—where he improved his skills. But more of him, and his return to the road, later.

Mobile cinema vans and cultural centres: the authorities' growing involvement in cinema (the 1930s to the 1950s)

Parallel to private entrepreneurs, colonial administrators began organizing mobile film screenings in a bid to reach as many colonial subjects as possible outside the main towns. These screenings played a role in introducing people to cinema, even if for most spectators they were a one-off occasion. The authorities' screenings were organized in schools, where a screen was set up, in administrative buildings and cultural centres, or outdoors. Given the rarity of new distractions, the public flocked to the screenings, but they did not necessarily respect the categories devised by the authorities. In Senegal, for example, where one tour was specifically designed for young people, 'it was difficult to limit the number of spectators in places where there is no cinema and where people know the show is free.'[4] Spectators thus imposed their own will.

Public screenings were held in all the colonies, but they were most common in the British territories, followed by the Belgian Congo. They were part of a wider rhetoric about colonial audiences and particularly Africans, who, it was believed, required films corresponding to their intellectual capacity and cultural specificities (see Chapter 2). Colonial authorities thus thought it necessary to produce both documentary and fiction films, and to organize a circuit to distribute them. This was first put into practice in Central Africa in 1935, with film distribution in mining camps. Organized by the BEKE (Bantu Educational Kinema Experiment), a body funded by the International Missionary Council, the Carnegie Foundation, and the Colonial Office, this has been the object of a number of previous studies (Ambler 2004; Burns 2002b; Reynolds 2015; Smyth 1983a, 1983b, 1989). Major Leslie Allen Notcutt and Geoffrey Latham made films within this framework, but it ceased activity in 1937. World War Two rekindled an interest in film propaganda, leading to the creation in 1939 of the Colonial Film Unit (CFU), a metropolitan film production body that aimed first and foremost to promote the war effort. Branches of the CFU were then opened in each territory, with about twelve local branches operating in eight colonies between 1945 and 1950. Its journal, *Colonial Cinema*, devoted several articles to the mobile cinema: 'The Mobile Cinema Van in the Villages (contributed by an African)' (1945), 'The Mobile Cinema Van is a New Weapon in Mass Education' (1949), and 'Mobile Cinema Shows in Africa' (1951).

With its branch of the CFU run by the doctor William Sellers, Nigeria was a forerunner in this domain. Convinced of the power of images, Sellers produced and screened hygienist documentaries in the north (see Chapter 2). He popularized simplistic film codes, the premises of which were condescending and even racist: simple narratives, easy-to-follow action, linear plots, overbearing moralism, and clear, direct shooting (Burns 2002b). The paternalistic moralism of these films marked the experiences of the first generations of spectators (Larkin 2008). UNESCO's discourse was hardly any different in 1949. The same prejudices were found, confusing illiteracy with lack of intelligence, which, it was believed, required adapting films to 'backward peoples' and 'unsophisticated minds', expressions that were recurrent in *The Use of Mobile Cinema*. In the vast territory of Nigeria, where only four vans were in circulation in 1948, film shows drew 2,000 people on average, and at times the astonishing number of 15,000. The network later expanded.

Mobile cinema practice took on another meaning in the south-west of the country when the political context changed. By the early 1950s, Chief

Obafemi Awolowo, the Yoruba leader of the Action Group and first prime minister of the West Region's local government from 1954 to 1959, used mobile cinema screenings to promote his education policy. He concluded a deal with the Marconi firm, which provided technical aid and programmes—prominently featuring westerns—before films in Yoruba were available. Awolowo was the first leader in West Africa to found a television channel in 1959, using the power of images to build a sentiment of regional and national unity.[5]

In Ghana, mobile cinemas of course showed films produced by the local CFU, but they screened comic short films too, which were often cut by the censors. Scenes that were considered incongruous in an African context were also cut (such as snow scenes, or scenes featuring a dentist's chair), as well as those that mocked the authorities, police, or clergy. During the war, in a bid to boost the war effort, newsreels were used to emphasise connections with local soldiers sent to fight far away in Asia. Film shows were free, or at least very cheap, to attract the public. They were a mix of propaganda, education, and entertainment. One Ghanaian's description of a show in early 1945 gives an indication of the atmosphere that ensued when the mobile cinema van pulled up. In its tow was a machine for cracking palm nuts and a mobile Post Office and savings bank. Directly addressing his readers, the author writes:

> Now those of you who live in a town like Accra are accustomed to cinema shows. You pay your money, you sit down and relax, and the show begins. The operator has no more arranging to do than to fit the film into the projecting apparatus and press a switch. But a cinema show out in the 'bush' is quite a different matter. Do you know what happens in the villages, when the van arrives?[6]

He goes on to describe the Fanti villagers' fear on seeing a policeman guarding the post van, their questions concerning the use of the machine, and their surprise on hearing the wireless broadcasting in different languages (Hausa, Twi, Ewe). Spectators nonetheless had to wait a long time before seeing *Charlie the Rascal*, the comedy which was to be the climax of the evening:

> Gradually it becomes dark. The cinema performance will soon begin. The screen is fixed. Regimental marches are played and the amplifier makes them echo through the village. When the music stops, a speech is made by the interpreter on the urgent need for the people to practice saving. And then the cinema operator starts his part of the show. Newsreel films are seen, and there is a series of pictures about the palm-kernel drive in the Gold Coast. They were filmed by the Cinema Office of the Gold Coast.

And no village audience is satisfied until, at the end, they see some comic film, such as *Charlie the Rascal*. I often wonder if Charlie Chaplin knows how many ardent fans he has in the Gold Coast.[7]

It was thus only after being subjected to a postal savings promotion film and a documentary about palm-kernels that the villagers were able to enjoy Charlie Chaplin.

The writer also transcribes certain spectator dialogues—more of them about the newsreels than the feature film—and the chief's thanks for this screening, which recalled the previous year's and looked forward to the next. This mobile cinema van did not travel the whole country, as there were only four vans in circulation in 1945, but news travelled by word of mouth. In 1947, the chief of the Tongu Confederacy, created in south-east Ghana's Ewe zone in 1945, begged the government to equip his little town, Volo, with a 'static cinema'. He noted that his subjects had 'not yet realised the importance of the Mobile Cinema Vans because we all live along the Volta River and there is no motor road in our district except the Launch'.[8]

Building the road necessary for its passage was a lot to ask for the sake of mobile cinema, but this request clearly shows widespread demand. Geographically speaking, access was of course uneven, but it was developing: viewership was estimated at approximately 3.5 million spectators across 12,281 localities between 1949 and 1955.[9] In 1957, Ghana had about twenty vans in operation, evidence of a dynamic policy. Other changes took place in the 1950s. Under the leadership of Sean Graham from 1948 to 1957, the CFU produced films that moved away from the stereotype of intellectually limited Africans. At the same time, an effort was made to train local technicians, although screenplays were still always written by Europeans. This evolution reflected new attitudes which were also expressed in a 1952 study by British anthropologist Peter Morton-Williams, who refuted the essentialist racial vision of Sellers and insisted on the need to take local cultures and circumstances into account in order to make cinema's message more effective (Blaylock 2011).

While information is available concerning the practical organization of mobile cinema and the colonial discourses that surrounded it, information about audience reactions and the impact of these tours only materializes through snippets, such as the account cited above, that more often than not constitute counter-sources. The central CFU, which until Independence remained characterized by paternalist perceptions and a blanket approach to all audiences, sought to control representation and to create modes of screening that were identical throughout the colonies, calibrating their duration, standardizing the content of screenings, and giving strict guidelines to commentators who spoke vernacular languages. In so doing, it dismissed the reactions of the spectators about whom it knew so little, their interactions with organizers, and, notably, the involvement of African intermediaries who played an increasing role in the 1950s, but whom the authorities did not know how to control due to lack of funds and linguistic incompetence.

There was, however, a clear conflict between the CFU's project to make films and shows adapted to an African audience and their profound lack of knowledge of local cultures. Sitting children at the front of screenings, for example, often accompanied by their mothers, seemed to be a strictly pragmatic measure when it in fact carried strong social connotations and in certain regions provoked the opposition of the male population. More fundamentally still, certain signs revealed underlying tensions that the authorities tried to anticipate, as indicated by a situation described in 1943:

> The report explained that a lamp had been fitted to the screen 'to reduce any slight tendency to friction in audiences'. Isolated trouble makers ... are thus exposed to the general gaze and come under the censure, unmistakably expressed, of the main body of the audience (Rice 2016: 381).

This apparently innocuous measure speaks volumes about the way in which spectators took advantage of the darkness to express themselves freely; a mark of defiance that the authorities attributed to a handful of rebels who would be called to order by their compatriots.

The reality, however, was often very different. The authorities soon became aware of the ambivalence and impact of shows held at night. More than the film, it was the screening itself that needed to be controlled, which compromised the growing autonomy that the authorities sought to grant colonial subjects in the 1950s. This was particularly clear in Kenya where, in the context of the Mau Mau uprising, all gatherings were considered dangerous, film shows included (Rice 2016; Ambler 2011). Moreover, the inability to understand commentaries given in local languages inverted power relations and put the colonizers in a paradoxical position of weakness. Intended propaganda sessions transformed into potentially subversive environments. This unforeseen complication destabilized the mechanisms of indoctrination.

In addition to the British colonies, public and parapublic mobile film shows were common in the Belgian Congo, operated by the Information Service and the missionaries. The latter organized screenings in the countryside for audiences of up to 5,000 spectators. They carefully selected films for screening or produced them themselves so as not to take any risks, in keeping with their perception of what was 'good' for Africans. This perception was based on a similar logic to that deployed by the CFU and UNESCO, as described above. Yet over the years spectators became more demanding. Born in 1907, Father Cornil, a government-employed missionary, noted that 'once they have seen films for Europeans, they consider it contemptuous when we offer them mainly films destined for Africans' (*Clergé Africain*, 1957, cited in Ramirez and Rolot 1985: 277). This remark says a lot about the style of the films produced in the Belgian Congo by Cornil, who was one of the colony's most committed film-makers (Convents 2006). Indeed, while audiences were initially limited in their choice of what to watch, access to information and to the cinema itself was growing, thanks to news of the films screened in towns, the rural exodus, links between urban and rural areas, the organization of screenings by mining companies that were hardly concerned with propaganda, and so on.

The same evolution can be observed in the French colonies, where the authorities proposed mobile film shows with two objectives: to educate a larger audience about general questions and, in the 1950s, to steer young people away from Independence campaigns. The screenings organized by the authorities generally drew a lot of spectators. Rarely presented with the opportunity to watch films, people took what was offered, happy for the break from their daily lives. The films' didactic dimension did not preclude their entertainment value: screenings of health or farming documentaries about France and its Empire were often preceded by short comic films to attract the rural populations, or followed by reports on folklore or agriculture. Félix Iroko recalled the mobile cinema's visits once or twice a year during the dry season in his little town of Allada in Dahomey, where he was a primary school pupil in the 1950s. He described seeing documentaries on daily life in Africa. The screenings were free, and attracted a wide audience of all ages and genders, who sat on the ground to watch the films at nightfall.

Bernard Cornut-Gentille, the Governor General of FWA from 1951 to 1956, set up cultural centres which were inspired by his experience in French East Africa, and also became screening venues. In 1955, the centre in Forécariah, a small town in Guinea that had no cinema of its own, rented films (thrillers, westerns, and Egyptian films) from the Vox cinema in Conakry and screened them three times a week, consistently opting for entertainment films.[10] Not able to equip all communities, however, the Social Affairs service organized film tours. In 1954, during a month-long tour of the forest region in south-east Guinea, 38,110 spectators attended travelling film shows.

Audiences, which were varied, had a range of different expectations, affecting the reception of the films. The twenty-five-minute short film *At the Service of the African Farmer*, made by the federal Social Affairs Service to train farm managers, met with a mixed reception. While farmers appeared interested, students demanded films of a different kind: 'Films about Africa are of interest to the uneducated; the educated want films about the rest of the world' (see Chapter 5).[11]

This was the dilemma that cinema faced in the colonies: the more audiences diversified, the more specific tastes emerged. As time passed, contention grew. These different audience responses, which ranged from enthusiasm to criticism, also reflected contrasts between two groups: on the one hand, pupils and students who were home on holiday and frequented the Maisons de Jeunes (youth clubs), which were more autonomous organizations than top-down cultural centres; and on the other, village audiences who were less aware of questions of representation and were above all looking for entertainment.

However, this desire for entertainment did not stop villagers from expressing themselves very clearly if and when images shocked them. The authorities were not very good at anticipating such reactions, which were highly variable from one culture to the next. What went down perfectly well in one region could generate misunderstanding or even rejection elsewhere:

> Of the last batch of films you sent, 'Images of Fulani Country' was generally the most popular. It must be pointed out, however, that when it was screened in Kouroussa, the circumcision scene—a ceremony that is strictly forbidden to women and uninitiated boys in Malinke country—caused quite a furore in the audience, echoes of which reached the Territorial Assembly. I have given instructions for precautions to be taken in the future when films of local interest are shown.[12]

This documentary, made with the backing of the social services, had circulated in Senegal and elsewhere in Guinea without provoking any particular reaction. The local representatives' interpellations, and thus the possibility that the Ministry would be informed, worried the administration in a context of ongoing challenges to colonialism.

Despite their overt political desire to use films to educate and entertain local populations, the overall results for the French Empire, which ultimately devoted few resources to these tours, were limited. Jean Rouch writes of the shortcomings of both their programmes and their equipment. In the late 1950s, Ivory Coast had only a 'beaten-up Power Wagon that was almost definitively inoperative and an old projector belonging to the Cultural Centre, whose usage was fatal to the copies screened' (Rouch 1962a: 24; republished in 1967: 395).

Missionaries also contributed to the spread of cinema (Gangnat et al. 2013). Born in Atar, a small town in Mauritania that had no cinema, film-maker Med Hondo saw his first films at mobile screenings organized by the White Fathers. Conditions were very simple and equipment rudimentary; a sheet and darkness were all that was required. Like others, Hondo remembers not the films themselves, but rather the 'phantasmagoria' of the astonishing discovery of the 'Whites' images' that 'we did not understand at all' (inter-view, Strasbourg 2008). People were intrigued by the technology: 'the chil-dren went behind to see what was there', and invented their own makeshift cinema out of bits and bobs. The colonies in which the authorities' or mis-sionaries' mobile screenings were the most developed were also those where the fewest independent entrepreneurs operated; their demand for images was apparently already satisfied. Yet there was a very fine line between official and private screenings, with travelling entrepreneurs screening both propaganda and fiction films.

From trains to vans: a sharp increase in demand, and the vicissitudes of tours (the 1950s)

Technical advances, yielding lighter equipment, and the—albeit relative—improvement of road infrastructures, along with the demand for modern lei-sure activities, encouraged the travelling entrepreneur trade, especially in FWA. After World War Two, requests to operate mobile cinemas drastically increased, with approximately fifty of them in 1953 alone. The authorities responded to this upsurge with concern, but their vision of an unbridled inva-sion was a reflection more of their obsession with control than of reality:

> An excessive recourse to mobile cinema does not seem to be the case in Guinea, for there are very few enterprises of this kind, and it is indeed one of the reasons why basic education through cinema was a certain success in villages in the bush from the outset.[13]

Such an observation was the norm. In 1960, there appear to have been only ten mobile cinemas, six of which were in Ivory Coast and one in Upper Volta. While there were indeed many such projects, it was rare that they actually came to fruition, for they were often unrealistic, economically fragile, or launched by amateurs with little knowledge of the local situation. The proce-dure was always the same: candidates wrote complex proposals stating their motivations, their financial means, and their civil and moral status (nationality, police record). These applications were then examined. The candidates were reminded of the regulations that were in place, the tax rates, and the need to have the list of films to be screened approved—films which, moreover, had to have a *visa d'exploitation* (film distribution certificate). Sent to Dakar, sometimes accompanied by a recommendation from the Ministry of Colonies, applications would pile up on desks in the colonial offices. Standard replies were usually sent back:

> It is my duty to inform you that, in addition to the number of enterprises of the same nature already in operation in the Federation, an initiative of this kind is likely to involve certain risks for you. For this reason, I hereby request that you send me all the relevant details concerning the means you dispose of to properly carry out this enterprise.[14]

This appears to have been fairly dissuasive. Moreover, when applicants sought to obtain authorization for the whole of FWA, they were informed that they had to file a request with the governor of each territory. Indeed, local authorities conserved the power to ban a film, according to their local situations—pertaining, for example to religious sensibilities or political activism—even though the Dakar censorship board was given a hegemonic role in 1954. This burdensome procedure discouraged multiple applicants.

It is interesting to consider the profiles of the applicants. Some had already practised the profession in France (such as Marcel Feret, who ran a small cinema in northern France, 1954) or in Polynesia (such as Jean Maestrati, a 'travelling filmmaker in Tahiti who ran a canvas cinema', 1956).[15] Others were traders or growers who wanted to diversify their activities. Others still were soldiers in the colonies seeking to change professions thanks to their knowledge of the milieu and their connections.

That was the background of René Lequeux, whom the archives mention several times, although information about his tours is incomplete.[16] Born in 1914, he was a captain in the reserve force who trained in Kati and knew French Sudan well. Arriving from Dakar in August 1948 with a 'van equipped for screening cinematographic films', he lodged in the African quarter of Kayes with a former *tirailleur* (colonial infantryman), Makan Kanté. His movements and activities were watched, as this note indicates: '[he] only took a few meals at the Hôtel Lamé, where he was always seen in the company of Africans.'[17] Close contact with the African population was hardly appreciated by the authorities. Lequeux was stuck at the time, due to the heavy rains, and could not follow his ambitious schedule, which was to take him to Nioro and

Bamako, then to Ivory Coast, Upper Volta, and Dahomey. He did, however, successfully manage this journey the following year, in 1949–50.

He returned to Kayes in 1951, after travelling back to France, where he repaired his equipment. His arrival on 'the express train on 4 October 1951' was noted, as was the fact that he spent the evening at Lebanese tailor Fouad Abiad's house. The company he kept was therefore monitored again, at a time when residential and social separation was the norm, but the report nonetheless concluded that there was 'nothing abnormal to report'. In 1953, his status changed. Under the title of Director of Cultural African Cinema (CINAC), exempted from paying a deposit and directly enjoying the backing of the French Overseas Ministry, he was granted an authorization to tour the entire Federation of French West Africa to 'present documentary films about Metropolitan France and the French Union'. The various lieutenant-governors were told to facilitate his passage, but he, like everyone else, had to follow the law and foot all the costs. Finally, by the late 1950s, he was the head of a permanent cinema in Divo, a small town in Ivory Coast, where his business is said to have been ruined by that of a dynamic entrepreneur, Yacouba Sylla (see below), who transported spectators for free to fill his own newly opened cinema.

Other applicants fell into this trade by chance, or as a result of their life experiences in Africa. One application states that:

> Colonialists in small towns and trade centres totally lack entertainment activities. The cinema ... shows very old films. That of course breaks the monotony a little, and serves as a topic of conversation for a few days. Mobile cinema, showing a few good films, would have been welcome and would still be a real blessing today.[18]

This individual experience of boredom—a kind of inadvertent market survey—thus appears to have motivated the application, which was never followed through. In another instance, a widow in Gao was granted authorization after a very lengthy procedure, but there is no trace of her following activity, which would have been very uncommon at the time for a woman on her own.[19]

The authorities sought to retain control at all levels, monitoring the routes taken, the films screened, and the entrepreneurs themselves, whose profiles were scrutinized, especially those of any non-French entrepreneurs suspected of anti-French intentions. Touring film projectionists had to submit their planned circuit in advance, along with the list of films to be screened, their distribution certificates, and the certified approval of the local censorship board. The authorities were afraid that these projectionists' mobility would make control difficult. A grower from Guinea's forest belt was refused authorization because 'controlling films and policing community halls is practically impossible in the bush'.[20] Local wariness sometimes even extended beyond that of the official censors; a circle commander in Guinea commented in 1950 that: 'The screening of certain films (the exploits of thieves and bandits, notably) is, in my opinion, harmful enough in the town of Mamou, without needing to spread its effects to the bush.'[21]

Applicants thus strove to highlight their loyalty: 'May I specify ... that I only screen French films and, moreover, that I am responsible for running one of the best organized mobile cinemas in French West Africa,' wrote Dominique Bocogano. Granted authorization for the Zinguinchor district in Casamance, Senegal, in 1953, he expanded his operations to the whole of Senegal in 1955. Now he was seeking authorization for all of French West Africa so that he could adapt his circuits according to the rains and their corollary difficulties, thereby making his enterprise more profitable.[22]

The national origin of films was thought to be a guarantee of their patriotism or morality. Village audiences were often perceived as fundamentally naive and impressionable, in line with general prejudices about African spectators. Observation, of course, countered such attitudes. Ultimately, these commercial tours, whose routes and frequency were unpredictable, by no means reached all rural areas. They did, however, spark a desire to reproduce the experience in those who had enjoyed the opportunity of seeing a mobile show. Ndiaye Youssoupha Amadou described his burgeoning passion for cinema, which he was finally able to satiate when he moved to Dakar: 'In 1948, a mobile film show came to Tamba[counda] from Dakar. I was eleven years old. My discovery of cinema was a disaster; I stopped focusing on school ...'[23]

To discover more about these extraordinary events, which were synonymous with festivity and escape, let us consider the examples of three popular mobile cinema operators. Their paths take us beyond Senegal, a colony where many mobile cinemas circulated in Casamance and in the peanut-growing zone, where profits from the cash crop provided the necessary income to pay for this leisure activity. Manifestly, despite clear regulatory procedures, controls were not always that rigorous due to the authorities' frequent inability to implement them. There were many hitches on the part of the operators, too, and audiences were often demanding.

MOBILE CINEMA AND TRAVELLING ENTREPRENEURS

Popular circuits in French West Africa: Marcel Rochefort, Raymond Borremans, Jean-Paul Sivadier

Only a few names emerge from the archives and accounts; the profession was not easy and required many skills, including driving, operating technology, and managing human relations. 'Mobile cinema was an arduous and dangerous activity,' in the words of the man who held the longest record in the field: Raymond Borremans. Let us look more closely at three figures who predominated in the 1940s and 1950s: Marcel Rochefort (1948–56), who sold his van to Jean-Paul Sivadier (1956–59), who in turn crossed paths with the aforementioned Raymond Borremans (1937–74) in Sikasso, Mali, in 1957. Their itineraries sometimes crossed, although they avoided this where possible to guarantee cost-effectiveness. However, while they organized their tours independently, they were dependent on one or the other of the two hegemonic distribution networks—the COMACICO and the SECMA—for renting films. The information available offers a more or less precise record of their work. Very little information exists about Rochefort, but Borremans gave an account of his activities in 1985 (cited in Retord 1986), and Sivadier meticulously archived all of his documents.

After an interruption imposed by the war (see above), Borremans set out on the road again on a long tour in 1946. Departing from Abidjan, he did not return there until 1951, after stops in Ivory Coast, Mali, Senegal, and Guinea. This long tour was not without its difficulties and inventive solutions. To get from Dakar to Conakry, Borremans sent his van by boat while he took the plane, a new means of travel. On the return journey, he lost a van in Banfora (southeastern Upper Volta) when a bridge collapsed. In this new phase of his career, he found himself among a new generation of tour operators, as it was now necessary to use projectors designed for non-flammable film. In Ivory Coast, he lists, in no particular order:

> Spencer, Anglo-Portuguese, based in Bongouanou and around Katiola; a member of the Yacouba Sylla family; Mr Bruno in the Dimbokro region; Mr Antoine in Daoukro; a camp manager in Bouaflé; a part-advertising cinema run by Mr Rocheford [sic], distributing Bastos cigarettes [made in Dakar] during screenings and which, from 1949 to 1951, thus destroyed the other tour operators' market (Retord 1986: 17).

His account gives a lively image of his activity. He describes setting up in a village, the influx of viewers, and the at times rowdy ambiance:

> After showing my authorization documents and presenting myself to the representative of the local administration, I would set my equipment up in the market

place. My helper—for many years a young Guinean called Douraba, now based in Katiola—and I would put up posts to stake out a spot in the market place, and fix lengths of hessian (cheaper than tarpaulin) to the posts, then would set out rows of benches in front of the screen, itself set up in the van. We would announce that night's screening, at 8 pm, and that is when the problems would start: we would recruit guards, who in principle were meant to stop cheats from slipping under the hessian to get in, but they in fact often let them in for half the ticket price (Retord 1986: 19–20).

This experience was subject to a few conditions: administrative control, building the screening venue with material transported in the van (seating, the screen, etc.), and, finally, securing the space to prevent fraud. This was not easy, as demand was often greater than the number of seats—a proof of success. The space staked out as a cinema could host about 300 people—in other words, less than the overall local demand—which caused a crush outside and a rowdy atmosphere within:

> We also had guards inside to stop other cheats from peeping through the hessian after cutting holes in it with little knives. We also had to handle those who, angry at not having been able to get in, threw stones over the hessian, or tore it. We had to handle this even bigger throng outside than in, and any power cut or breakage of the film bordered on a state of panic (Retord 1986: 20).

It is well imaginable that all incidents needed to be handled quickly to avoid degeneration into chaos. The trade thus necessitated both technical and social skills. Borremans screened a mix of fictions and documentaries, taking on a pedagogical and moralizing mission, as his pre-war refusal to screen westerns demonstrated (see above). In Guinea in 1947, he screened 'after-school educational and recreational films' that were well-received in regions not yet familiar with cinema, such as the forest zone. The district officer wrote: 'He put on three shows at Macenta, which were a great success among the African population who, for the most part, were totally unfamiliar with cinema. There were no incidents to report.'[24]

Surveillance was thus *de rigueur*, but the authorities were, on the whole, happy about this innocuous entertainment, especially as schoolchildren were able to go for free. There were two categories of ticket price: twenty-five and fifty francs in 1946, the latter of which rose to 100 francs in 1950–51, before falling back to fifty francs due to the fluctuation in the price of export crops (cocoa, coffee). Although Borremans was able to restock his COMACICO-supplied *Spécial-Ciné* programme when passing through the cities of Abidjan, Bamako, and Dakar, one can suppose that the French newsreels were out of date after touring for a few months. Borremans has less to say about the films he rented and the audience reactions, however, although certain anecdotes are highly revealing of colonial tensions: 'I never showed boxing matches between black and white fighters where the white fighter lost, as the audience would become delirious and risked smashing everything up, even in the furthest-flung places. When the white fighter won, there was deathly silence' (Retord 1986: 19).

This account deconstructs any stereotypes about naive or passive villagers. It also demonstrates the audience's identification with black actors, for whom positive roles were few and far between in this period of hegemonic colonial and Hollywood productions. As a result, even portraits of black people that reflected colonial ideology but depicted strong personalities were a hit, such as the roles played by Paul Robeson (1898–1976), the African-American actor, singer, and activist. The 1935 British film *Sanders of the River* continued to circulate long after its initial release, even though Robeson played the archetypal African at the service of imperialism in the film.

Slavery, too, was a sensitive theme and provoked antagonistic reactions, as Borremans describes:

> *La montagne verte* [1950 documentary], a feature film about the life of Victor Schoelcher, included a scene showing a slave market in which the slaves' teeth were shown to show off the quality of the merchandise. The Africans did not appreciate this, whereas the Europeans did not like the slaver scenes. I avoided screening this type of film (Retord 1986: 19).

To avoid conflict, Borremans and others favoured Tarzan, Laurel and Hardy, Charlie Chaplin, Fernandel, or Zorro action films and comedies, which audiences loved. Indian films full of intrigue and romance were also screened. Borremans specifies that the latter films 'were often subtitled, but never dubbed'. This poses the question of the audience's understanding of the plot, beyond the fights, songs, and dancing. Borremans's account includes a list of films submitted to the Dimbokro (Ivory Coast) police commissioner in February 1956, which confirms the types of films screened, but also the obligation to inform the authorities 'in case any of these, to your knowledge, are partially or totally banned by the Territory's Censorship Board'. Respectful of the law, but also not wanting to create any difficulties for himself, Borremans wrote: 'I wish to signal that I have personally expunged all my newsreels of any political and socially or internationally contentious subject that could cause confusion or be wrongly interpreted by the African public' (Retord 1986: 34).

This personal censorship is in part a reflection of Borremans's own personality. He liked touring for the freedom it gave him but, above all, it was a means to meet people and to collect information for his planned encyclopaedia. Yet he lived alone, was of an 'antisocial temperament', and was relatively unconcerned by the upheavals of his time—and notably unconcerned by the political implications of the reactions to his screenings in this decade of the fight for independence.[25]

Borremans's testimony is typical of the mobile cinema phenomenon, which, in his case, was remarkable for its duration of over thirty years, albeit with several interruptions. Marcel Rochefort was more or less a contemporary of Borremans. He founded his Cinéma Circuit Africain (CCA) in 1948, based in Kaolack (Senegal). In 1949, he toured in Guinea; from 1951–52, he could be found in the French Sudan. Like all of the mobile cinema operators, he was the object of close surveillance:

> 5 March, 1951, ROCHEFORT Marcel, born 9 March 1906 ..., cineaste, and ASTIER Edmond, born 16 June 1910 ..., mobile cinema manager, reach Kayes from Kaolack. Associates operating a mobile cinema known as the Cinéma Circuit Africain, put on several shows in Kayes met with great success.
>
> Circus-type installation with tarpaulin, high-quality equipment, perfect sound and luminosity. A power generator.
>
> In Sudan for 1st time; usually only tour in Senegal.
>
> Plan to put on shows all the way to Bamako, then return inland via Nara, Nema, etc.
>
> Left for Macina on 11 March as plan to give one or more shows before continuing on way to Bamako.[26]

This confidential colonial intelligence service report reveals the simplicity of the installation, but also the quality of the equipment and the screenings in this medium-sized town, which was introduced to cinema in the 1930s (see Chapter 1). If they stayed for six days, it was likely because there was an ongoing interest in cinema there. Some brief citations in the archives mention him and his movements—notably in association with the sale of Bastos cigarettes, thus recalling that mobile cinema was sometimes linked with advertising campaigns to increase revenues. One could obtain a cinema ticket on purchasing a packet of the cigarettes, a practice virulently denounced by Borremans (see above). After almost a decade, Rochefort, by now aged forty-eight, decided to end his enterprise and to sell his equipped van.

At that time, Jean-Paul Sivadier, who had come to Dakar in late 1949 for his military service, dreamed of running a cinema hall, but he would end up running a mobile cinema instead. Ironically, his name features nowhere in the colonial archives, but Sivadier himself carefully archived all his documents, yielding a detailed account based on his letters sent home to France; his account ledgers; correspondence with his distributor, the SECMA; the list of films he screened; photographs; and so on.[27] The documents provide an overview of his short but rich experience. After accompanying Rochefort on his final tour for a brief apprenticeship in March to April 1956, he toured French Sudan, Upper Volta, Senegal, and southern Mauritania for three dry seasons:

- 24 March 1956 to 12 June 1956 (joined Rochefort's tour and completed it alone): c. 4,828 km.
- 15 November 1956 to 6 June 1957 (with his brother, Jacques, for part of the tour): 8,028km.
- 10 November 1957 to 16 May 1958 (with a woman friend; the tour was cut short when he fell ill).
- 15 November 1958 to 31 May 1959 (with his wife): 7,077 km.

Sivadier's experience confirms what has already been stated: the population's love of cinema; the difficulties caused by the state of the roads and bridges; the fluctuations in revenues depending on the time and place; and the gruelling nature of the job, engendered by rudimentary accommodation, constant travel, the physical toll of setting up the 'cinema', equipment breakdowns, and so forth. He also added some new elements, notably precise information concerning hiring costs, turnover, the routes taken, and the films screened. The documents also shed light on the often tense relations with the distributor; both parties attempted to maximize their profits, one by raising the hiring costs, the other by negotiating the rate or the duration of the hire—a ploy that the distributor was most certainly not fooled by.

While it is difficult to evaluate any profit made, the information concerning the mobile cinema's functioning, the nature of the journeys, and audience diversity and expectations is interesting. Let us pause to look more closely at various aspects of mobile cinema, starting with its supply of films. What clearly transpires is the difficulty of obtaining a film on time, and of picking up the new film reels from a shop, post office, or railway station on the way through a town. Sivadier thus recounts his mad rush by van, then by scooter, to reach the Kayes post office before closing time on New Year's Eve. Implicit rules governed where the mobile cinema operators could stop. They could not stop in towns that had a cinema; they would of course have found it hard to compete with cinema theatres for reasons of comfort and visual quality. The opening of a cinema in Tambacounda (Senegal) thus deprived Sivadier of a profitable port of call. Conversely, Sikasso (Mali), which had previously had a cinema hall, was profitable because a film-going clientele already existed. Sivadier was able to stay there for about ten days, as opposed to an average of two to three elsewhere. However, this required him to juggle the programme:

> A rate of two films a day required eighteen films to stay nine days in one place. The number of films rented was six. Rochefort had long found a trick: he would get hold of pirated copies well-known to the clientele. These for the most part were old westerns and other action films, the most famous of which was *King Kong*.[28]

This additional stock of pirated films allowed the travelling projectionists to pull off a rapid rotation of films, a feature common to cinema halls and mobile cinemas due to their limited pools of spectators.

The mobile cinemas also had to avoid competing with one another; if one operator was already present when another arrived, the former was given priority. One anecdote illustrates this: in November 1957, Borremans reached Sikasso, where Sivadier had already set up his cinema. But, as he was sick, Sivadier was unable to work even though he had a film that 'was a huge hit with the clientele': an American version of the 1954 Japanese film *Godzilla*. They came to an agreement: Borremans screened the film and shared half the takings with Sivadier. This film, which the SECMA rented to Sivadier for the high cost of 10,000 francs a week, compared to the usual 5,000 francs, stayed in his repertoire for a long time.

Generally speaking, films shown by the mobile cinemas were much older, the distributor having long recouped their costs. The poor quality of old copies at times rendered the film incomprehensible and triggered negative reactions on the part of the audience, who accused the operator of censoring the film. On Sivadier's first tour, all of the films bar one were over ten years old:

Beau Hunks (a Laurel and Hardy comedy), USA, 1931
Arizona Whirlwind (a western), USA, 1944
The Gaucho War, Argentina, 1942
Salon Mexico, Mexico, 1949
Fares el Aswad, Egypt, 1954

This list reflects the usual range of action films and comedies. With a few exceptions, Sivadier operated in modest towns or large villages. He noted the audiences' different expectations, as shown by a conflict concerning the Indian film *Albela* (1951), which the SECMA wanted to rent for 20,000 francs a week, compared to 9,000 francs for the others, because it was deemed 'an absolutely extraordinary film'.[29] Sivadier retorted that the villagers barely made a distinction between the different Indian films, and that, for them, *Mangala* (1952) was the picture that everybody talked about.[30] Rare were colonial films set in Africa, such as *Paysans noirs* (1948), based on a novel by the administrator Robert Delavignette.

As with other mobile cinemas, Sivadier's programme comprised several parts: a short film (one reel), followed by twenty minutes of advertising (Valda lozenges, Fly Tox insecticide, Gibbs toothpaste) and a feature film (two to three reels). Advertisements were part of the contract, and a log book signed by the local authorities certified their screening. Altogether, this produced an approximately three-hour show, with no intermissions in a bid to avoid disorder. Newsreels were rare. In 1958, however, the federal colonial authorities requested that Sivadier screen a documentary showing General de Gaulle's journey throughout the Territories before the French constitutional referendum. It was reported to have been a hit. Sivadier generally rented three double bills for his tours, combining a short and a feature film, plus the corresponding, often well-worn, posters which announced the films, even though the population was already alerted by the arrival of his big red van.

Tickets were sold just before the show by the light of a hurricane lamp, and their sale often caused a crush. Delimited by a three-metre-high tarpaulin, the cinema could take up to 800 people, although that was rare. A certain amount of precaution was required: 'Our clients so manhandled their banknotes that they were often torn in several places. They would stick together pieces that weren't from the same note, and the banks would refuse to take these mismatched bills.'[31] The average ticket price varied according to competition and location. In Senegal, for example, Sivadier did not have the monopoly: 'There is a lot of competition in Senegal, and I am the fourth mobile cinema in some villages. I have to align my prices with the African cinemas.'[32] He offered two rates, high and low; the distinction between them was completely random. His average prices rose from twenty-five and sixty CFA in 1956–57 to thirty and seventy-five CFA in 1957–59, which was on a par with ticket prices for African spectators in Dakar's cinemas.[33] The CCA van travelled in both Muslim and Christian regions, some of them inhabited by villagers who had ample monetary resources (the groundnut growing zones of Senegal, the Office du Niger in Mali), and others much poorer areas. However, it met with the same successes everywhere, as well as the same technical, climatic, and economic vicissitudes. Accordingly, 'takings fell after harvest revenues had been spent and during the Ramadan.'[34] As he was very busy with the screening itself, and keeping a look-out for fraudsters, Sivadier had little time to really observe the spectators, but there is no doubt that his mobile cinema drew many villagers, to whom, for the space of a few hours, he offered an escape from daily toil. Once the screening was over, Sivadier left as quickly as possible, travelling at night to avoid the heat, but also to guarantee the maximum possible number of working days. During his 1955–56 tour, he worked thirty days in December, thirty-one in January, twenty-seven in February, thirty in March, twenty-seven in April, and twenty-six in May; in other words, with very few breaks.

Sivadier decided to bring an end to his mobile cinema tours in 1959. There were several reasons for this: a fall in revenue which, according to him, was due to the exorbitant price of renting films; competition from fixed venues; and the crippling fixed overheads. However, he also made this decision due to political changes: 'Since the last season, a lot of villages we stop in have become communes and have introduced often abusive taxes.'[35] Moreover, to the usual vicissitudes (such as sunken ferries, and mechanical and electrical break-downs) were now added 'political rallies, that do or don't end in fights, Magals, night prayers that keep our clients away, when the authorities don't purely and simply ban us from screening.'[36] While in the throes of negotiating another tour, he hurriedly sold his van, without finding anyone to take over the cinema, and returned to France when Mali became independent.

Jean-Paul Sivadier was not the only projectionist to travel the countryside. Sometimes, these mobile screenings constituted a preliminary stage before the opening of a cinema, either to test the set-up before a cinema was constructed and build up an audience, or to make film hires profitable. There were many such examples in Senegal in the early 1950s: Pierre Palombi, who ran a cinema in Sédhiou, requested authorization for a tour, as did El Hadj Alioune Sow, who ran a cinema in Kaolack and wanted to expand his activities, and Jean Subrini, a forestry operator and owner of a cinema in M'Bour. Similarly, in Guinea, Jacques Demarchelier, owner of a cinema in Labé, wanted to put on screenings in the neighbouring town of Pita, and Yacouba Sylla in Ivory Coast put on mobile screenings before the opening of his cinema and as a parallel activity afterwards. These screenings gave villagers, hungry for escape, a taste for film, but, for the majority of them, the illusion offered was fleeting, lasting only as long as the film itself.

Independence did not put an end to this nomadic practice, which instead took new directions. Faced with difficulties in distributing their films, which resulted mainly from blockages on the part of the distributors, certain African filmmakers organized their own screenings. This move also reflected a desire to be closer to their audiences, as Maryse Condé recounts after accompanying Ousmane Sembène on one of his tours of his own country, Senegal, in the mid-1960s:

> His arrival sparked a celebration every time. We would wait for night to cloak the main square before starting the screening. Some villagers would sit on mats in front of the huge screen, others on benches, others directly on the ground. While awaiting the first images, the dignitaries would dignifiedly chew their tooth sticks. Seated in the front rows on the ground, the children would be still. First, the griots would sing, accompanied by the balafon. Acrobats would juggle and do summersaults. Then, silence would fall. When the screening had ended, a debate, generally moderated by a student from a neighbouring school, would ensue. Ousmane Sembène would generously answer all the questions, never tiring (Condé 2012: 313–14).

In true militant style, Sembène transformed screenings into 'night schools', as he termed them. The filmmaker also went to Guinea to promote his 1968 film *The Mandate* (*Mandabi*) in the early 1970s. These activities left traces in the memories of many spectators, and helped cinema to flourish.

In its 1949 report, cited at the start of this chapter, UNESCO saw mobile cinema as an interim measure, preceding the generalized installation of movie theatres throughout African nations. Mobile cinema initiatives were numerous but unsystematic, and the entire swathes of the continent lying beyond their circuits thus remained deprived of images, knowledge of which only reached them through distant echoes. From the 1940s to the 1950s, however, the number of screening venues and of towns touched by cinema grew, radically changing the nature of this leisure activity and making it accessible to a wider audience.

Palladium, built by Alfred John Ocansey (1889–1943) in Accra,
Ghana 1920s, photo John Collins, 1970s

Sikasso, Mali, photo Jean-Paul Sivadier, 1956

Rex, Saint Louis, Senegal, 1943, postcard, private collection

Vox, Saint Louis, Senegal, 1943, postcard, private collection

Vox, Kindia, Guinea built 1954/55, photo Odile Goerg, 2005

Queens, Ibadan, Nigeria, photo Jean-Luc Martineau, 2011

Palace, Conakry, Guinea, photo Odile Goerg, 2003

El Mansour, built in the 1950s, transformed into a shopping centre, Treichville, Abidjan, Côte d'Ivoire, photo Odile Goerg, 2017

4

A WINDOW ON THE WORLD

Screens from Dakar to Accra to Léopoldville played pictures from all over the world that had no correlation with the daily lives of their local populations. Despite this, cinemas in the region had to establish, attract, and retain members of the public. In the early days of cinema, audiences did not choose which films they went to see, as very few towns had more than one screening venue. Not caring what was billed, people 'went to the pictures', generally on a Friday or Saturday night, as a sort of consecrated rhythm and ritual. The rapid turnover of films meant it was not always possible to know the programme in advance. In the early days, information spread by word of mouth; later, advertising methods were gradually introduced: posters displayed in front of the cinemas, or in different sites around the town; megaphone announcements made by cars driving around the neighbourhood; human billboards; and musicians, as in Grand Bassam in the 1930s (Dadié 1971: 38–39).

The press played a limited role, designed specifically for the educated few. From 1931 to 1936, the *Gold Coast Times*, which reported prolifically on sports events and conferences, did not print one film show announcement, even though the cinema industry was vibrant in the Gold Coast. Contrastingly, *Paris-Dakar*, created in 1933, devoted a column to cinema. Initially reaching a small readership but later more prominent, it was made up of adverts and film reviews. This newspaper mainly targeted a European readership, as did the *Madagascar illustré* in Madagascar. A specialized press also emerged in Dakar, the films' port of arrival and the headquarters of the distribution companies.

The freely distributed *Courrier cinématographique de l'Ouest Africain Français* described itself as 'the African Coast's first film and advertising weekly'. An organ of the Compagnie Marocaine Cinématographique et Commerciale, or the COMACICO (see Chapter 1 and below), it was first published episodically in 1934, and later more regularly. A little later, *L'AOF-Ciné* had a similar function for clients of the Palace, an upmarket cinema affiliated with the rival distributor, the Société d'Exploitation Cinématographique Africaine (SECMA). In 1937, the Dourlot Brothers' cinemas offered the same service in Ivory Coast, publishing *Abidjan-Ciné*.[1]

These sources indicate which films were shown to the public, but do not give any indication of how they were chosen. Selection indeed took place earlier, and depended on both anticipated profitability and the stereotypical vision that cinema owners had of African spectators. This raises the question of import mechanisms, although audiences very quickly demonstrated their preferences by filling or deserting the cinemas, thereby influencing programming. Spectator opinions were rarely given voice in the laconic official sources, which simply reported expressions of enthusiasm or rejection. In the darkness of the cinema house, spectators—young men, for the most part—at times seized the opportunity to speak out, something they were rarely able to do in public. This prompted the authorities to react. *Storm Over Asia*, banned 'in the colonies' by the French film censorship board in 1931, was still screened in French Equatorial Africa but was ultimately censored there too in 1938. This 1928 Russian silent film about the young herdsman Bair, who is believed to be the descendant of Genghis Khan and fights against the British army in 1920s Mongolia, showed scenes of the British torturing 'natives', which prompted angry reactions in cinemas.

From the pioneers to the creation of distribution circuits

While in the early days cinema depended on the ad hoc initiatives of daring entrepreneurs, such as Raphaël Fumey in Togo or the Lisk-Carew Brothers in Sierra Leone, its development brought change in the way films circulated. Film reel was initially sold by firms, but was available for hire from 1910. This change occurred later in Africa, due to distance and the need to create specific distribution circuits. At the time of his death in 1930, Fumey left behind fifty or so silent films in Lomé; these constituted his considerable stock, from which he selected for his screenings. Denis Tétévi Lawson owned about twenty, and Albert John Mensah just six. Similarly, Madame Mähl in Bamako owned a few films by 1932, including the silent movies *The Three Musketeers* and *L'Atlantide*. Neighbouring cinema operators would swap copies. These personal collections were completed with imports. Fumey imported films directly from Germany, Britain, and France. A former colonial power, Germany remained the main supplier, which testifies to both its enduring ties with Africa and the dynamism of German film production. Parallel to this, circuits began to take form in the 1920s. The company Cinémas Maurice supplied both Madame Mähl in the French Sudan and the hotel owner Aldo Gariglio in Lomé. It had exclusive rights for the American company Metro Goldwyn Mayer in French West Africa and, as a result, only distributed MGM films. Pathé and Gaumont newsreels were also imported.

These ad hoc initiatives were marginalized by the operations of two French entrepreneurs, Maurice Jacquin and Maurice Archambeau (see Chapter 1). After arriving in Morocco in 1924, Jacquin set up a film hire and sales agency, before moving to Dakar in 1926. There, he expanded his operations and set up the COMACICO in 1933. This company soon established the biggest film circuit in French West Africa (FWA), and also became the owner of multiple cinemas there. It later changed its name (keeping the same acronym), multiplied its local branches, and increased its capital. In parallel, Archambeau developed his own enterprise and in 1936 founded the SECMA. These two companies very rapidly came to play a central role in cinema in the region. The COMACICO became firmly established in all the major cities of FWA, and in particular Senegal, where it ran many of the cinemas from 1936 onwards. The same year, the SECMA also set up there.

The British colonies did not have an equivalent centralized distribution system. Each cinema owner acquired their own supply of films directly, juggling both imports and film stocks. In the Gold Coast and Nigeria, cinema operators owned stocks of films, or, not limited by the language barrier, obtained works directly from the American distributors.

In Central Africa, the Palace-Parlant circuit predominated, supplying Brazzaville, Pointe-Noire, Léopoldville, Matadi, and Stanleyville (now Kisangani): in other words, both the Belgian Congo and French Equatorial Africa. Thanks to these circuits, it was possible to frequently renew the selection of films billed, which was crucial given the limited pool of spectators.

Films were generally screened for only two to three consecutive days, and usually at weekends. This rapid turnover answered the spectators' demand for new films, but audiences also enjoyed watching the same films over and over again, to the point that they knew the dialogues and songs by heart. This explains the regular scheduling of successful, and sometimes old, hits. The pleasure of knowing a film well was a key characteristic of audiences' relationship to cinema. Birago Diop, who had already seen Julien Duvivier's *Un Carnet de Bal* (*Life Dances On*, 1937) at least three times in France, returned to watch it in Bamako in 1939 just to see the 'wonderful scene between Jouvet and Marie Bell' again.

In the absence of a local film industry, the distributors and cinema-owners chose from a common catalogue of Westerns and from the 1930s onwards, to a lesser degree, Egyptian and Indian films. Some importers selected these non-Western productions to meet the audience demand for more familiar images, or to develop different tastes, but the role of these films was limited in FWA for a long time. In East Africa, Indian cinema owners imported films from India—a major producer—first and foremost to cater to their own community (Fair 2018).

A compromise was gradually established between the authorities, who were attentive but mainly non-interventionist, the distributors, and cinema owners; together, they favoured works likely to be a hit, and thus a source of profit. The importers and authorities did not necessarily share the same criteria, but a certain consensus seems to have reigned. Censorship measures taken in the West stopped potentially subversive or shocking films from reaching the African market, as the limited number of films banned locally, even in this period, demonstrates. The aim of making an economic profit often led to the importation of inexpensive old films, whose costs had already been recouped. This was confirmed in a 1946 survey which described the French Empire's unsuitable programmes, made up of 'old cowboy or romance films [which] do a disservice to the colonizers', worthless documentaries, and 'preposterously out-of-date' French newsreels (Lacolley 1946: 4).

This hardly flattering picture describes a situation which was nevertheless common in the late 1930s. Indeed, it comes as little surprise given the limited repertoire of available films and the slowness of transportation between Europe and Africa, and even more so inland Africa. Planes were rarely used. In 1936, therefore, there was a three- to four-year delay between a film's release and its screening in Bamako or Kayes. The oldest film showing at the time was a 1926 police comedy by Julien Duvivier; the most recent were four films dated to 1935. Of the fifty-eight films identified, the majority were over two years old: fourteen were dated to 1932, thirteen to 1933, and fifteen to 1934. In Dakar, the COMACICO boasted of screening Jacques Feyder's *Le Grand Jeu* in July 1936, a 'film classed first in the 1935 French questionnaire', but the film had been released in 1934. It also claimed to have negotiated the exclusive distribution rights to over eighty recent French works, but did not hesitate to screen the 1926 silent movie *L'Homme à l'Hispano* in 1936. Only a few cinemas in the colonial residential Plateau districts of Dakar and Abidjan, which targeted a predominantly European clientele, actually offered 'first-release' films, which were advertised in the press. In Ghana, the prevalence of low-quality old films appears to have been one of the reasons that the elite turned away from the cinema, once its initial curiosity factor had worn off (McFeely 2015). The proliferation of cinemas and their clear hierarchical rankings gradually accentuated the differences between individual cinemas' programmes, while also leading informed audiences to become increasingly demanding in the few well-equipped towns.

On the screen and in the cinema

What atmosphere reigned at the pictures, both inside and out, and before and during, the show? The experience went beyond the simple viewing of a film. This scene, which took place in Bamako in 1937, gives an indication:

> A crowd flocked in front of the large gates, waiting to be allowed in to buy a ticket. Among the waiting crowd, some ambled aimlessly, others chatted amicably, others shouted out. Young hawkers, crates on their heads, touted their wares, crying: 'Get your sweets, cigarettes, matches, dates! Get your cola, lemonade, peanuts! Stock up! Stock up! Soon it'll be dark and you won't be able to buy anymore!' ... 'Tickets!,' yelled the seller ... A short while later, the spectators, blinded by the electric lamp light, started looking for something to do while waiting for the show. ... Suddenly, the lights dimmed and came on again. It was the signal to go back to one's seat ... A deathly silence fell ... Strange noises broke the silence and beams of light sliced through the dark (Bâ 1967).

Interactions before the show—the purchase of food and tickets, general conversation—filled the void before the screening started. The hubbub described by Bâ was also characteristic of the film shows at the Empire Cinema in Freetown. Tickets were sold beforehand, but spectators would rush to grab the best seats as soon as the doors opened (Anthony 1980: 138). Other accounts by African or European spectators complete the picture.[2] Beyond the size of the cinemas, and thus their potential audience, they reconstitute the ambiance and elements of the audience's behaviour.

Once inside, the spectators would take their seats and continue their discussions in an atmosphere that was undoubtedly closer to that of working-class cinemas—as depicted in Giuseppe Tornatore's film *Cinema Paradiso* (1988), set in a Sicilian village—than to the reverent mood that the gentrification of screenings progressively imposed in Europe, as they left the fairground and entered the comfortable Rex and Palace theatres. Rare are the images of spectators tightly packed on wooden benches, circulating between the rows—of the pleasure on their concentrated faces, the lively commentaries, or the expansive gesticulations. As an imported media, the cinema unquestionably disrupted social and cultural practices, but it nevertheless integrated with certain existing forms of sociability; the spectators' interaction with events on the screen reproduced the dialogue between public and storyteller during village gatherings, or the call-and-response exchanges between audiences and actors in Mali's Koteba theatre. Indeed, cinema was referred to as *tiyatra* (the local pronunciation of 'theatre') in Mali (Haffner 1978). Gesticulations and commentary punctuated film shows. In the interwar years, then, a cinematic culture emerged that surpassed the movie theatre and incorporated existing spectatorship practices into the behaviour of audiences before, during, and after the show.

A typical show at the Gariglio Hotel in Lomé would follow a specific schedule, starting with Pathé-Revue newsreels, followed by a dramatic film in several episodes, and then a comedy. In the same city, Lawson would screen a comic short film, then a dramatic feature film, and finally another sentimental or comic short film. Shows that followed this fragmented structure, which alternated short films, burlesque, fiction, and documentary, were all the longer due to the intermissions imposed by the need to change reels. Just as in the West, then, a show would comprise several types of films, a practice that was reinforced during the 1930s slump when double bills were introduced, showing two feature films. Film shows went on late into the night—another argument for keeping women away. The poor quality of copies, precarious screening conditions, inexperienced staff, and, at times, the inversion of reels could add to the confusion. Shows and spectator relations took on a particular character in the face of such mishaps: exclamations and remarks; running commentaries on the dialogue; connoisseurs revealing the action before it took place; angry reactions and protests. People went to the cinema as much for this excitement and for the experience of sharing a story as for the film itself. However, this was still an important part of the event, and elements of the films were subsequently integrated into language, behaviour, and daily discussions. Film shows created at times ephemeral, at times lasting social ties, particularly for young people, who found a space of freedom here, far from the eyes of adults. This process was just beginning in the interwar years, but would flourish after 1945.

Even if Bâ exaggerated his anecdote about the 1908 screening in Bandiagara with his talk of 'devilry', it is easy to imagine the rupture that this technology represented for various social groups, whatever their culture or religion; it offered a completely different relationship to visual culture and to narration. Moreover, with the exception of the rare individuals who had attended colonial schools or travelled to Europe, for African audiences the films portrayed a totally foreign environment.

Given their cultural baggage, how did these spectators interpret these images? For certain administrators, such as the Gold Coast Native Affairs Secretary, the answer was clear:

> it is obvious that a film which is considered suitable for Europeans, who know at a glance whether it deals with fact or fiction, may be glaringly unsuitable for exhibition before an audience composed of perhaps 5 per cent of people who can read the titles and all of whom probably believe that the lurid scenes flashed on the screen depict the ordinary events of everyday life in Europe.[3]

How, indeed, to tell the difference between fictionalized stories, or characters on the screen, and real life when this 'real life' is not part of one's own experience? We get a sense of the general mechanism: audiences projected their own codes onto images and reacted according to their own interpretative schema. Some of these were similar to Western codes: for example, the appeal of heroes or chiefs, which possibly explains the success of Abel Gance's *Napoleon* (1927). However, many other Western codes, notably lifestyles and gender relations, were very different from those of African cultures. Relationships to time and space, which influence narrative linearity or non-linearity, and the role of myths, were important too. And, ultimately, it was also necessary simply to understand film language. One anecdote, which evokes the early screenings of the Lumière Brothers' 1895 film *The Arrival of a Train*, testifies: 'One of my cousins had us in tears of laughter: in one scene in which a train thundered across the screen, she jumped back, yelling, grabbing hold of Father, certain she was already under its wheels' (Diallo 1997: 65).[4]

It is not surprising that already-familiar scenes were more accessible and better appreciated. Hence this reflection on the part of an administrator who, in 1937, indubitably minimized the audience's ability to understand:

> Cinema only plays the evocative and educational role that it does for European audiences if it signifies something to the native, if it enters the domain of the

native's preoccupations and familiar horizons. Hence the major interest, in the Sudan, of filmed reports and exotic cinema.[5]

But 'exotic' cinema—understood here as colonial documentary representations of Africa—was not often screened in commercial cinemas in FWA. Made by Europeans, such films met with the same misunderstandings as any others, as illustrated by an example in the Belgian Congo when images of a dead chief caused terror among audiences (Ramirez and Rolot 1985: 273). A proximity of experience was, in contrast, one of the reasons for the success of the Egyptian films shown in the mid-1930s, well before sub-Saharan African films began to emerge in the late 1950s.

How to imagine concretely the atmosphere of screenings in the silent movie era? Were there musical accompaniments or sound effects? Doctor Sultan mentions the balafon players who accompanied screenings in Guinea in the late 1920s, entertaining spectators during the intermissions. A few years later, a gramophone player replaced them at the École Normale William Ponty while films were being rewound. It is hard to say whether these musical interludes continued during the screening. Probably not, apart from in a few hotels where pianists played. The lack of competing sound most likely made the interjections, laughter, and exclamations particularly conspicuous. Is it feasible to imagine that audiences gave a running commentary on top of the generalized intertitles? What proportion of spectators would have been able to read them anyway? The emphatic acting and exaggerated displays of emotion probably allowed the majority of viewers to follow the plot without too much difficulty—all the more so given the repetitive, simplistic nature of the storylines, which were often full of gags or chases. Other more sophisticated fictions proposed more complex narratives, however, with ellipses and flashbacks.

The transition to sound cinema naturally modified audiences' relationship to film, but they still had to use their imaginations to understand the plot; they also needed to understand a foreign language if they were to follow the dialogue. Whether silent pictures or talkies, films were powerful cultural conveyors, disseminating gestures, behaviours, and social practices. Their role in the circulation of music and fashion in South Africa has been studied; while silent movies popularized certain dances and theatre forms, talkies triggered a craze for tap dancing (Coplan 1992: 191). Similarly, in the Gold Coast, local theatre incorporated various influences: in addition to the ideas relayed by sailors and traders circulating between the Gulf of Guinea and Britain, silent films played a significant role in this process. Williams and Marbel, a comic dancing and singing minstrel duo, took their inspiration in part from vaudeville and cowboy films. In 1923, when Ocansey opened the Palladium in Accra, he invited the duo to perform a show every Saturday night, thereby enhancing the link between cinema, artistic performance, and the music hall. These different elements made up the elites' concert parties and the musicals which, in the 1930s, spread beyond the capital and into more working-class milieus (Collins 2009: 230). Whether directly or indirectly, onscreen images thus influenced all of urban society.

While silent movies and their intertitles limited film dialogue to the strict minimum, the talkies necessitated a greater mastery of a spoken foreign language, recognizing its various accents, the nuances of exchanges between characters, the rhythm of speech, and so on. Having attended primary school for a few years did not suffice. Can it be deduced that the talkies addressed a different audience? In Algeria, the advent of the talkies appears to have reinforced the elitist nature of filmgoing: it was above all the literate and the young who now went to the cinema (Carlier 2012). This observation may be refined, however, if we note that the spread of the talkies was contemporaneous with a general growth in audiences which was linked to other factors—notably the increase in cinema houses and the albeit limited rise in school enrolment. The importance of linguistic skills also needs to be questioned, as films can be read on different levels. Many of us have had the experience of watching a film in a vaguely understood foreign language with no subtitles, nonetheless managing to follow the broad lines of the plot, or even inventing alternative versions. African spectators' experiences would have been similar, and they undoubtedly filled the cognitive or narrative gaps for themselves. Several testimonies thus mention such and such an illiterate spectator interpreting the onscreen story, or female spectators relying on the imprecise explanations of theoretically literate viewing companions.

The advent of the talkies manifestly did not turn audiences away from cinema; the opposite was true, in part due to the songs that they introduced in addition to dialogue. But they did inaugurate a new learning process and produce a range of varied interpretations, depending on audiences' levels of linguistic comprehension and familiarity with the situations portrayed, and individual spectators' own finesse. They also influenced choices made by the distributors, who opted for the works that were the most accessible to the majority: in other words, films without complex dialogue, with a resulting preference for action films.

Adventure films, vaudevilles, and westerns

One text written by a European conveys the atmosphere that reigned in Dakar in late 1932, but also the racist prejudices of the time:

> It is, as is fitting, a sound cinema ... for Dakar has moved on from the silent movies. The recently constructed building has a capacity of 600 seats. The clientele is both European and black, for the natives, won over by the Seventh Art, assiduously frequent the establishment. They form a captivated audience, arriving on time and not missing a moment of the show. While they are little interested in documentaries, they love adventure films, full of movement ... and romance films full of pathos, which even the blacks cannot resist.

> Shows begin with three-month-old newsreels, forming a sort of retrospective. Then follows the feature: a popular melodramatic talkie steeped in insipid sentimentality, washed up here after having toured the world, been cut, and stripped of its foreign language subtitles.

> Tonight's screening soon turned out to be defective, to the point that the characters began talking in a stilted, incomprehensible language, accompanied by scratching and grating sounds.

> The black spectators, who find anything funny, burst out laughing, while the more demanding Europeans reacted, protesting loudly and shouting in unison above the din: 'Refund! Refund!' The owner, an alien resident, strove to calm everyone down, requesting that they be patient. The show was interrupted, before starting again more or less smoothly fifteen minutes later.

> Black people truly love the cinema. They all come out after, their faces joyful, delighted by these funny stories, the shallowness of which makes you want to cry. For a few hours, they forget their troubles, the crisis, and the material burden of their existence (Burthe d'Annelet, c. 1932–33).[6]

While attesting to the success of cinema in Dakar, this text also highlights the poor screening conditions there, and the misunderstandings that can arise from the interpretation of a film through local lenses and with limited command of the colonial language. Looking beyond the racist stereotypes embedded in this narrative, one can learn about the attitude of the audience in the dream palace (respectful silence before the show starts, laughing and relaxation), but also the function of cinema: to provide a safe outlet within an oppressive everyday existence.

In the French West African capital, the inherently cosmopolitan cinema offered images of a sometimes disconcerting elsewhere—especially when screening conditions were defective—which lay several thousand kilometres away from the films' site of reception. Although audiences were mixed, the above author saw them through the prism of the usual stereotypes and was unconcerned with the diversity of the spectators themselves, who watched films according to their own experiences and motivations. When the Second World War broke out, teenagers in Freetown rushed to join up and were amazed not to be enrolled; Farid Raymond Anthony recalls in his memoir *Sawpit Boy* that 'I could not see what age had to do with it, especially as we had acquired such a lot of experience from cowboy and war films!' (Anthony 1980: 156).

Anthony also recounts his enthusiasm for one of the first films he saw: Irving Cummings's *Poor Little Rich Girl* (1936), starring Shirley Temple. In general, romance and action movies were the mainstay of film programmes. It was to better evaluate audience taste that the French Ministry of Colonies launched its 1932 survey: 'It is indispensable ... to know what types of shows are favoured by the public, the subjects likely to meet their preferences'.[7]

But what is known of spectator preferences? To what extent did decisions taken higher up allow for a real evaluation of the tastes of a public whose choices were very limited? And did tastes change as talkies replaced silent films? Born in 1918, Moïse Alassane Traoré certainly had fond memories of the latter: 'There were also silent movies, the Archambaut cinema. Spectators would flock from all over town for them. The cinema was open-air, like the outdoor dances where we would dance the Charleston.'[8]

From 1927 onwards, the talkies spread slowly because they necessitated a new supply of films and equipment. In 1932, none of Nigeria's eight cinemas were equipped yet, whereas two cinemas in Accra—one for a mixed audience, the other for an African audience—offered talkies, which confirms this city's pioneering role. In 1937, five of the nine cinemas in the Gold Coast were equipped to screen talkies: three of Accra's four cinemas, and the cinemas in Koforidua and in Kumasi. In 1938, therefore, *The King of the Kongo* (Richard Thorpe, 1929), an American film whose poster declared it 'the first great talking wild animal serial', was screened in Ocansey's Palladium. *The Return of Bulldog Drummond* (a 1934 British crime film) was shown at Bart's, and two old silent films were shown elsewhere, including *The Hope Diamond Mystery* (1921).[9]

In 1932, a few synchronized sound films were screened at the Buffet de la Gare in Bamako, generally in English as they were supplied by Metro Goldwyn Mayer. In Togo, films imported from the Gold Coast were still silent, with their intertitles in English—the language of the trader elite. Another chronological milestone was the opening of the first sound cinema in Saint-Louis, Senegal, announced with great pomp in a governmental publication in 1935:

> On 5 January, Saint-Louis' first sound cinema was inaugurated. We wish the new cinema a brilliant career, for the immense pleasure of Saint-Louisans, deprived until now of this entertainment that has already been found for some time now in several other towns in Senegal, and in most of the capitals of the Federation's other colonies.[10]

This time frame is not unusual in the French context, which was characterized by the lateness of cinemas' conversion to sound. In 1934, only two-thirds of cinemas were equipped for sound in metropolitan France (Montebello 2005: 4; Bosséno 2002: 191). FWA was thus not particularly behind. The transition also took place in the mid-1930s in French Equatorial Africa, in competition with the neighbouring Belgian Congo. 'Brazzaville modernizes', announced the local newspaper in 1934:

> Last Saturday, the highly successful inauguration of sound cinema took place.' These 'open-air sound screenings' were held every Saturday in the gardens of the Hôtel Congo-Océan, a European social hotspot: 'The residents of Brazzaville can now enjoy an interesting show that, until now, they had to go to Kin for.[11]

Léopoldville, familiarly known as 'Kin' in reference to the African district of Kinshasa, was thus equipped before Brazzaville, a modestly sized regional capital.

The expansion of the COMACICO and the SECMA accompanied this transition. The cost of investments at a time of economic crisis, and the concentration of capital in the hands of a limited number of companies, modified the political economy of this new media. The growth of cinema, which had asserted itself as the leading urban leisure activity, increased certain spectators' range of choice between cinemas and films, and led them to become more demanding. Most people wanted to watch sound films, but much to the displeasure of these audiences certain cinemas continued to screen the old silent movies still in their stock, sometimes right up until the 1950s.[12] The two types of films indeed co-existed for some years.

That being said, both silent and sound films deployed the same registers of burlesque. Comic devices (repetitions, gags, farce) were a real success, and Felix the Cat, then Mickey Mouse cartoons, delighted audiences. Interviewees remember the major comic actors, such as Laurel and Hardy, Charlie Chaplin, and Fernandel, along with other actors including Maurice Chevalier, Jim Gerald, or the singer-actress Florelle. African-American singer and actor Paul Robeson garnered the public's enthusiasm and the concern of the authorities. The 1936 announcement that he was coming to Sierra Leone to shoot *Song of Freedom* created huge excitement among Freetown's film-lovers, and great disappointment when the trip was cancelled (Anthony 1980: 89).[13]

Audiences—and notably young spectators—had a penchant for adventure films, westerns, and cloak-and-dagger movies. Recalling his childhood in the late 1930s, Farid Raymond Anthony evokes his group of friends' passion for westerns: 'The boys in our group were all fond of film shows, especially cowboy films, and we would do anything not to miss Roy Rogers and his horse Trigger and the Sons of the Pioneers, or Gene Autry, or Gary Cooper' (Anthony 1980: 138).

Cowboy songs performed by Roy Rogers and above all by Gene Autry (already famous in the 1930s) were sung outside the cinema, and left their mark in people's memories. Westerns were not yet stigmatized by the authorities and the moralistic elites as a potential incitement to violence or deviant behaviour. The most popular genres varied little from town to town; here, the governor of Togo gives a clear indication of which films were successful:

> [The natives] particularly appreciate sports films (boxing, races, etc.), adventure films, crime movies, and comedies, in which there is a lot of movement. They are not fond of documentaries unless they have a lot of movement in them, such as work in factories, in mines, etc. As for dramatic films, they struggle to follow the plot and are only interested in the episodes that accompany it.[14]

Underlying this account was the idea that African spectators were incapable of understanding a complex plot. In French Sudan, the governor insisted on the enthusiasm of the 'native element': 'The latter love violent action, such as chases and fights, comic films and certain American films featuring coloured comedians. The prototype of a film that captures the natives' attention is, for example, *The Three Musketeers*.'[15] Birago Diop mentions this film with emotion in his memoir, *La plume raboutée* (1978): 'I still have in my mind's eye *The Three Musketeers*, Harold Lloyd, Max Linder, Pearl White, as well as Tancred and Armida.' It was also one of the films regularly screened by Madame Mähl in Bamako, along with *L'Atlantide* (Jacques Feyder, 1921). This colonial film, based on Pierre Benoit's novel, was the first feature film shot in Algeria and a big hit in Europe. Combining a military adventure set in the Sahara with the exotic romanticism of its mythical kingdom ruled by the ageless queen Anitea, the film's Orientalist vision mixes jealousy, power, and remorse. It would be fascinating to know how African audiences reacted to this story and its representation of a purely imaginary Africa.

These dominant genres were demonstrably popular in Bamako and Dakar, although the picture is admittedly complicated in the French West African capital by the demands of the European and African elites who frequented the cinemas in the Plateau district: announced in the daily *Paris-Dakar* newspaper, their programmes are better known than those of the low-end cinemas. On the Plateau, comedies and romance films predominated: *The Land of Smiles* (1929), a German film by Max Reichmann, with the tenor Richard Tauber; *The Story of a Cheat* (1936) by Sacha Guitry; *Carnival in Flanders* (1935) by Jacques Feyder; *The Well-Digger's Daughter* (1940) by Marcel Pagnol; or *Bouboule 1ᵉʳ, roi nègre* (1933) by Léon Mathot. This final film, which was full of the incredible adventures typical of Boulevard comedies, starred Georges Milton, aka Bouboule, a famous chansonnier of the interwar years. Typical of colonial cinema, it deployed all the usual condescending stereotypes about Africans, who are considered childlike and hopeless imitators of Europeans. It also reduced Africa to a backdrop, as demonstrated by the poster, which featured warriors armed with Zulu shields even though the adventure was supposed to be set in Senegal. Also among the dominant genres were musicals, crime films, and adventure films, such as the two American feature films *Lucky Boy* (1928) and *King Kong* (1933), which were also shown in the Médina district cinema—along with, of course, westerns. Curiously, however, Tarzan did not appear on Dakar screens until the early 1940s, whereas *Tarzan and His Mate* (1934) was screened in French Sudan in 1936.

Readily accessible plots, with an obvious distinction between 'goodies' and 'baddies', were appreciated by spectators who had limited fluency in the language of the film. This explains the public's attraction to action films. Enthusiasm for this genre did not wane in the interwar years. In French Sudan in 1937, we are told:

> Native audiences obviously prefer cloak-and-dagger films, crime films or pageant historic reconstitutions. The simplistic psychology of these scenarios, in which innocence, virtue and youth always end up triumphing over the doings of traitors and baddies, and where strength defeats treachery, suits them perfectly, and their reactions are more or less the same as a European audience's. But operettas, vaudevilles, and comedies of manners, or problem plays do not put them off, and while they more often than not react in the wrong places and roar with delight in the saddest parts, their assiduous attendance of screenings and concentration remain the same.[16]

While recognising that African spectators reacted 'more or less the same' to action movies, this analysis stresses the fact that the audience, confronted with films with a strong psychological component which required a good understanding of the dialogues, sometimes appeared to have misplaced attitudes. The remark concerning reactions 'in the wrong places' demonstrates Westerners' incomprehension of African audiences' behaviour; it refers, for example, to the laughter provoked by romantic behaviour that was culturally and socially unacceptable in most West African societies.

Even if action films' simple storylines and clear opposition between heroes and other characters appealed to spectators, other films did circulate more marginally: historical films about the lives of Christ or Muhammad; official documentaries (such as one about the Minister of Colonies' trip to FWA which screened in 1929 at Madame Mähl's); and ethnographic films. Referring to shows organized at the school in Aného, which 'aroused the curiosity of both children and adults', the governor of Togo noted: 'The most popular films were those that represented scenes of native life.'[17]

This observation was confirmed by the governor of French Sudan in 1937:

> It must nonetheless be noted that native audiences are highly appreciative of shows familiar to them, or with which they have affinities—shots of Africa and even North Africa, and generally exotic scenes and landscapes. ... An aerial shot of Bamako for example, or a shot of a local market, or a drumming session, fascinates them far more that the most sensational of spectacles.[18]

Analyses of how images are perceived stress a conception of the screen as a mirror, where the audience looks for representations of themselves. It cannot be said that the distributors heeded such local preferences. There were still few films shot in Africa, and those that were offered images of a purely imaginary and archaic Africa which echoed the colonial discourse.[19] These colonial films targeted metropolitan audiences and shaped their viewpoints, but rarely featured in commercial programmes in Africa. As for African cinema—that is, films made in Africa by Africans—it did not yet exist in the interwar years.

The more cinema spread, the more the range of films screened in each town diversified. Different audiences developed different programmes and interpretations, depending on the degree of mastery of Western language and culture, and on spectators' centres of interest. In Bamako in 1932, then, the films, prices, and clientele at the Buffet de la Gare were different to those at Madame Mähl's cinema. However, if specialized cinemas were to exist, there needed to be a potential pool of cinephiles. This was the case in Mauritius, observed as early as 1927, where three firms imported films: two targeted popular audiences, providing old adventure and crime films, while the third targeted the inhabitants of Curepipe, a town with a wealthy population who were used to cinema and demanded productions of a better quality.[20]

Less educated and unable to read the French intertitles, the majority of African spectators liked American crime and adventure films, which represented 90 per cent of imports. Even though they denounced the amorality and violence of such programmes, the censorship boards were conscious that there was a limited market for historical or educational films. They focused instead on maintaining social concord by censoring films that 'deal with race and colour [and] which would have offended various groups of the local population'.[21]

In Northern Rhodesia, too, going to the cinema meant watching 'the high-action products of Hollywood dream factories' (Ambler 2001: 85). As audience demand became more exacting, the colonial authorities found themselves in a bind: while they could limit the choice of films by censoring them prior to their distribution, or by banning or mutilating them with ad hoc cuts locally, they could hardly force audiences to watch boring shows.

The metropolises versus Hollywood

What a contrast between the discourses that insisted on the limited understanding of Africa's 'backward populations' and the growing success of Hollywood films in the 1930s! It was apparent that audiences loved cinema, whatever contemptuous onlookers thought. Indeed, that is precisely what worried the colonial authorities, as expressed here by Sir Henry Hesketh Bell, member of the Board of Control: 'To the vast majority of black, brown, and yellow people, the inner life which flourishes in centres of crime and infamy was unknown until the American films showed them a travesty of it.'[22]

Was this invasion of American films, denounced by the metropolises, a true phenomenon? Were national productions more moralistic than foreign ones, for that matter? This assertion resonated with the notion of a hierarchy between documentaries—thought to be innocent and less ideologically marked—and fictions. Such moralistic affirmations served as the official justification for the protectionist policy adopted by the British in 1927, which imposed a 20 per cent quota of British films; equivalent measures were introduced the following year in Italy.[23] In France, the 1928 Herriot Decree introduced the idea of protecting French films, at a time when nearly 90 per cent of films screened were foreign; it was not until 1946, and again in 1953, that a law was adopted which did so.

The situation nonetheless differed between the British and French Empires, for obvious linguistic reasons. The *Blue Books* provide detailed, but contradictory, annual statistics concerning the films imported to Britain's West African colonies. They show that 1927 was a pivotal year which also needs to be contextualized in relation to the debates raised during the various Imperial Conferences: it was from this year on that imports were classified by country of provenance, and that the Gold Coast specified the number of linear feet of Cinematograph Films imported, most of which came from Britain, the United States, and Nigeria.[24] At this stage, nearly half of films came from the USA; the proportion then fell, but these figures are underestimated, as American films also arrived via the metropolis and Nigeria. The structure of Nigeria's imports was different, with considerable variations from one year to the next: few films arrived directly from the United States, whereas the Gold Coast was a pole of regional redistribution. These statistics give an indication of import structures but only a vague idea of the distribution of American films, whose prevalence other literary or administrative sources nonetheless evoke. British productions struggled to rival Hollywood, but the British authorities hesitated to introduce a law to back the national film industry; they requested, rather, that it compete with American films commercially by producing hits.[25]

The situation was different in the French colonies, where no real control existed in the early 1930s, as highlighted by the governor of Togo: 'It is more or less impossible to establish figures concerning the nationalities of films, as all are screened several times.' A film's nationality was manifestly not a criterion of choice for the spectators; all that mattered was their interest in the film itself. However, after asserting that 'the natives seem to share the same taste for French and English films', the governor of Togo did say the following of 'French films shown in the neighbouring foreign countries': 'As for commercial French films, they have no chance of being favourably appreciated by the natives, who are more or less the sole clients of this cinema [in Accra]. French production companies, like the foreign production companies, show little concern for the tastes of the native clientele.'[26]

During the interwar years, French films were predominant in FWA, for reasons that were related to language as much as to distribution circuits. Of the sixty-one films clearly identified in the French Sudan in 1936, over half were French (62 per cent) and a third American (31 per cent). A similar proportion is found in the COMACICO's programme in Dakar on the weekend of 4 to 5 July 1936, during which three cinemas shared five films, two of which were American and three French. The COMACICO, for that matter, played on this Frenchness in its advertising of these films: 'The COMACICO is proud to announce the list of French films to which it has the exclusive rights.

A deluge of French films'.[27] In reality, some of the films announced had already been released in the metropolis two years earlier, which shows the lack of direct competition.

French productions were also predominant in Senegal (83 per cent of the films announced in *Paris-Dakar* in 1937), but the prevalence of American films was still considerable: they represented 79 per cent of so-called 'foreign' films, and did not just comprise westerns. *King Kong* (1933), and comedies such as *It Happened One Night* starring Clark Gable (1934) and *As You Desire Me* starring Greta Garbo (1932), were huge hits (Seck 2008: 88–89). In contrast, according to Ivory Coast's film screenings control registry, of the 280 films authorized from September 1937 to September 1939, over 90 per cent were American (Kipré 1985: 183). Was this colony a forerunner in a phenomenon that was to take off after the Second World War?

5

THE SPREAD OF CINEMA
(1945 TO THE INDEPENDENCE ERA)

At one end of the scale there are those who are only now hearing of the cinema for the first time, and at the other end, a town such as Lagos, with six or seven cinemas, and where some Africans ... go to see films four times a week.[1]

After the Second World War, cinema spread as a popular leisure activity, occupying more space both literally and in people's imaginations. Film shows became a common phenomenon, spectatorship grew, screenings took place daily, audiences expressed themselves more openly, and pressure groups became more active. But, as the above quotation shows, experiences remained highly diverse. Cinema grew to be a marker of the modernity to which young people aspired, and a feature of city life; however, it also expanded beyond town centres. In some cases, spectators had a choice between a range of screening venues. In others, a single show at the weekend remained the only opportunity to see a film. Commercial cinema remained the affair of private entrepreneurs, even if the authorities intervened by funding mobile cinema tours, or by encouraging the screening of films in certain organizations, such as schools or youth clubs (see Chapter 3).

Highly dynamic in the British colonies, local Lebanese and Indian business investors branched out into cinema construction and management, and into film distribution. This movement was more tentative in the French colonies, where European circuits set up in the interwar years predominated. A few new actors, who were often Lebanese and occasionally African, did nonetheless emerge. The entrepreneur and religious leader Yacouba Sylla was one such exception in Ivory Coast.

Making a slow but steady mark on the urban landscape

In the 1940s, over 60 per cent of South African city-dwellers, of all classes and conditions, went to the cinema once a week on average. This was unequalled anywhere else. While Dakar had a dozen cinemas in 1948, Mauritania and Niger each only had one 'real' indoor cinema. Similarly, towns in southern Nigeria and the southern Gold Coast were well-equipped, whereas in Freetown a second screening venue—the New Odeon—did not open until 1948, even though the town had a population of 65,000. In the 1950s, the number of cinemas and spectators grew across the continent, increasing from 1,683 cinema houses in 1950 to 2,168 in 1960: an increase of 23 per cent (Sadoul 1972). They were nonetheless concentrated in North Africa and South Africa. Starting out at a far lower number, the number of cinemas in sub-Saharan, or 'tropical' Africa rose from 400 to 614. This represented an increase of 54 per cent, but compared to the world's 160,000 cinemas, or as a ratio of the population, the number of cinemas and spectators nonetheless remained derisory at the time of Independence, as film pioneer Paulin Vieyra observed: 'An African goes to the cinema once every two years, whereas, on average, the French go ten times a year' (Vieyra 1958b: 96). Fellow filmmaker Jean Rouch was even more abrupt: 'Statistically, Europeans go to the cinema thirty to forty times a year. Indians and populations in the Middle East and North Africa go once a year. Africans go once every thirty to forty years and, in some African countries, once a century' (Rouch 1962a: 1, fn. 1).

These statistical averages, of course, mask stark contrasts in practice: in some areas, keen cinephiles went to the cinema almost daily, while other towns were only just discovering the medium. The coastal regions remained the best-equipped. Other determining factors included demographic density, economic dynamism, the state of road infrastructures and electrical installations, and, crucially, distribution policies. Thus, while the COMACICO and the SECMA's quasi-monopoly rigidified the film sector in French West Africa, competition between entrepreneurs stimulated it elsewhere.

The example of the Gold Coast, whose film trajectory remained dynamic, illustrates the fundamental role of competition. In 1962, it had the same number of cinemas as Nigeria—that is, about seventy—even though the latter was much bigger and more populated. The Gold Coast offered 80,000 seats for 7 million inhabitants, compared with 50,000 seats for 40 million Nigerians. Twenty-seven cinemas in the Gold Coast were equipped for CinemaScope.[2] Elsewhere, the quality of installations varied enormously. Good quality equipment was often hard to come by in the French colonies. After Independence, only sixty out of their 220 cinemas were equipped with more modern 16mm projectors (Rouch 1962a), and the distribution of cinemas equipped for standard 35mm remained very uneven. Two colonies predominated: Senegal, where fifty-six cinemas had 35mm projectors, and Ivory Coast, with thirty-three. Next came the French Sudan (fourteen), Guinea (twelve), and the Congo (eleven), leaving the others far behind.[3] But what can be said of the Belgian Congo, where few towns were equipped and cinemas were strictly segregated, but many villagers were exposed to cinema thanks to the missionaries who organized open-air screenings?

Whatever the situation, and whether cinema was a daily reality or a rare dream, it took root in people's minds well beyond the places where it was truly accessible: secondary school children talked about it in the holidays; official or commercial tours screened films in the countryside; migrants discussed them on their return to their villages. The walls of towns were emblazoned with posters and distributors took out newspaper adverts to announce their bills, extolling the performance of such and such an actor and promising plentiful gags and thrills. These initiatives naturally targeted a limited readership, but one that was growing. The size of the ads was proportional to the prestige of the cinema: a quarter page with a picture for a top-of-the-range venue or just the film title for a more modest one. The radio, too, embraced the cinema. *L'écran invisible* (*The Invisible Screen*), a radio show broadcast in Dakar from 1954 onwards, even played extracts from the films' soundtracks (Seck 2008: 127, 139). Few patrons of the working-class cinemas, however, informed themselves via these channels, as most of them had little formal education and limited revenues. They were targeted using other techniques: brightly coloured posters in front of cinemas, parading musicians, human billboards, and megaphone announcements. In one fictionalized account, an adolescent describes the call for the evening show at the Mamou cinema in Guinea: 'He scanned rue du Commerce, by which we were now approaching, and through the old, tinny microphone, the music of the West Indian Léardé announced that the screening would soon start' (Monénembo 1997: 121) In Accra, a bell-ringer known as Charlie Mask Man, after Chaplin's tramp character, walked the streets announcing films (McFeely 2015: 169).

In its different forms, cinema animated the towns, even for those who rarely went. Its ascendance was facilitated by changes in attitude from those in positions of power: adults who relived and shared the pleasure they had discovered in film in their youth; teachers who saw cinema as an educational tool; parents who treated their children; and associations which screened films to liven up their galas. In Muslim areas, some imams' initial opposition waned, especially as it was difficult to counter the powerful attraction that this leisure activity exerted. The affluence of spectators at cinemas in Sabon Gari—the southern migrants' district on the outskirts of Kano's old centre—attested to cinema's great success (Larkin 1998). Certain events had a major symbolic impact: in 1955, the imam of Dakar's central mosque, El Hadji Lamine Diène, attended his first screening, where he watched a carefully chosen film: *Zuhur El Islam* (1951), an Egyptian film recounting the birth of Islam. The event caused a stir, and was relayed by the press (Seck 2008: 166).

From entrepreneurial initiatives to administrative constraints; from town centres to suburbs

After 1945, the hierarchies between cinemas were accentuated in all towns, and with them the potential for division of audiences according to political and social status. Because of the growing awareness at this time of cinema's importance, more information is now available about it in records and archives: administrators carefully filled in the surveys launched by the colonial authorities, UNESCO, and the metropolitan agencies, and the first tourist guides provided lists of cinemas with their names, owners, and locations.[4] However, these sources reproduce a Western definition of cinemas as indoor buildings, whereas the majority of Africans watched films predominantly in open-air cinemas, or similarly rudimentary venues. The sources thus minimize the importance of this leisure activity. In 1948, for example, the lieutenant-governor wrote of 'the inexistence of veritable performance venues in Upper Volta, a designation that can only be applied with difficulty to Bobo-Dioulasso's open-air cinemas'.[5] A 1962 evaluation of the situation in Nigeria also reported only one entirely indoor cinema in Jos; the other cinemas were open-air and were used as car parks in the daytime. Screening conditions in these cinemas were deplorable; according to the American distribution circuit American Motion Picture Export Company Africa (AMPECA), set up after Independence: 'Most theaters were merely crude open-air enclosures and the films old and dilapidated ... despite great potential enthusiasm for this form of entertainment.'[6]

A dual phenomenon characterized the post-war period: an increase in the number of towns equipped with cinemas, and the equipping of the suburbs—due in part to the more modest size of French West Africa's townships—and thus a decrease in the time it took to walk or journey to see a film.[7]

Cinema certainly did not wait until the 1940s to expand outside of the capitals. Its spread beyond Accra continued in the Gold Coast, but there was still an acute regional disparity in the distribution of the country's seventy or so cinemas: most of the screening venues were concentrated in the Gold Coast Colony, slightly fewer were located in the Ashanti region, and very few in the Northern Territories and Togoland (McFeely 2015).[8] With its sixteen cinemas—none of which were located in the European sectors—Accra was well-equipped. In 1955, 42,000 tickets were sold a week, for a population estimated at a maximum of 400,000 inhabitants: that is, the same ratio as in France, a country where cinema was still very dynamic. With a fill rate that now stood at 70 per cent, the industry was ensured a certain profitability (McFeely 2015: 55, 170).

As in Sierra Leone, this leisure activity, in which the bourgeoisie had ceased to show much interest, attracted the working classes. This accentuated the hierarchy between first-release cinemas and the rest, which were often situated near busy spots, such as markets or stations. Considered insalubrious and turbulent by the authorities, the old districts of Jamestown and Ussher Town were home to many a leisure venue. Here, the early Palladium stood proudly alongside new cinemas such as the Opera, which was opened just after the war by the Lebanese Captan family; they went on to build the Odeon, the Orion, and the Roxy. There were also many cinemas in operation along the coast: six in the twin towns of Sekondi-Takoradi, two in Cape Coast, three in Asamankese, and three in Sewdru, near to Accra. In 1951, Kumasi's second cinema, the Rex, opened. With a capacity of 1,500 seats, it was one of the biggest in the country and belonged to the Barakats, another Lebanese family active in Accra. Ten years later, Kumasi had seven cinemas, mainly located in the Zongo, the foreigners' district. In the far north of the country, however, opportunities to watch a film were rare.

Access to cinema was just as unevenly distributed in Nigeria, where distance, which influenced access to film supplies, also affected the distribution of cinema houses. The southern part of the country was better equipped: there were ten cinemas in Lagos, four in Ibadan and Port Harcourt, three in Aba and Onitsha, and two in Enugu, Benin City, and Sapele.[9] The major towns of the north were not without cinemas, however: there were four in Kano, three in Kaduna, two in Zaria, and one each in Maiduguri and Sokoto, which notably catered to demand for cinema by migrants from the south. Screening conditions and comfort levels varied enormously from one venue to the next, but access to films was largely possible.

In the less populous French West Africa, cinema remained rare in the smaller towns and was generally concentrated in the regional capitals in the immediate post-war years. Its expansion further afield varied from one colony to the next. In Senegal in 1948, in addition to Dakar and Saint-Louis, there was a cinema in Thiès, the home of the railway workshops. Ten years later, there were cinemas in twelve Senegalese towns, notably throughout the Atlantic coast's peanut growing region and in Casamance (in Ziguinchor, Kolda, and Vélingara). The situation in the French Sudan (Mali) is particularly interesting, as it suggests that cinema followed the development of economic activity: active in the interwar years in Bamako and the railway terminus of Kayes, cinema progressed inland and, in 1948, could be found along the Niger River in Mopti and Ségou, and to the south in Sikasso. By 1958, Sikasso's cinema had closed down, while Gao and Koulikoro, near to Bamako, now had cinemas. Growth was thus minimal, progressing from five to six equipped towns.

In Guinea, medium-sized towns were equipped, but often in a rudimentary fashion, and screenings were not daily. Cinemas were operational in five towns in 1947, and their number had doubled by 1958. In addition to Conakry, it was possible to watch films in Boké, and Kindia; in Mamou, Dabola (where a mobile cinema put on three shows a week), Dalaba, and Labé in Fouta-Djallon; in Kankan in Upper Guinea; and, in the far-flung forest zone, in Beyla (twice a week), Macenta, and Kissidougou. Even though there were only about fifteen cinemas for 2.5 million Guineans, cinema made an impact upon an entire generation. Conakry was the best equipped city: the suburbs included, its population reached over 50,000 inhabitants around 1955, of whom 3,000 were Europeans. The most prestigious cinema was the Palace, which lay on the road leading to the governor's palace. On his return to Conakry after studying in Dakar and assiduously frequenting its cinemas, Doctor Sultan described the situation in 1947: there were no matinees, but there were two screenings a night, at 9pm and 11pm. Screenings began with newsreels, followed by a short film, then the feature. The programme alternated between French films and westerns. In the intermission, an iced sweets seller would walk up and down the aisles (interview, Conakry 2005).

The Triomphe, near the Chamber of Commerce, also attracted a wealthy clientele of Europeans, Lebanese, and the literate elite. The Rialto by the central market, on the other hand, screened westerns and detective films for an almost exclusively working-class African audience. Similarly, the Vox, right at the heart of the African neighbourhood of Sandervalia, was rarely frequented by Europeans. In addition to these cinemas were the Club on the outskirts of the town, and a large tent installation on Perrone Beach in the European district, frequented by Europeans and Africans alike. Audiences could not choose the bill, but 'it was joyous', recalls Mrs Walter, who lived in Conakry from 1949 to 1953 (interview, Strasbourg 2006). It was not until the late 1950s that the first cinema was built in the suburbs, in Coléah, a residential development for African civil servants.[10] In the inland towns, cinemas were built on the initiative of Europeans or Lebanese, who combined their activities as trader-planters with entrepreneurial ventures. Certain cinemas made their mark on people's memories, such as the Ranch in Labé, owned by Jacques Demarchelier, which was not only a major leisure venue but also a venue for political rallies; the Rex in Mamou, run by the Lebanese Raffi family; or the Vox in Kindia, opened in 1955 by a Lebanese woman trader Mme Veuve Chediac.[11] With their wooden and metal benches imported from Europe, the 700-seat stalls were separated from the slightly raised balcony at the back, which was equipped with ninety-six armchairs.

Cinema also prospered in Ivory Coast, increasing from a dozen screens in the early 1950s to twenty-four in 1955, and over thirty in 1960. The south was best equipped, notably Grand Bassam and Abidjan, where cinema was active in both the city centre and the working-class districts of Adjamé and Treichville. Bouaké also cut a fine figure with its Vox and Rex cinemas. Yacouba Sylla (1906–88), a Muslim leader and dynamic entrepreneur, made his mark on the west of the country. Deported from the French Sudan in 1930 for his religious activism, he settled in Gagnoa after his release in 1938 and, in parallel to his activities as a transporter and a planter, founded seven cinemas from 1950 to 1965 in the centres where his religious community was established (Gagnoa, Daloa, Divo, Sinfra, Oumé, Soubré, and Adzopé). After an initial period of mistrust due to 'the person in question's belonging to the Hamallist milieu and his political influence, and, secondly, to the possibility that Mr Yacouba Sylla organize, or allow the organization of, public meetings in the cinema', the authorities backed Sylla, who provided entertainment to migrant workers and to the local populations in a region where no European investor had considered setting up a cinema (Goerg 2019).[12]

Elsewhere, the cinema remained limited to the major towns, such as in Upper Volta, where only Bobo-Dioulasso (which boasted cinemas the Rex, the Normandie, and the Eden) and Ouagadougou (which had the Olympia, near to the main market, and Naderciné, opened in 1952) were equipped in 1958.[13] In Togo, beyond Lomé where cinema was popular, only the inhabitants of Aného, the former German capital, and Sokodé and Atakpamé in the north were able to go to the pictures. In Atakpamé, screenings took place in an open-air bar, drawing many spectators as they were the only local entertainment. A drummer, displaying the film's poster, would walk the town crying: 'Tonight, cinema at Akapki bar'. Similarly, in Dahomey (today's Benin), only Porto-Novo and Cotonou—respectively the administrative and economic capitals—had cinemas. In Parakou, the terminus of the railway line stretching 430 kilometres from the coast, films could be viewed twice a week in the community hall.

Despite the increase in cinema houses, then, going to the cinema was often only possible in the main towns. Those that offered a range of cinemas, from the town centres to the peripheral neighbourhoods, were rare. Dakar, which had a population of over 400,000 inhabitants at the time of Independence— comparable to that of Accra—was particularly well-equipped: the town had eight cinemas in 1945, but there were seventeen (16,311 seats) by the mid-1950s, and about twenty by 1960. The two main operators predominated: the COMACICO had ten cinemas (9,924 seats) and the SECMA had four (3,182 seats), with entrepreneur Abdou Karim Bourgi running the remaining three (3,205 seats).[14] In the town centre, the oldest, partially covered cinemas (the Palace, the Bataclan, and the Rialto)—originally the most prestigious— coexisted with more recent indoor cinemas, such as the Vog and the Studio, which targeted Europeans and sought to separate themselves from the increasingly sizeable African clientele. The social geography of cinema evolved as the years passed and more cinemas opened. The Vox, which lay outside of the central Plateau district, lost its prestige amongst the Europeans, who continued loyally to frequent the Rialto and the Palace, whereas the Rex and the Lux catered to a mixed audience comprising mainly Senegalese, but also Lebanese and French spectators. Other, less comfortable, cinemas in the Médina, or on the outskirts of the Plateau district, specifically targeted a more working-class audience, as did the Rio and the ABC. In parallel, the periphery districts were increasingly well-equipped, such as the new Point E residential district where the COMACICO built the vast El Mansour with its 17-metre screen, the only cinema equipped in CinemaScope; middle-class districts, such as Fass, were becoming better equipped too.

The population of Dakar thus had a wide range of venues at its disposal, varying in proximity, price, programming, and comfort levels. In general, for practical and financial reasons, people nonetheless stayed in their own neighbourhoods, which greatly limited the social integration that cinema otherwise enabled: 'For reasons of convenience, I stay in my neighbourhood, but that does not stop me from going to other cinemas when they put on a good film.'[15] In Saint-Louis, a new cinema—the Pax (later renamed the El Hadj)—was established to serve the suburban Sor district, adding to the earlier Vox and Rex cinemas located on the island.

The opening of new cinemas depended on demographic factors, of course, but also on administrative constraints or incentives, and on the economic and cultural landscape. In the Gold Coast, different factors explain the longstanding dynamism of the film sector: entrepreneurial activity, a strong entertainment culture (highlife music, concert parties), the cosmopolitanism of the elites, the level of school enrolment, and international circulation. This film sector underwent a major transformation. It was dominated in the interwar years, along with a British entrepreneur, by local businessman Alfred Ocansey; when Ocansey died in 1943, Lebanese and Indian traders entered the sector, taking advantage of their networks throughout the British Empire. In 1962, five main operators were active in both cinema management and film distribution. In 1956, the West African Pictures Company (WAPCO), set up by the Lebanese Barakat family who were also active in Nigeria, was taken over by Ghana's government, run by the Convention People's Party (CPP); its five cinemas were included in this takeover, but their management was left to the Barakats. The other four operators were Captan Films, Nankani Films, Broadway Films, and Advani Films (Balogun 1987, McFeely 2015).[16] The competition between them influenced the development of both cinemas and film import strategies.

While the British authorities encouraged private initiatives, the French were caught up in top-heavy regulations and a contradiction between their desire to grant free reign to independent businesses and their obsession with control. Locally, some administrators were aware of the negative impact of monopolies (a paucity of programmes, low investment, the degradation of equipment) and encouraged diversification, aware that the restrictions came above all from the cinema owners and distributors, who feared competition. In the colonial microcosm, the administrators' personalities and their personal relationships to cinema, as well as their ties with the local entrepreneurs, played a major role. Some entrepreneurs, who had been in place since the 1930s, maintained their position by accommodating and flattering the administration. To avoid the opening of rival cinemas, they evoked security, public order, or even patriotism.

This lobbying often came up against the authorities' legalism, however. In 1947, while certain Europeans opposed the opening of a cinema in Bamako, apparently for fear of the noise and crowds in the town centre, the head of the Public Works service affirmed:

> It would even be desirable that a cinema offering correct conditions of comfort especially, and well-chosen bills of French productions be set up in Bamako, helping us to erase the memory of the films screened for many years, which, ninety-five times out of a hundred, are an old, or very old, garish load of rubbish.[17]

Surpassing merely technical concerns, this engineer revealed a lot about the monopoly hitherto exercised in Bamako and openly promoted commercial competition. In Guinea, too, the authorities were favourable to competition. In Kankan, the district officer estimated in 1948 that: 'With 20,000 inhabitants, two cinemas are possible.' The second cinema, the Vox, built by a Lebanese proprietor, was inaugurated in 1955; it had 600 seats, a bar, and a dance hall. In Mamou, both the administrator and El Hadj Almamy Ibrahima Sorry Dara Barry, head of the province and member of the French West African Grand Council, backed this request made by a Lebanese trader in 1951: 'The opening of a second cinema is most necessary in Mamou; film-goers will have the choice between two cinemas, and the owners will do everything possible to make their cinemas more comfortable and more welcoming.'[18] However, even though the authorities gave a favourable response, the project did not come to fruition. At the time of Independence in 1958, the Rex, opened by the Raffi family in 1945, remained the only cinema.

The decision to create—or not to create—a situation of competition depended on complex stakes which need to be individually examined, and concern politics, economics, and, secondarily, cultural considerations. Expanding the range of cinemas did not resolve the question of the two film distributors' almost complete monopoly, however. Depending on their location and available communication networks, some towns even depended on just one circuit. In Guinea, the COMACICO predominated in Conakry, Kindia, and Mamou, while Kankan, further inland, benefited from its proximity with Mali and Ivory Coast, receiving films from both of the major COMACICO and SECMA circuits. On the whole, the administration protected them and was wary of foreign investors. In 1955, reacting to the rumoured arrival of an American circuit, the French Overseas Ministry insisted that the choice and distribution of films should remain in the hands of the French.[19] In 1961, the two circuits controlled two-thirds of cinemas: the COMACICO controlled sixty and the SECMA forty, and almost all of the independent cinemas depended on them for their supply of films.

Some rare private cinema owners nonetheless managed to import films directly. In Dakar, several Lebanese cinema owners—first Abdou Karim Bourgi, followed by Albert Bourgi and Ibrahima Réda in 1953—organized themselves to satisfy a taste for Arab films among their approximately eight thousand compatriots.[20] The representatives of the existing circuits did not appreciate these entrepreneurs. At the time of the Suez Crisis in 1956, the president of the federal Censorship Board did not hesitate to emphasise Abdou Karim Bourgi's mixed French-Lebanese heritage in an attempt to curb his activity. Similarly, in Ivory Coast, a nationalistic and moralizing chord was struck to denounce Yacouba Sylla, who was accused by a member of the French West African–French Equatorial African–Togolese–Cameroonian cinemas union (CINESYNDIC) of importing films without federal visas.[21] An administrative enquiry denied these insinuations and affirmed that Sylla 'presented himself to the Directorate for Political Affairs and readily agreed on the need to follow the common rule.'[22] Sylla's legalism—a key quality emphasised within his religious community—thus protected him from these accusations, and allowed him to become a major figure in cinema in western Ivory Coast.[23]

Regulations regarding the circulation of films, censorship, and cinema safety standards were tightened after the Second World War. In addition to the genuine fire prevention concerns, there were worries about preserving the image of certain towns. Cinema houses' visibility in the urban landscape, the forms of night-time socializing that they encouraged, and their tendency to spill over into the public space caused crowds, fights, and noise, and sometimes even a stench. One report described the streets around a cinema in Dakar as 'urinals'. In 1951, the manager of the Triomphe in Conakry was ordered to stop the 'disorder' both inside and outside the cinema, as complaints had been made about the din.[24] As places to gather at night, cinemas might also, it was thought, indirectly encourage petty crime.

In 1949, the regulatory requirements for running an entertainment venue were standardized across the whole of French West Africa. These were tightened in 1950 with the classification of cinemas as dangerous establishments, which meant that an administrative and technical enquiry had to be carried out before authorization for a cinema was granted.[25] The regulation was modified in 1955, making it still more constraining. This judicial complexity contrasted with the rudimentary character of the majority of venues, and limited the opening of new cinemas.[26]

Measures were also taken in the British colonies to make cinemas safer, but the regulations were not always followed. Blocked emergency exits were thus responsible for the 1951 El Duniya tragedy in Kano, Nigeria, in which over 300 spectators died (Larkin 1998). This tragedy made a huge impact on the public and fuelled the imams' condemnation of cinema, but nonetheless did not hinder the growth of the leisure activity's popularity in Kano. A 1954 regulation reinforced earlier guidelines, requiring the presence of firemen at cinemas and the payment of a licence. Elsewhere, fires regularly demonstrated that cinemas were risky places: a fire broke out at the Dakar Vox in 1950, a stock of films went up in flames in Accra in 1956, and so on. In Diourbel, Senegal, there were several victims when a burning dustbin caused a panic, marking local memory and putting people off cinema for a while (interview with Thioub, Amsterdam 2010). Other incidents threatened security, such as the crush caused when 'spectators in the open-air seats came barging into the first-class seating area [at the back] when it threatened to rain'.[27] The regulations adopted to avoid tragedies (emergency exits, fireproof materials, extinguishers) did not suffice, as inspections were infrequent and the administrative services very often shut their eyes to irregularities, worried more that cinemas would be turned into places of social disorder or protest.

To each their own cinema: different atmospheres and experiences

Although cinemas by no means catered to all areas, they were a landmark for town-dwellers and symbols of modernity, as one canton chief in Upper Volta affirmed in 1956: '... in town, one must follow the ambiance of the milieu, dress accordingly, go to the cinema, go to dances; in other words, be fashionable.'[28]

Questions of modernity were inherent to cinema as an activity, but also to its buildings. Only the most prestigious town centre cinemas displayed their status as modern temples through their architecture or the quality of their fittings (such as projectors and seating); the others looked more like warehouses or enclosures. Particular attention was paid to these prestigious cinema houses' facades, which were visible from afar, and to the entrances where people waited before the show. The Palladium in Accra was particularly fine, for example. In Saint-Louis in Senegal, the ticket offices at the Rex and the Vox were improved over the years, while the buildings remained partially open-air. In the 1950s, the Rex in Abidjan and the Colisée in Dakar had imposing facades and canopies. In Brazzaville, the architecture of the prestigious Vog cinema in the town centre contrasted with the five cinemas in the poorer districts of Poto-Poto and Bacongo. A Gabonese high school student in this town in the 1950s recalls the clear distinction between these relatively cheap, rowdy open-air cinemas frequented exclusively by Africans, and the indoor cinemas where the public was mixed. His host family encouraged him to go to the better-reputed cinema in the town cinema (interview with Owono Nguema, Aix-en-Provence 2010). Most cinemas had a bar, which served as a place to meet people from beyond the usual family or neighbourhood circles. These amenities were also found in front of the working-class cinemas. Inside the front courtyard of the Vox in Kindia, for example, were market stalls and a covered bar alongside the ticket office. Clients who were not going to the cinema could also access these spaces.

Through their very presence, cinemas thus created new spaces and new modes of sociability. In major municipalities such as Kano, Accra, or Dakar, and even in smaller towns, cinemas became landmarks at the level of the post office or the market. People would meet there or hang out without necessarily going to see a film. Hawkers sold their wares on the pavements outside. People ran into acquaintances they might not have seen otherwise. Social control was less rigid in these spaces. Relationships between men and women, between people of different social classes, religions, or origins, between individuals and groups, between young and old, and even between black and white were renegotiated.[29] Codified in the professional world and the urban space, the distance between colonizer and colonized was also redefined within the frame of this leisure activity. In the mid-1950s, the director of the SECMA noted 'certain cinemas in Dakar and Abidjan whose clientele was 90 per cent European', these being cities with large foreign populations.[30] At this point in time, prices for cinema tickets were determined according to the clientele; there was a controversy about ticket pricing in 1957, as the COMACICO distinguished between two groups: 'Africans' and 'First Class'.[31]

However, the sociological evolution of the European population in the 1950s—exemplified by the diversification of jobs, particularly for women, and increasing politicization—tended to broaden experiences and mindsets. The often young, white population had already developed a taste for cinema in France, and did not hesitate to go beyond their limited circles to frequent mixed cinemas. Although the working-class Vox cinema in Conakry was outside the habitual areas, or even the recognition, of the majority of Europeans, it was readily frequented by those sympathetic to the Guineans' political demands (interviews with Lagache-Blanchet, Conakry and Paris 2005, and Ghussein, Conakry 2005).

In addition to the social and aesthetic contrasts between cinemas, there were also significant differences in cost. Variable from town to town and venue to venue, some ticket prices could exceed those of the cheaper cinemas by four times or more, barring the majority of the town's inhabitants from more prestigious cinemas, or keeping them out of the best seats. However, over the course of the 1950s, the proportion of Africans frequenting the first-release cinemas, or buying tickets for the most expensive seats, rose: 'I choose the seats for reasons of comfort and convenience. It is too squashed on the benches, you cannot see as well, and the people are too noisy.'[32]

Increasing school attendance and the beginnings of Africanization in the managerial classes engendered the emergence of intermediary social groups, who asserted their right to access cultural facilities. University students, graduates, well-off traders, and lower-ranking civil servants were attracted by a wide range of films—for their entertainment value, of course, but also as a means of broadening their knowledge. Some would go to the cinema as a couple. Parents might go in the evening or send their children to enjoy outings at the matinees (anonymous interview, Dakar). The cinema 'created a platform for husbands and wives to bond and have their special moments', stated one old man in Accra.[33]

As several historians have shown (Bickford-Smith 2000; Burns 2002b; Fair 2018; Goerg 2017; Larkin 1998), the material conditions of the venue determined the atmosphere both inside and around the cinema. The mood ranged from quasi-reverence in the first-release cinemas to an animated din in working-class movie theatres (McFeely 2015: 273, 279–80). According to Jean Rouch, the din could even render the dialogues incomprehensible, because of the level of noise: 'In the darkened cinemas where films were shown, the sound played no role, so drowned out was it by the shouting of the crowd' (Rouch 1958: 92).

Accounts and interviews affirm the rowdy atmosphere in cinemas, where the public talked loudly, commented on the action, sang along with the songs, or spoke the lines before the characters, having already seen the films. Nafissatou Diallo, a teenager at the time, describes a show at the Corona, a working-class cinema in Dakar, thus:

> It was an Arabic film, starring Raba, a famous singer of the time. We couldn't follow much. There were lots of cuts, the film was old, the projector often broke down and the spectators were noisy. Some were watching the film for the dozenth time and knew the songs by heart, which they sang along to with the actors. Others smoked, threw peanuts at or called out to one another, or exchanged rude remarks (Diallo 1997: 65).

The more well-to-do audiences of certain Plateau district cinemas, be they European or African, would not have appreciated such rowdiness. Other spec-

tators, on the contrary, sought out this lively atmosphere for reasons of pleasure or activism—among them Cheikh Anta Diop, author of *Nations nègres et
cultures* (Black Nations and Cultures, 1954), who used to enjoy going to a
working-class cinema with his friends (interview with Diagne, Paris 2006).

Their location in the cinema also determined the atmosphere and attitude
of the spectators, ranging from the animated stalls to the more regimented
balcony, or the section at the back of the cinema. The front rows right at the
foot of the screen were the site of lively exchanges between the generally
younger spectators. Sometimes called the 'goat pen' in Dakar (interview with
Dieng, Dakar 2005), this unruly zone was also designated by metaphors taken
from westerns. In Guinea, the distinction was made in working-class cinemas
between 'the pit (the cowboy area, as it was commonly known), and the one
or two rows of the Indian area (that is, the cheapest part of the cinema)'
(Monénembo 1997: 189). In Bamako, the 'cheapest seats [notably for] young-
sters, sat on the floor or on low benches' were termed the *indiennat* ('Indian
land'), in reference to 'Indians hidden behind bushes' (Haffner 1978: 169);
others, however, took this to indicate the 'Indian whoops' of the children in
the audience (interview with Bakary, Ouagadougou 2008). This noisy, joyous
atmosphere was an integral part of the cinema experience, but sources written
by elites failed to capture it, as McFeely suggests: 'Elite commentators domi-
nate the surviving narrative of audience behaviour in large measure because
they populate the official and newspaper archives in ways that less literate
viewers could not unless their voices were sought out and recorded by aca-
demic or journalistic observers' (McFeely 2015: 287).

The cinema attracted viewers because it was by far the cheapest form of
entertainment. In Dakar in the 1950s, prices ranged from forty to sixty francs
in the working-class cinemas, to seventy-five to 150 francs in the mixed cinemas. That the Théâtre du Palais was expensive (200 to 250 francs in 1955) is
hardly surprising given that it was an elitist venue, but the same went for the
major football matches (150 to 200 francs for the final of the French West
Africa Cup in 1957) or for certain nightclubs, such as the Jockey, an African
dance hall, which cost 100 francs in 1955. In Accra, too, the cinema was
cheaper than certain clubs or concert parties (McFeely 2015: 157).

Cinema was thus accessible to all who could afford it. Children, who benefited from a cheaper rate, thus spent their meagre pocket money on cinema
tickets, while city youths found ways of scraping money together for a show.
Fraud, practiced everywhere, attests to the existence of a keen but penniless
potential audience. The El Duniya tragedy, in which the cinema's emergency

exits were blocked, indicates that the cinema owners, aware of the problem, chose to sacrifice security to beat the fraudsters. Other strategies were invented: people passed round one ticket, sneaked in through back entrances, or, according to historian Emmanuel Akyeampong, clubbed together: 'Children in Ghanaian cities would pool their change to raise enough money to buy a single movie ticket for the one boy or girl who could be counted on to absorb the film and describe in detail the hero's dress and gait and repeat his memorable phrases' (McFeely 2015: 299; Akyeampong cited in Ambler 2001: 94).

Beyond the images themselves, it was the imaginary conveyed by films and their narratives that adolescents truly latched onto. During the late colonial period, cinema's success and its relative reach created a diversified audience that was less and less controllable, far from the contained circles of the early years. Both through the films they saw and the fellow spectators they mingled with, the cinema took individuals out of their daily lives and their normal milieu. The expansion of audiences accentuated this dimension of cinema-going, although these observations must be qualified: above all, social homogeneity and a limited range of film genres depending on the cinema remained the norm. Moreover, different groups' patronization of the same space did not necessarily mean shared conviviality, but rather parallel experiences. Nonetheless, cinema was not a neutral space in the eyes of either the African authorities (including elders, men, the first elected representatives, administrative chiefs, and dignitaries) or the colonial authorities and European spectators. It permitted expressions of both joy and violence. Critiques unleashed in the cinema took on all the more significance when the audience was mixed, and rowdiness frequently transformed into direct confrontation with colonial oppressors. Police reports highlight the hostile atmosphere often witnessed: 'Observation of the crowds' enthusiastic reactions generally leads civilian and military Europeans to regret the screening of such films before an indigenous population.'[34]

Some Europeans recounted the commentaries heard in cinemas, which at times became vehicles for vehement anti-colonial sentiment. But these reactions also meant that cinema served as a form of safety valve. Indeed, the surveillance of cinemas tightened as the proportion of working-class and notably young spectators increased; these demographics were deemed more turbulent or dissenting, and 'quick to speak out and be uncivil'—behaviour reported in Bobo-Dioulasso's open-air cinema.[35] The shared space of the cinema at times generated the formation of visible solidarity groups. This new sociability worried the authorities, who sought to prevent these groups from taking root and to restrict the social function of cinema buildings. Hence the complex negotiations between young people, who had extremely quickly appropriated this mode of entertainment and its spaces, and the administrative authorities, who tried to exert their control over it. It is thus no longer on a scale of towns and cities, but one of neighbourhoods, or even cinemas themselves, that cinematographic experiences and the complex factors that surrounded them need to be assessed. These considerations, however, must not obscure the fact that unruliness in cinemas was not always of a political nature; rather, it was often festive, and film shows were, for the most part, entertaining and trouble-free. As a result, they often left limited traces in the police archives, and even in spectators' memories.

6

THE INDEPENDENCE GENERATION

FILM CULTURE AND THE ANTI-COLONIAL STRUGGLE IN THE 1950s

We should do as the French in Paris and not be afraid to shed our blood for our country and our freedom.[1]

This call to struggle, pronounced in Niamey, Niger, at a screening of René Clement's *La Bataille du rail* (The Battle of the Rails), reflects changing political circumstances. Although this film celebrating the French Resistance was screened in Dakar at the time of its release in 1946, it was a screening in 1949 that provoked this heartfelt reaction from a Rassemblement Démocratique Africain (RDA, African Democratic Rally) militant, and revealed how unprepared the colonial authorities were for resistance. The film was immediately banned. Gustave Borgnis-Desbordes, Superior Commander of the French West African land force, drew an immediate parallel between the film's events and the colonial situation, fearing that it would offer dangerous knowledge to the colonized:

> Films about the Resistance constitute very thorough and highly varied lessons on ways to clandestinely fight an established order, smuggle arms, organize secret meetings, and carry out sabotage. It seems to me absolutely counter-productive to give such lessons to those who see us as occupiers whom they wish to throw out.[2]

In the years that saw the unravelling of colonial domination, the cinema was at the centre of important questions: films proposed alternative modes of action and reflection; demands could be voiced in cinemas openly and without punishment; and censorship incarnated the authorities' illusion that tight control would stop the march of history and limit activists' perception of colonial authoritarianism. Censorship was a matter of difficult compromise. In 1958, for example, it was lamented that certain westerns judged to be 'lessons in rape, murder and immorality' were shown to 'an audience that still believes what it sees'.[3] This was not the opinion of a colonial administrator concerned about public order but of Daniel Ouezzin Coulibaly, Vice President of the Governing Council of Upper Volta, who was worried about young people's behaviour in the light of his country's coming independence. His remarks reflect the contemporary debates that animated the emerging postcolonial societies, which were torn between attachment to the past and modernity, African values and Western depravity. In Ghana, the elite, who were very active on the censorship board, expressed the same desire to remove images that might encourage reprehensible behaviour from screens in working-class areas.

Throughout the 1950s, cinema was the site of tensions between audiences, the authorities, and the rising elites, while at the same time remaining, fundamentally, a place to relax. For both African politicians and the administration, films seemed to contain a subversive dimension beneath their unassuming air of entertainment that needed to be combatted. As the colonial territories opened up to the world considerably thanks to the increasing circulation of people and information (through written press, radio, and education), the authorities were caught between their fear of disorder and protest and the acknowledgement of spectators' ability to judge filmic content; between rowdiness in the cinemas and the activism of pressure groups with diverging aims.

Beyond Western cinema?

> When I think of my own childhood, it's cinema that first comes to mind, its very premises even. It symbolized the town more than anything else: a town wasn't a proper town unless it had a cinema house. As a child, it was the place where you could escape into your imagination (Monénembo 1998).

Multiple witnesses emphasise that to go to the cinema was to 'escape into another world; it was a celebration you got dressed up for, a magical moment' (interview with Diakité, Conakry 2005). The distributors responded to this escapist impulse with the same range of films as before, addressing audiences made up primarily of adolescents and young men through action and adven-

ture films (including westerns, crime movies, and fantasy films) and comedies. Throughout the continent, they drew on the same pool of films. Sharing
the same language as the world's greatest producer, the United States, considerably facilitated the circulation of films in the British Empire; no dubbing
was necessary, although the use of American slang was frowned upon. Arab
and Indian entrepreneurs nonetheless broadened the spectrum of films available, while also satisfying the demand for the American films that the public
loved watching over and over again. Despite a slight increase in school enrolment, more complex films and narratives raised the problem of audiences'
variable proficiency in the colonial language. Only a small sector of the population demanded such films. However, the images that did play in cinemas, if
often limited, created the impression of contact with the wider world and
access to a global culture, some of whose gestural and linguistic codes or
clothing were appropriated. On the whole, films had little overlap with audiences' daily lives; following the plot thus required complex mental gymnas-
tics, or a vivid imagination.

The post-war years saw an influx of American films, with increasing quanti-
ties of old pictures imported for reasons of profitability, but also because a
large stock was needed to ensure the rapid rotation of films. Some cinema
owners in Ghana boasted a stock of over 200 films; collections of this size
were made impossible in the French colonies by their centralized distribution
system (McFeely 2015: 13, 284, 295).[4] What criteria determined the distributors' choices? Did they select films in terms of their own prejudices, or did
they refuse to risk censorship? We can, at any rate, safely imagine that the
quest for profits was a key criterion. Distributors thus screened the same films
across their cinema chains, with no choice on the part of local cinema managers—a cause for protest. Crates of films were, for example, sent from
Léopoldville to tour the entire Belgian Congo, and even Ruanda-Urundi
(today's Rwanda and Burundi) (Convents 2006). The same was true of French
West Africa. Film importers reserved first-release films for the prestigious
cinemas in a bid to draw European and elite African spectators, but were less
attentive when it came to working-class audiences. In small towns with a single cinema, screenings of more unusual films were rare, due to both the distributors' lack of effort and the composition of the audience. As one
distributor stressed: 'How many spectators in Niamey could understand and
appreciate Jean Cocteau's film *Orpheus*, which did show in Dakar? ... It was
experimental, addressing a limited audience, even in the Metropolis. How
could one hope to recoup the costs of such a film in Zinder or Niamey?'[5]

American films with a focus on pure entertainment thus predominated in both British and French colonies. Georges Balandier summarised the programme of Brazzaville's working-class cinemas in the early 1950s: 45 per cent of films were westerns and epics, some of which dated back to the 1930s, 23 per cent were comic films (Laurel and Hardy, Fernandel, and the like), 19 per cent were romantic comedies, and the remaining 13 per cent was made up of diverse works, including crime films (Balandier 1985: 256). The proportions reported in this analysis reflect the general situation across West Africa.

Westerns, which were already popular in the inter-war years, found an extremely enthusiastic audience in the new post-war cinemas, particularly among adolescents. Indeed, westerns remain present in everyone's memories; witnesses cite the names of actors such as John Wayne and Gary Cooper and the titles of films such as *The Lone Ranger* (1938), watched many times in the 1950s by one inhabitant of Saint-Louis at the Sor district cinema (interview with Diagne, Paris 2006).

Even though the young Nigerien migrants in Abidjan who featured in Jean Rouch's 1959 docudrama *Moi, un Noir* took the nicknames Eddie Constantine (aka Lemmy Caution), Edward G. Robinson, and Dorothy Lamour in reference to film noir, their environment was above all marked by westerns: including posters on walls, clothing styles, and catchphrases. These references circulated smoothly between different cultural environments. During a *goumbé* in Rouch's film—a festivity that brought together the Nigerien community—acrobatic tricks are executed on a bicycle symbolizing a horse, by men dressed as cowboys.[6]

Although they were by this point being targeted by the administrative and moral authorities—based on critique that was circulating well beyond the African continent—westerns were popular for their simple narratives and clear-cut moral messages.[7] Their visual elements made it possible to rapidly situate the action and identify 'goodies' and 'baddies' through their clothing (such as cowboy outfits, dark suits, and the stern dresses worn by the pioneer women), their attitudes, or their clearly hierarchical modes of transportation (horse, mule, and foot). The narration left space for personal and culturally localized interpretations; the dialogue, for example, was not essential, which was useful given spectators' often imperfect understanding of the film's foreign language, and the ambient noise that often permeated the soundtrack due to poor film quality. However, this did not stop spectators from imitating the cowboys' accents and expressions. Teenagers mimicked the heroes' blatant virility. In the two Congos, 'Bills' strutted about; in Rhodesia, they called themselves the 'Copperbelt cowboys' (Burns 2002a; Convents 2006: 16; Gondola 2009, 2016). *Cowboiadas* ('cowboy films') were a huge hit in Angola, as they were in West Africa (Moorman 2001; Goerg 2012–13). Their eventful adventure narratives, easily identifiable heroes, and draconian systems of justice echoed the narrative codes of local oral tales. This favoured the identification process and facilitated the appropriation of specific elements into daily, local existence thousands of kilometres away from the places represented on the screen.

A real culture of the western emerged, with a corpus of references shared by an entire generation. Young people appropriated this culture in a manner that related both to their passage to adulthood and their environment of colonial contestation. Westerns met their need to assert themselves as individuals or as members of groups. The nicknames of their leaders, the tunes they whistled, their passwords, subjects of conversation, and modes of group initiation: all revolved around the westerns. Adolescents imagined themselves as valiant cowboys with boots, hats, chaps, and guns; they adopted an easily assimilated model of manhood, parallel to the masculinity portrayed in peplum films, and soon to be accessible through Kung Fu films as well. The paraphernalia of a recreated Far West allowed youths to carve out a place for themselves in towns and to stand out from other adolescents—most notably those who attended school—but also to position themselves in relation to adults. Westerns and crime films became ways of contesting elders' authority, as suggested by McFeely: '... the core issue was not always the content of films but rather the threat that cinema-going, with its boisterous, even disrespectful, local tradition of talking back to the screen in some venues, might represent to existing authority' (McFeely 2015: 296).

The popularity of westerns may seem surprising given that the cowboy/ Indian divide metaphorically mirrored the dominant/dominated paradigm clearly found in the colonial context. However, young Africans manifestly identified with the brave cowboys. Only a political awareness that was rare, or unlikely, given the age of the group concerned, made it possible to surpass the alienation induced by a context of colonial domination. In accordance with classic psychological reactions to narrative, young spectators identified with the powerful. Various witnesses presented this anti-Indian stance as self-evident: 'We didn't understand' (interview with Dieng, Dakar 2005). It would take the politicization of the 1950s to challenge this identification. The same process was at play regarding the *Tarzan* films, which were big hits in working-class cinemas, despite their perpetuation of racist clichés.

In addition to westerns, other Hollywood films circulated, conveying negative representations of black people. French films were just as full of racist content. As the evolution of censorship demonstrates, the public increasingly reacted negatively to the images put before them.

Other genres began to appear more often on screens, alongside the films from the West that were favoured by the distributors. Dynamic players in the film market, Egypt and India both saw their productions take off after the introduction of sound cinema and musicals. These films revolved around song and dance but also foregrounded epic plotlines, whose recourse to heroism and magic opened spectators up to new cinematic horizons which were culturally and sociologically closer to home.

While Indian films spread along the east coast early thanks to Indian traders who initially imported them for their own communities (Fair 2004, 2009, 2010, 2018; Reinwald 2006), they met with certain success over more or less the entire continent. In Ghana, their popularity was cemented in the second half of the 1950s, and some cinemas—such as the Dunia in the Nima district, which was home to migrants from the north—specialized in Indian films. The Nankani family played a key role in importing them.

Female audiences enjoyed not only these films' gestures, clothing, and music, but also their treatment of emotions and relationships, while young men often scorned their sentimentality:

> – Are you telling me that *Bahut Din Huwe* or *Mother India* are rubbish films? retorted Benté.
>
> ...
>
> – Not at all! It's because there's too much music and weeping in Hindi films, while in cowboy films ...! Have you seen *Warlock*?
>
> (Monénembo 1997: 137).

The most famous Indian films were consistently billed and constantly rescreened: *Aan* (*The Savage Princess*, 1952) was shown in Dakar throughout the whole of 1955. It was also billed at the Lomé Rex in 1959, along with the equally famous *Mother India* (1957) (Zimmermann 2008: 111). These films' images and songs left their mark on spectators' memories. They were mostly screened in working-class cinemas, but also circulated in the countryside.

Arab films were another popular import, particularly in Dakar where the approximately 8,000-strong Syrian-Lebanese community guaranteed them visibility in the prestigious cinemas. They were more widely distributed in the French colonies, particularly those with larger Muslim populations, than in

Ghana, Nigeria, or British and Belgian Central Africa, where they were rare. Their success reflected the growth in Egyptian production, which rose from nine films a year between 1927 and 1945 to fifty-one a year between 1945 and 1963 (Sadoul 1966: 283; Shafik 2007; Wassef 1995). Lebanon contributed marginally to this production. *Arouss Lubnan* (*The Bride of Lebanon*, 1951), the first Lebanese film, was screened by the Dakar Vox in 1953 at a gala event. Audiences loved Arab films, and the distributors—most notably the Lebanese who operated in Dakar, but also the two dominant companies—met this demand. The COMACICO put up the posters with the following text in Arabic and French: 'COMACICO is proud to present *Bellal* to Black Africa's Muslims, the most grandiose film production about the birth, triumph and glory of Islam'.[8]

Nafissatou Diallo's account of audiences singing along to them testifies to the popularity of the films' songs (see Chapter 5). This singing along suggests that the film in question had been seen many times, but also implies at least phonetic familiarity with Arabic, the language of Quranic schools.

From 1953 to 1954, Arab films made up 13 per cent of the 767 films screened in Dakar (Seck 2008: 162). A comparable percentage was found in Upper Volta, with strong variations depending on the cinema: they represented about 10 per cent of films shown at the Rex in Bobo-Dioulasso but very few of the films at the Normandie, a cinema adjacent to a hotel frequented by a mainly European audience. In Gao (French Sudan), 'Arabic films from Egypt' made up between a third and a quarter of the 1957 summer programme of the Askia, the only cinema in this little town.[9]

Their sentimental plots, the familiar sonorities of their music, and their socio-cultural familiarity, in some instances reinforced by a shared religion, explain why these films touched African spectators while meeting with incomprehension, or even contempt, among the Europeans and parts of the local elite. Women were particularly receptive to this genre, as one female Dakar resident demonstrates: 'I only like Arab films, as they are close to my religion and always include song and dance. I particularly liked *The Thief of Bagdad*, *Leïla*, *Zuhur El Islam*, etc.'[10]

Men were not absent from audiences for these films, however, either because they were accompanying their wives, or because they openly enjoyed the genre. The films evoking Islam were a big hit. In 1953, *Zuhur El Islam* (The Dawn of Islam), the first historical film about the birth of the religion, drew a total of 24,000 spectators in Dakar over the nine days that it was screened in five cinemas. Shot in 1951 by Ibrahim Ezz Eddine, the film was regularly rescreened, particularly during Muslim festivities or Ramadan. During screenings, some spectators would show their enthusiasm by chanting 'Allahu Akbar', provoking the wrath of the colonizers. Already strictly censored in Egypt, the films nevertheless did not give the colonial censors much cause to intervene. As one administrator remarked: 'They are generally of a high moral standard and stigmatize vices such as debauchery or drunkenness which, it must be said, are rightly or wrongly considered by the Islamized populations to be European importations.'[11]

Arab films thus did not arouse particular suspicion on the part of the authorities, who saw them as innocent entertainment. This view changed after Nasser took power and film production became a vehicle for nationalism and pan-Arabism. A note by the Intelligence Services specified this in 1954:

> Very popular with the Africans, these films generally include music, song and dance scenes, interspersed with dialogues, and it is not unusual, at a certain point, to hear an actor slip in a few lines to smear colonization and, for example, to express Muslims' interest in grouping together to constitute a confederation of Arab states in the future.[12]

The authorities thus sought to ban Egyptian films by applying the 1953 French film quota decree and demanding a full translation of their texts, including their song lyrics, in 1956. A battle of cinematic images was thus initiated at a crucial historical moment, when the colonized were seeking political models. Previously authorized films, such as *Zuhur El Islam*, were censored on the grounds that:

> the political context has changed our point of view ... this eulogy of Egypt is currently inopportune. As for the essentially religious action, it can be seen as a glorification of holy war. The battle scene between the people of Mecca and Medina may be censored due to its violence.[13]

Opting for bans, which elicited protests from distributors who had already imported the films, was nonetheless a swansong for the waning empire. It was certainly undermined by France's weakened position after the Suez Crisis (Goerg 2013).[14]

Although Egyptian films were made in and set on the same continent, they were no substitute for the 'African films' that many spectators called for: 'I impatiently await the birth of an African cinema, not to see people dance the waltz in it, or to see African cowboys, but to learn the true history of my country, the history radically denied by the majority of historians.'[15]

Contrary to these wishes, which were also reflected by official enquiries such as one carried out in Nigeria in 1951, the desire for films that spoke to the lives and experiences of African viewers had no impact on the film industry or the colonial authorities. With its distorted image of African societies and its condescending, even racist messaging, colonial cinema did not meet this demand. It mainly targeted metropolitan audiences and was, in reality, rarely screened in Africa's commercial cinemas (Bloom 2008; Burns 2002b; Reynolds 2015). Occasionally, some colonial film units made films with local technicians. However, these films represented ambiguous progress; although their stories featured Africans, the films were conceived of and supervised by Europeans. Nevertheless, the first feature fiction shot in Ghana, director Sean Graham's *The Boy Kumasenu* (1952), was a hit, as spectators were happy to see people who resembled them onscreen (McFeely 2015: 48).[16]

In the Belgian Congo, films were shot by the missionaries, most notably Father Cornil, using Congolese actors but conveying overriding prejudices, to the point that it was inconceivable to screen some of them in Belgium as 'they would be likely to accredit the tenacious legend of the congenital stupidity and dishonesty of the Congolese race', and would shock 'evolving or evolved [populations] who [would see] them as an attack on the entire black race'.[17] At the other extreme, the Belgian–Congolese Cultural Group, which founded the Léopoldville cinema club in 1950, aimed to make 'original Congolese works', but its means were limited (Convents 2006: 156).

In the French colonies, initiatives of this kind were exceptional. The expectations of the Fifth Amateur Film from Overseas France National Competition in 1958 confirmed the abyss between the vitality of the independence movement and the vision of the French Overseas Ministry:

> It would be preferable for competitors to choose subjects showing the evolution of the material and moral living conditions of indigenous populations under the influence and help of France, whose efforts and sacrifices made in favour of the said populations are too often unknown abroad and even in our country.[18]

Colonial propaganda was thus still the focus for the administration, even at this late date. There was very strong resistance to giving the colonized the technical and financial means to make their own films. Nevertheless, *Afrique-sur-Seine*, considered the 'first sub-Saharan African fiction film', was shot in Paris in 1955 by the Groupe africain de cinéma, which included the Beninese filmmaker Paulin Vieyra—the first African student to attend L'Institut des hautes études cinématographiques (IDHEC), the French national film school—Mamadou Sarr, Robert Caristan, and Jacques Mélo Kane (Haffner 1992: 189; Vieyra 1975). Barely distributed at the time, it sought to give Africans an alternative perspective to the one conveyed by colonial discourse.

Yet the group struggled to obtain even a tiny grant in 1957, despite being 'the only organization bringing together Africans who had truly studied cinema and who knew their trade; the organization was backed by neither the authorities nor private funders'.[19]

In 1958, Mamadou Sarr, author of the above remarks, wrote a memorandum entitled *Première histoire du cinéma et du théâtre africains* (First History of African Cinema and Theatre) advocating the birth of African cinema and requesting the backing of the authorities.[20] The question was discussed during the International Meeting on Sub-Saharan African Cinema, held in Brussels in July 1958. Vieyra spoke, clearly expressing the need for Africans to take matters in hand: 'Each time Africans have been able to give their view on their destiny, they have always done it in a very different way to that imagined by the Europeans' (Vieyra 1958b: 15).

At the same conference, David Acquah, the Head Welfare Officer of the by then independent Ghana, denounced 'the prevalent idea that an illiterate person had the mentality of a child' (De Heusch 1958: 11). Even though this position was supported by figures such as Jean Rouch, other retrograde voices continued to speak out. William Sellers, former Head of the Colonial Film Unit, 'thought that Africans could play a larger part in African film production, especially in those films destined for African audiences. At the same time, he thought that films made for overseas audiences were best left to Europeans' (De Heusch 1958: 17).

This obstinately tone-deaf view is strange considering that Independence was approaching. At the Second Congress of Black Writers and Artists in Rome in 1959, Vieyra insisted on the political dimension of the prospective African cinema: 'This cinema must obviously be African, otherwise how can it contribute to forging national consciousness in Africa?' (Vieyra 1959: 307). Film content was indeed a key issue in the 1950s, both for African militants and for the authorities. However, African cinema would only truly emerge after Independence.

Censorship in the period of anticolonial struggle

Audiences did not only express their pleasure at images on the screen; their interjections also sometimes challenged colonial dominance at a time when freedom of speech in public spaces was still muzzled after the war. Spectators felt protected in cinemas. The audience at the Rex in Dakar thus reacted strongly to the line 'It makes you ashamed to be French' in André Berthomieu's

Peloton d'exécution (Resistance, 1945): 'These words were vigorously applauded by the majority of the African audience. Orders were given for the passage in question to be cut from future screenings.'[21]

The censors had clearly not anticipated this reaction, but the police were never far away. Informers gave daily reports, describing the atmosphere and audience comments. The darkness and relative anonymity of these vast spaces with their several hundred seats—or even a thousand at the Rex—facilitated individual and collective expression: comments, rowdiness, shouts of joy, whistling, the scraping of chairs, and the throwing of objects. The surveillance of cinemas did not diminish the prevailing sentiment of impunity. Informers kept watch for material that provoked a reaction: usually nudity, romantic scenes, political discourse, racist behaviour, and dialogue. These reactions were not specific to the colonies alone, but the restrictions on freedom of expression, the contempt shown to the colonized, and the scarcity of other meeting places made the cinema an ideal space for exuberance, joy, and critique.

Surveillance was all the more intense given that the first political meetings were held in cinemas. Reported to have taken place everywhere, this practice blurred the line between entertainment and militancy. Connections between progressive parties and working-class cinemas were evident: in Conakry, the Section Française de l'Internationale Ouvrière (SFIO, French Section of the Workers' International) and the Rassemblement Démocratique Africain (RDA, African Democratic Rally) held meetings in the Vox and the Rialto as of 1946, while the more upmarket Triomphe hosted the Gaullist Rassemblement du Peuple Français (RPF, Rally of the French People) in 1951. Cinema owners' personalities played a role: in the interwar years in Dakar, Maurice Jacquin, founder of the COMACICO and an active member of the SFIO from 1936 to 1939, lent the Rialto to his party. Similarly, in Guinea, RDA sympathizer Jacques Demarchelier lent the party his cinema in Labé as of 1947.[22] In Gagnoa, Ivory Coast, rivals used concerns about cinema owners' political partisanship to attack Yacouba Sylla in 1950, as he supported the RDA (see Chapter 5). McFeely also notes this use of cinemas as meeting places in Ghana (McFeely 2015).

To avoid having to ban films already in circulation, censorship boards attempted to spot elements of the films that had made it past the metropolitan censors which might provoke an audience reaction in a West African political context. It must be remembered that the distributors already restricted the choice of films coming into Africa, and that censorship measures in West Africa affected everyone, whether African or European, literate or non-literate, male or female. The only distinction between groups came with the introduction of an age classification.

The political activity of the 1940s and '50s necessitated a rethinking of censorship. Faced with films whose images contradicted the model of the ideal citizen, the authorities became conscious of their inability to control the screen; they also became aware of the need to adopt a particularly careful approach as the cinema reached an increasingly broad range of demographic groups, some of whom were considered more susceptible to the power of images. The gaps between the legal texts, the objectives of censorship boards, and the practical application of regulations remained significant. Censorship was often applied *a posteriori* in response to audience reactions, which demonstrates the lack of anticipation also shown by the examples of *La Bataille du rail* and *Peloton d'exécution* (see above). Censorship exerted once a film was already billed was politically more dangerous, because it was more visible; it revealed precisely what it sought to hide from the eyes of the colonized, and exposed the arbitrary power of the authorities and their attempts to prevent access to certain images.

The centralized approach adopted in French West Africa contrasted with the autonomy given to the censors in each British colony from 1931 onwards. An early advocate of film regulation in the 1920s (see Chapter 2), the Gold Coast was also at the forefront of the contrasting movement away from censorship. After a brief attempt at firmness in 1947 when eight films were banned, and before the explosion of anti-colonial political activism in the Gold Coast—represented most notably by Kwame Nkrumah's Convention People's Party (CPP)—the Cinematograph Exhibitions Board of Control soon became aware of the counterproductive nature of a repressive approach. It was not possible to negotiate the transition towards self-government while at the same time treating Ghanaians as childlike, in accordance with the rhetoric of the time (McFeely 2015: 126; Goerg 2012). The logic of censorship reflected this infantilizing mindset, through which 'each colony fell on a spectrum of views regarding the intellectual capacity of the local audience to process what was depicted onscreen and to (self-) regulate its behaviour in ways that were acceptable to the colonial rulers' (McFeely 2015: 70).

Moreover, given the considerable time that cinema had been active on the continent, the old argument about audiences' inability to distinguish images from reality no longer applied, as spectators had by now acquired a genuine cinematographic culture that equipped them to understand film. The Gold Coast's new policy emerged after the 1951 legislative elections, which confirmed the elected representatives' direct participation in government. The Board of Control thus adopted a more moderate attitude, and in 1955 only sixteen out of 869 films were banned (McFeely 2015: 130). As elsewhere, however, the elite remained concerned about the impact of films on young people and the working classes, attributing to both groups a more limited critical capacity. Different audience demands and different programming according to cinema and neighbourhood made it possible in part to remedy such concerns. The social conservatism inherent in this approach was accentuated after Independence, in the name of national morals. Censorship became stricter again, except when political tensions necessitated the reduction of pressure in at least one domain: that of leisure.

In French West Africa, too, the censors were forced to reconsider their original firmness. The Laval Decree remained the legal basis for both the screening and the shooting of films. It was reactivated by the Vichy government from 1940 to 1942. High Commissioner Pierre Boisson reaffirmed the need to preserve the image of white people:

> Cinematic films that portray conflict between races must, in general, be excluded from the screens in French West Africa. The problems that they evoke, albeit sometimes with a generous intention, but one which almost always risks being misunderstood, are a dangerous source of misinterpretation among natives and the mixed race that it is better to avoid.[23]

Predictably, certain elements were targeted by the Vichy government, such as critiques of the clergy or mentions of the *Marseillaise* or the Republic, which were cut from films. If Nazi films such as *Jud Süß* (*Süß* the Jew, 1940) were banned, however, it was not in condemnation of their anti-Semitism, but so as not to show the conflicts which were tearing white people apart (Ginio 2003).[24]

Overwhelmed by the influx of films, the Provisional Government (1944–46), and later the Fourth Republic, fumbled ahead.[25] Their approach was indecisive, granting primacy alternately to a single federal censorship board in Dakar and to local boards, which were often overwhelmed but knew the specificities of 'their' populations better (including cultural and religious factors and political contexts). These fluctuating policies also applied to the mandated territory of Togo (Zimmermann 2008: 87). Both pragmatic considerations—such as the impossibility of viewing films given their rapid turnover—and more theoretical concerns—unity of the Empire, equality between film spectators—explain this indecision, which endured until 1956. At this point, the *loi-cadre* (framework law) transferred jurisdiction to the local assemblies.[26] Before this, the lieutenant-governors were entitled to ban films themselves, but they did not appreciate not knowing the reasons for, and thus not being able to justify, federal censorship. The governor of Ivory Coast thus wrote in 1949: 'It would be opportune if the decisions of the Senegalese Cinematic Censorship Board that are regularly communicated to me indicated the motives for cutting or banning a film.'[27] Similarly, the Guinean authorities protested in 1952: 'Very recently, a film screened in Conakry (*Massacre in Lace*) had had so many cuts and mutilations that it was incomprehensible and its screening provoked the justified protest of the audience.'[28]

Irrespective of distribution certificates awarded by the metropolis, cinema was still subjected to control and censorship at the colonial level. Formalized in French West Africa by the general decree of 15 December 1948, this practice was hotly contested by the African deputies; they denounced their differential treatment and the restriction of their freedom of expression, which went against the 1946 reforms that had given them political rights. Represented by Nigerien Boubou Hama, the Grand Council of French West Africa demanded the decree's abrogation.[29]

Hackneyed stereotypes were employed to justify this double censorship. It was still common to draw parallels between African spectators and children who needed to be protected. This belief was firmly expressed in the Belgian Congo in 1954, for example:

> Several members showed their approval for the impetus behind the project: the tightening of regulation on representations destined for natives and non-adults. ... Films that are suitable for adults in the metropolis can have a regrettable influence on the uneducated natives, who are incapable of measuring the part of fiction in them.[30]

What attitudes and objectives were prevalent in these final days of Empire? Studies have shown how film sought to shape spectators' behaviour, and have analyzed the impact of historic films on self-representation and protest— notably in India, where foreign and national productions were screened side-by-side (Grieveson and MacCabe 2011a, 2011b). Interviewees rarely have strong memories of censorship. This is not as unlikely as it may at first seem, given, as already stated, that selections were made before films even arrived in the colonies, which meant that few potentially subversive images ever reached audiences.[31] Moreover, screenings were often interrupted due to the poor quality of the reels; in these circumstances, it was difficult to tell the difference between the jump cuts that resulted from the cutting of censors and the many technical hiccoughs. In such conditions, only spectators who had already seen the film, on release in the metropolis or further afield, could have been aware of local censorship. It is rare, then, that this subject comes up, although one Senegalese witness mentioned the censorship of Chris Marker and Alain Resnais's 1953 film *Les Statues meurent aussi* (Statues Also Die). The film was indeed banned in both the colonies and France, as was the 1950 film *Afrique 50* by René Vautier.

The censors equivocated between the habitual rhetoric which affirmed the supposed naivety of the public, and an increasing awareness that racist lines or certain scenes now provoked angry reactions. Instructions nonetheless remained imprecise: 'We haven't a yardstick to go by,' affirmed K. W. Blackburne, Director of the Colonial Office Information Service, in 1948.[32] As in the early years, attention was focused on potential incitements to crime and violence, and sexual morals were scrutinised. These were the priorities in the Gold Coast, in contrast to settler colonies such as Kenya, which were above all concerned by racial tensions. Films that legitimized revolt were also targeted. Among the films censored in French West Africa, then, were: *Bengal Brigade* (1957), about the Indian Rebellion of 1857, *Riot in Cell Block 11* (1954), *We Were Strangers* (1949), *Rififi* (1955), and *Wings of the Hawk* (1956).[33] The last of these was about 'an insurrection against the established order and risks giving "fans" a whole host of ideas and "technical" advice on how to triumph in an insurrectional movement'.[34] This was also the verdict on *20,000 Years in Sing Sing* (1932), an old American film that was banned in 1950 as 'prisoners sentenced to death are portrayed in it as kinds of heroes'.[35]

Some films nonetheless slipped through the censors' net. In 1950, therefore, *The Mystery of the Black Jungle*, a film about a revolt that overthrows a white ruler, met with the enthusiasm of the spectators at the Bouaké Vox in Ivory Coast, and with the concern of the military:

> If this film of mediocre quality is without danger for broad, informed minds, the same cannot be said of the local indigenous populations. By their reactions during the screening, the natives of Bouaké clearly demonstrated how much they appreciated the scenes in which European soldiers were massacred, and were delighted at the final victory of the rebels.[36]

The atmosphere was indeed tense, as the army had just repressed demonstrations in favour of the RDA. In 1955, a warning of the same order was issued concerning *Tarzan's Savage Fury*, despite the fact that the film had been authorized: 'I draw your attention to the fact that this film, which initially is as naive and improbable as the rest in its series, portrays Europeans in an African country, in contact with a primitive population, in an unfavourable light.'[37]

Central to the colonial situation, the question of gender relations also became eminently sensitive. Any immoral behaviour on the part of a white man or woman, and any image of violence against 'native' women—especially if committed by Europeans—tarnished the representation of the colonizers.[38] In 1951, then, the Guinean censorship board demanded that a scene from *Méfiez-vous des blondes* (Beware of Blondes, 1950) be cut: 'a very short passage (at the start, when the gangster removes his belt to hit the blond woman) ... provoked some murmuring in the cinema.'[39]

In the colonial context, this was less a question of morality than one of potential destabilization. Nothing was deemed more pernicious in this context than the portrayal of interracial relationships. The governor of Niger therefore denounced the authorization given in Dakar to *Plages éternelles* (Lifelong Beach), which included 'Paris nightclub scenes between Blacks and Whites'.

Forced to make concessions to audiences, the authorities attempted to eliminate racist dialogue. In 1957, the governor of French Sudan stated: 'It quite often happens, in French Sudanese cinemas, that unfortunate reflections in films provoke protest and diverse movements among the spectators.' He gave two examples: '*Auberge rouge* [The Red Inn, 1951] (remarks about "savages") and *Rumeur publique* [Public Opinion, 1954] in which it is said in defence of the accused: "at least it's not a Negro who raped one of your girls".'[40]

Such lines provoked an angry uproar. While normal by the standards of the colonizers, they had become unacceptable by the 1950s. The same went for criticism of Islam, but reactions varied depending on the colony. As modes of circulation diversified, fears of uncensored films reaching screens increased. The administrator of Kankan, the second largest town in Guinea, thus worried that the American film *Home of the Brave* (1949)—which showed the racism suffered by a black soldier during the Pacific war and was banned in Senegal—might be screened in his town, after entering the country via French Sudan.[41] Similarly, in Niger, films reached Zinder via Niamey, and the administrators and the local police did not have the means to control them.

Ultimately, while exerting a certain control, the authorities were conscious of cinema's role as a safety valve: it would have been unwise to deprive spectators, and especially young spectators, of this form of escapist entertainment, which, in a colonial setting, was an outlet for their pent-up energy. Yet we can try to evaluate the weight of censorship, despite the paucity of sources. As in the Gold Coast, the number of films banned was ultimately marginal: in Togo, in the space of over a year, 'the exploitation of 545 films was authorized and twenty-two [approximately 4 per cent] were banned. A certain number of cuts were prescribed.'[42] Likewise, in French West Africa over a period of fifteen months (1955–56), the federal Board banned approximately 4 per cent of the films that were put before it. In the Belgian Congo, from 1949 to 1958, the Léopoldville Censorship Board censored approximately 13 per cent of the films destined for the Congolese public; 5 per cent were cut, and 8 per cent were banned outright (Convents 2006: 40).

The issue is not so much the actual number of films banned, as the widespread belief that the colonial authorities implemented an arbitrary policy, in this domain as elsewhere, and restricted colonized populations' access to films. In all cases, cinema censorship had to account for the differing objectives of a range of local actors, not to mention pressure from importers. At the same time, cinematic images were increasingly a basis for protest, and revealed the underlying tension of societies.

Forging the nation, shaping the youth

Beyond its continual reference to the supposedly childlike nature of African audiences, discourse on cinema voiced a concern, shared by the African political elites, about cinema's impact on young people, and particularly young males, who made up a significant proportion of the audience. Scholar Manthia Diawara, saxophonist Manu Dibango, and many others evoke the cinema of their youth with enthusiasm, as did one ordinary spectator in Bouaké: 'We just followed the vibe; we didn't know we would be questioned about it' (interview with Coulibaly, Bouaké 2017). Without knowing it, they were part of the new 'youth' category that was appearing in sociological surveys and demographic data. A specific policy was formulated for this young demographic, notably with the instigation of an age category in film classification, generally situated at 16 years old—a measure not unique to the colonies. This became official in the Gold Coast in 1952; in Britain, the 'Universal' and 'Adult' ratings had been operational since the 1920s (Low 1997: 57). In France and its colonies, the ban on under-sixteens was inherited from the Vichy regime. This blanket age requirement did not suffice to define the category of 'youth', with its highly diverse socio-cultural bearings, nor to control practices of cinema-going.

While colonial authorities worried about control, dignitaries and the new political elite thought in terms of forging the new nation. The cinema was accused of fuelling rising violence and delinquency. In 1948, Amadou Doucouré, senator of the French Sudan, complained of 'the harmful influence on young Africans of the screening in the Overseas Territories, and in particular in French West Africa, of numerous French or foreign adventure films'.[43] In 1950, the Ouagadougou Youth Movements in Upper Volta echoed the discourse of the politicians:

> Considering that too many films screened introduce the country's youth to scenes of banditry, murder, rebellion, or even adultery and lead it to believe that it is only capable of criminal acts and murky sentiments ... Anxious to preserve a sound, patriotic and strong youth in the country, who will be needed tomorrow ... [we] thank the Government for all the complete or partial bans that it has pronounced against certain demoralizing films in the territory of Upper Volta.[44]

Politicised young people thus requested further film censorship, showing themselves eager to participate in the building of the nation to come.

Colonial authorities in Ghana displayed similar concerns. In 1954, the Department of Social Welfare carried out a survey in Accra and Kumasi entitled *Children and the Cinema*, which denounced the negative influence of certain films, going so far as to recommend prohibitions on cinema-going as a punitive measure within the criminal justice system (Burns 2013: 210; McFeely 2015: 299, 302). The same year, the High Commission of French West Africa went further still:

> Public opinion has indeed rightly expressed concern about the potentially harmful effects on the African public in general, and on youth in particular, of the screening of certain films, whose subjects are too often inspired by the world of crime and prostitution, or which portray characters whose example can only be pernicious (westerns and gangster films, notably).[45]

Westerns in particular were consistently singled out in these denunciations. It was rumoured in the Belgian Congo that youths had tried to derail a train after seeing a similar deed in a film (Ramirez and Rolot 1985: 274). Depriving this irrepressible audience of its favourite leisure activity was risky, however, and attacks on cinema remained largely verbal. It was unusual that westerns actually got banned—*Apache*, directed by Robert Aldrich and starring Burt Lancaster, was one rare example, banned in 1955 for its overly Manichean opposition between the Apache and the Americans.[46]

At the centre of these struggles for influence, young people were seen as a hope for the future but also as a driving force for social and political protest. They were caught between the attentions of the colonizers, who made them the prime target of their cultural policy, and the strategies of the nationalists, who worked to mobilize them but worried about their frivolity, in a fashion not dissimilar to the various deputies who were anxious to preserve their morality. In spring 1954, French West Africa's territorial assemblies coordinated their efforts to demand a tightening of censorship, 'given the damage that the screening of dramatic films inflicts on the minds of the African youth; given the fact that sequences in certain films are contrary to the moral principles prescribed by the traditions of this country', to cite Fily Dabo Sissoko, representative of French Sudan.[47]

The reform of the Dakar Censorship Board in July 1954 was a response to the demand of the territorial assemblies. The Board now comprised representatives of the College of Physicians, cultural centres, and family associations.[48] It also demanded that bans on underage spectators be clearly posted in front of cinemas and enforced by their owners. This nonetheless appeared insufficient, and the distributors returned the responsibility to the authorities:

> The ban on certain films for juveniles (under-16s) should suffice as a restrictive measure for the protection and morality of young people. Its application is the responsibility of the police officers in control of each cinema; the box office cashiers cannot know if tickets sold to an adult are intended for juveniles. Moreover, it is not possible for us to ask every spectator's civil status, which, for that matter, does not exist in Africa.[49]

In responding thus, distributors highlighted the impossibility of monitoring spectators' ages in colonies where no official papers existed.

Activists also spoke out on behalf of Christian associations. In Sierra Leone, the youth section of the United Christian Council of Freetown, founded in 1947 and made up almost exclusively of Africans, attacked the selection of films for screening and demanded a change.[50] This contributed ten years later to an amendment to the Cinematograph Ordinance which increased the Board's powers in order, notably, to better protect children.[51] In Dakar, Cyrille Aguessy, a doctor from Dahomey and President of the Catholic Film Committee in Senegal, announced the creation of an African Catholic Film Committee in 1954. The idea was to guide fellow worshippers in their choice of films, acknowledging both 'the civilizational wealth that cinema can offer Africa's advancement, and the dangers that it also presents to its human ascension'.[52] Even if their work was more discreet, some Muslim groups engaged in similar projects. In Dakar, Majhmout M'Bengue, President of the Dahiratoul Islam (Muslim Circle), thus alerted the governor, also in 1954, that: 'Our association wishes to promote efforts to sanitize young Muslim milieus by fighting against certain films harmful to their education, which are very often screened in the Medina.'[53]

Dignitaries, the first elected representatives, the educated, and militants all shared these moral concerns with the colonial authorities, even if their objectives were not the same. Each had their own motivations: public order and controlling the youth for the colonial authorities; the vision of a new society and, often, social conservatism on the part of the new political elites; a desire to broaden horizons for intellectuals and the educated. Their platforms were nonetheless limited: elected assemblies, associations with relatively autonomous statutes, trade unions, political organizations, the press, and sometimes the meetings of censorship boards. Whether in the name of religious values or political struggle (both reformist and progressive), controls on cinema were considered essential as a means of banning indecent or violent spectacles, stopping films from dumbing down young audiences and spectators in general, or choosing and promoting films of educational value. There were dissident voices, of course; these similarly reflected positions across the political spectrum, from the allies of the colonial administration to its detractors, many of whom were intellectuals, anticolonial activists, educated youth, and students.

The latter, some of whom had studied in Europe, criticized the mediocrity of the films on offer, arguing that they distracted youth from the urgency of political action. Defying the attitudes of their often socially conservative elders, they demanded unrestricted access to images, notably contesting the 1954 policy on cultural centres in French West Africa, which were developed and strictly controlled by the authorities. To attract young people, who had by and large received a limited education, these cultural centres screened documentaries, but they also showed fictions conforming to the local moral and religious codes and magnifying the colonial enterprise, such as Baroncelli's *L'Homme du Niger* (African Diary), a 1939 film that was still in circulation in the 1950s.[54] The Senegalese youth called for a boycott; some proposed the creation of cine-clubs in order to develop a critical approach and a film culture. Submitted in 1954, the statutes of the Dakar Cine-club worried the authorities; the club 'aim[ed] to show classics, non-commercial films, *and those whose public screening is banned by the censors*' (original italics).[55]

Suspicions of the arbitrary application of censorship by the authorities were deeply entrenched. The attitude of these students mirrored that of the elites in general: from Senegal to Ghana and beyond, they accused films of poisoning the youth and masses but demanded unbridled access to all films. This combat was particularly pronounced in the Belgian Congo, where cinemas remained segregated and the implementation of censorship differed according to audience. The tiny elite sought to prove its loyalty to the administration and to stand above the rest of the population, while at the same time claiming to protect it. Nevertheless, the government did not trust this elite class, and considered the 'evolved' Congolese less qualified than the Europeans to judge the film scenarios created for Congolese villagers (Convents 2006: 97). Elsewhere, the existence of a wide range of cinemas, which targeted different audiences and thus adapted their programmes accordingly, tempered challenges to censorship.

Ultimately, even if the spread of cinema was far from ubiquitous, cinema halls and films highlighted pressing dilemmas within the emerging postcolonial societies, negotiating both local dynamics and globalized demands, and reflecting a background of urban expansion and multi-faceted modernity. Censorship and the debates around spectatorship did not represent a coherent, rational policy, but instead revealed constant improvisation and adaptation to circumstances under the pressure of both audiences and political actors. The authorities were wary of disorder, while audiences reacted negatively to their surveillance. Not every film show turned into an anticolonial demonstration, of course, but tensions could rapidly flare. Some moments of intense friction punctuated this period both in the immediate post-war years, whose mood of hope was inspired by promises of a better future and the foundation of political parties, and in the mid-1950s, which were marked by the emergence of protest movements, Arab nationalism, and the first independent African nations. Confronted with the forces of change in society, the authorities attempted to slow down this progress towards 'modernity', and sought local allies. This situation transcended the African colonies, also affecting other countries such as India (Jaikumar 2004). Everywhere, short-term alliances between the colonial authorities and local elites were formed, but they were based on a misunderstanding because the protest that expressed itself through cinema was as social as it was political. The building of a nation certainly required the advent of sovereign institutions, but it also involved changes in the societal role and character of age relations, gender relations, and relations between various other statutory categories.

As Independence loomed on the horizon, certain voices spoke out to radically challenge the dominant colonial discourse on cinema: if Africans were truly incapable of grasping the language and significance of film, how to explain their flocking to watch westerns and other commercial films rather than the simplified fictions produced specially for them by ad hoc bodies? Rather than the purported inexperience and naivety of Africans, was it not the producers and distributors' total ignorance of African societies and their desires that was astonishing? This argument was put forward by Nigerian writer and critic J. Koyinde Vaughan in a selection of work by intellectuals and artists published in *Présence Africaine*: 'Besides the preoccupation with this false exotic, there is the other attitude to Africa, an attitude that has greater currency in Britain. It is that Africans should be patronised, uplifted, and governed' (Vaughan 1957: 211). Similarly, filmmaker Paulin Vieyra ironically remarked:

> A lot of clichés have been spoken of Africans ... It has also been said that cinema needed to be adapted to Africans' level of understanding. I find the concern shown to us very touching. But I will simply recall that when cinema began in Europe, no one worried whether or not people understood its technique (Vieyra 1958b: 95).

Such reflections would nourish the African cinema that was born soon after Independence, both on an institutional level and in terms of the often highly militant and educational approaches of emerging filmmakers.

CONCLUSION

In the half century under discussion here, cinema underwent an unstoppable ascent in West Africa, albeit at varying rhythms depending on the country and, above all, on the region. A predominantly urban phenomenon, it profoundly influenced spaces and minds. It offered opportunities to escape a daily reality marked by colonial domination while also serving as a medium for contestation. The love of cinema momentarily transcended social status and, in part, gender. This leisure activity was thus socially and politically subversive. Its arrival coincided with colonization, but its story did not end with Independence: cinema still had new developments and triumphs to come. In every town, in every neighbourhood, people wanted their own cinema. The major shift from 1960 to 1962 during which most territories gained their sovereignty did not cause a rupture in the popularity of cinema-going.[1] Cinema continued its rise, taking on national inflections depending on the political regime and the local context. In Guinea, for example, the national anthem—a symbol of the new sovereignty—now played at the end of screenings:

> We arrived in front of the cinema. *The Hanging Tree* had finished. We heard the final credits and the long caterwauling of the reel. Then came the national anthem, and the whole street stood to attention ... New era, new customs! Two years ago at the same time, you would have heard being boasted the merits of Gillette, Kronenbourg, Bonnet Rouge milk, or Superior Job cigarettes ... (Monénembo 1997: 136).

Africa's golden age of cinema lasted from the 1950s to the 1980s, straddling the Independence era. Its postcolonial history largely remains to be written, beyond the many analyses devoted predominantly to African film itself. The specificities of cultural policies and national forms of film consumption are still barely documented, even though this collective leisure activity has continued to nourish imaginations, strongly influencing the Independence generation, who were fervent fans of Hollywood cinema, particularly westerns and other action films. One anecdote tragically attests to this: a political prisoner held at Camp Boiro, the Sékou Touré regime's detention centre in Guinea, related how he told stories to boost his fellow prisoners' morale, 'animating cell 14's film nights'.[2] In such a context, films fully played their role: 'When night fell, we needed to sing, to tell films as, more than ever, we survivors needed to escape, if only in our thoughts, for they at least could not be kept in a cell' (Gomez 2007: 77).

The adoption of nicknames from films also continued after 1960: the Guinean filmmaker Baldé Mamadou Alpha was known as 'Marlon' after Marlon Brando, the rebellious 1950s actor. Other nicknames taken from television dramas later became popular, with *Ninja* and *Cobra* replacing the cowboy names and entering the fray of Congo's civil war (Bazenguissa-Ganga 1999).

However, many aspects of cinema changed post-Independence—firstly, the film landscape itself. As African cinema steadily took off, the hegemony of foreign distribution circuits was contested. This was particularly true of former French colonies where foreign distributors had been predominant, in contrast to the British Empire's more diverse system, where American companies had set up circuits including the American Motion Picture Export Company (AMPECA) and the Motion Picture Export Association (MPEA) in Nigeria and in Ghana.[3] Firstly, in Guinea, Ghana, and Upper Volta (Burkina Faso), policies were gradually adopted to nationalize distribution circuits and cinemas or to fund film production. The same went for pan-African organizations, such as the Carthage (JCC) and Ouagadougou (FESPACO) film festivals or the African filmmakers' association (FEPACI).

Ethnographic films and the exoticizing stereotypes of Africa that abounded in Western fictions were also criticized.[4] Previously prevented from making films under colonial hegemony, a generation of African filmmakers emerged in the 1960s and 1970s, portraying other visions of Africa and Africans. Speaking about Western films set in Africa, Ousmane Sembène denounced the 'incredible stupidity of their stories, alien to our lives. And if, by chance, a black person features in one of these films, it is more often than not as an extra, or in the role of a servant or a clown' (Sembène 1964: 165). He added: 'It is essential to have our own cinema, that is, to see ourselves, to grasp ourselves, to understand ourselves in the mirror of the screen' (Ibid.: 166).

African cinema offered spectators representations of themselves, by them-selves—an alternative to foreign images—and gave its own reading of the his-tory of Africa and its societies, far from the versions conveyed by the cinema of the West. The first generation of filmmakers remained attached to the collective screening experience, to the magic of cinema as a moment of sharing, and felt that cinema had great potential to educate and raise national awareness.

The development of local productions, which were usually poorly distrib-uted, did not stop the continued dominance of screens by foreign films, nor the endurance of globally popular film genres, which reflected the evolution of global production, Africa's place in the globalized world, and underlying economic stakes. Kung Fu fighters replaced the heroized figure of the cowboy among teenagers but worried authorities just as much and led to further state surveillance of the cinema. The new states feared the subversive power of images as much as the colonizers had.[5] Pierre Haffner summed up this fear of film's potential for dissidence: 'The camera, and thus the screen, are far riskier [than paper and writing], eyes and ears very quickly learning the language of images and sound' (Haffner 2002: 149).

Censorship measures were generally reinforced, based on similar criteria to the previous colonial regulations: immorality, sex, violence, and incitement to rebellion. However, studies of each individual country would be needed to understand the logic of these policies fully and to evaluate their impact. In Nigeria in 1993, for example, criteria included: 'Does it expose African people to ridicule or contempt? Does it promote Nigerian Unity? Nigerian Culture?' (NFVCB 1996: 27). However, just as in colonial times, surveillance mecha-nisms and, notably, preventative measures were often lacking or inadequate, and new technology enabled films to circulate via other channels.

What of today? Times have changed considerably since the golden age of the 'dream palaces'. Anyone now wandering around a town is unlikely to come across a cinema; bar a few rare exceptions, they have shut down one by one, giving way to shopping malls, warehouses, or Evangelical churches (Olufunke 2012). The reasons for this are diverse. Firstly, from the 1970s onwards, cin-ema found itself in competition with other avenues or mediums of film distri-bution, such as the first national televisions and VHS tapes. Moreover, urban sprawl increased distances, and thus costs and travel time, from homes to the cinema. More recently, increasing urban insecurity has dissuaded city-dwellers from going out to the movies at night. Finally, various curfews have damaged the operations of the rare cinemas still open, stamping out nightlife: in Ghana under Rawlings in 1981, for example, or in Ivory Coast in 1999.

Yet films have never been so present, diverse, or readily accessible. Images from all over the world—as well as a vast range of West African titles, thanks to the rise of local production—are omnipresent.[6] They have found their niche in private courtyards and homes, or circulate in the plethora of cheap, easily accessible video parlours that have spread throughout towns (Ndiltah 2015).[7] And village or neighbourhood life abruptly stops when American series or Brazilian *telenovelas* appear on the television.

Recent years have also seen the opening of exclusive top-end cinemas in malls and hotels, targeting a bourgeois minority seeking comfort and their own sites of sociability. Cultural centres and outdoor festivals recall the collective nature of screenings.[8] The sense of communion before the moving image has nonetheless waned; as Gareth McFeely writes, 'The collective experience of the cinema belongs to an increasingly distant past for most Ghanaians' (McFeely 2015: 320).

This collective thrill is now procured at football stadiums, wrestling arenas, rap concerts, or even political rallies. Technological evolutions have guaranteed the immediacy of the circulation of films, and streaming has led to the individualization of viewing. With the development of satellite distribution, censorship measures are often either futile or highly complex. The arrival of the digital era and the Internet has improved access to images for an increasingly large portion of the population. At the same time, locally filmed productions have met with great success, and, in turn, find themselves screened internationally: globalization is truly at play.

NOTES

INTRODUCTION

1. Born in Bouaké (Ivory Coast) in 1941. Interviewed on 15 February 2017, in the Boukrou district of Bouaké.
2. This is particularly true of English-language publications (in the USA and Great Britain especially), where frontiers between fields are more porous. One may notably cite: N. Frank Ukadike, Imruh Bakari, Kenneth Cameron, Mbye Cham, Manthia Diawara, James Genova, June Givanni, Josef Gugler, Sada Niang, Françoise Pfaff, Femi Shaka, Dina Sherzer, David Henry Slavin, and Melissa Thackway. French academics have tended to focus on the film industry, cinema as a media, and variations in national production (Olivier Barlet, Denise Brahimi, Claude Forest, Pierre Haffner, Pierre Pommier, and Jean Rouch). These historiographies, of course, also need to be situated within their chronological contexts.
3. Barrot 2008; Şaul and Austen (eds) 2010; Meyer 1999, 2015; Haynes 2016.
4. The present work is a modified and updated adaptation of my book *Fantômas sous les Tropiques: aller au cinéma en Afrique coloniale* (Vendémiaire, 2015), to which a chapter on mobile cinema has been added. I thank my publishers Vendémiaire for having made this translation possible, and the Centre d'études en sciences sociales sur les mondes africains, américains et asiatiques (CESSMA) for funding it in part.
5. A doctoral thesis defended at the University of Bouaké (Ivory Coast) includes cinema in its study of leisure activities (Ouattara 2018).
6. Notably Jancovich, Faire and Stubbings 2003; Stokes and Maltby (eds) 2004; and Maltby, Stokes and Allen (eds) 2007. Concerning France see Bosséno 1996; Montebello 2005; and Chaplain 2007.
7. The Sahara does not, of course, constitute a divide, especially as all shared the colonial status, whether directly or not (in the case of Egypt). On these zones, see Armbrust 1996; Carlier 2012; Corriou 2011; Shafik 2007; and Wassef 1995.
8. For the cowboy archetype in West Africa, see Goerg 2012–2013.

9. I warmly thank Laura Fair for allowing me to consult extracts of *Reel Pleasures* before its 2018 publication.

10. While it is not possible to mention everyone here, I would like to thank the colleagues who drew my attention to precious snippets of information in the archives, novels, and iconographic collections, notably: Marie Rodet for Mali, Susann Baller and Mamadou Lô for Senegal, Yves Marguerat and Sophie Zimmermann for Togo, Clément Verfaillie, and the *Images & Mémoires* association. My discussions with James Burns greatly contributed to this work, as did those with the filmmakers Med Hondo (Mauritania), Gaston Kaboré (Burkina Faso) and Moussa Kemoko Diakité (Guinea). In his novel *Cinéma*, which evokes cinema in his teen years in Guinea, Tierno Monénembo brings to life these moments of great sociability. Our interview in Conakry in December 2012 confirmed his passion for the movies.

11. Film shoots to make either ethnographic documentaries or fictions set in Africa took place in the African colonies very early on. See, for example, Gehrts 1915.

12. For examples of these pioneering studies, see Ambler 2004, Burns 2002b, Convents 2006, Powdermaker 1962, Ramirez and Rolot 1985, and Smyth 1983b.

13. Pierre Haffner, for example, assiduously frequented the El Hadj in Bamako in 1972 and wrote an illuminating analysis of the experience: 'Le journal du Hadjiste', Haffner 1978, pp. 157–83.

1. FROM UNDER THE STARRY SKIES TO THE CONFINES OF THE MOVIE THEATRE: THE INTERWAR YEARS

1. See Chapter 3 on travelling screenings in the countryside or small towns.

2. *Report of the Colonial Films Committee*, 1930, p. 15. Cinema took off rapidly in South Africa due to urbanization (with 23 per cent of the population living in an urban area in 1911 and 31 per cent in 1936, compared with 2.5 per cent in 1920 in tropical Africa), strategies to control workers' leisure activities, and the presence of European settlers. At the other end of the continent, there were also a lot of movie theatres in North Africa.

3. Report of the Colonial Council, Saint-Louis, meeting of 8 November 1927.

4. *Guid'AOF*, Dakar, Agence de Distribution de Presse-Agence Havas A.O.F. (1948, 1950, 1951, and 1955 editions).

5. Archives Nationales du Mali (ANM), ANM 1D 62, 24 June 1932 report.

6. In addition to the 1932 report (ANM), see Zimmermann (2008) and the accounts concerning the 1920s in Marguerat and Pelei (1992).

7. *Guide du Tourisme en AOF et au Territoire du Togo sous mandat français*, 1939, p. 153. The spelling of this surname varies depending on the source: Archambeau/ Archambaud/Archambault/Archambaut.

8. Postcard found in private collection: Ganamer collection, Dakar, no. 37, Boulevard National et Café des Nations, signed 'Albert', sent in 1910.

9. Highlife was born out of a blend of different local and international influences and demand from a dynamic bourgeoisie made up of traders and planters, who established clubs and other social spots. The name refers to this elite's 'high life', from which musicians were, ironically, excluded. Highlife was an immediate hit in towns, and soon spread to the countryside and well beyond the Gold Coast.

10. ANM 1D 62, 24 June 1932 report.

11. Public Record Office, London (PRO), Colonial Office (CO) 323/1122/3, Recommendation of the Federation of British Industry (Film group) Scheme, 1931.

12. PRO, CO 323/1122. Letter from the Governor of Nigeria, dated 5 February 1932.

13. The press is a valuable source concerning the first screenings. *Sierra Leone Weekly News* (*SWLN*), 27 February 1909.

14. *SLWN*, 2 November 1912.

15. *SLWN*, 19 April 1919.

16. Among the different sources, see: *The Sierra Leone Guardian*, 24 April 1914; *The Colony and Provincial Reporter*, 19 October 1912 (Culver); *SLWN* 12 December 1914, 17 & 24 April 1915, 19 April 1919 (West African Cinema Circuit); 21 August & 13 November 1915 (Nicol), etc.

17. *SLWN*, 18 June 1921; *The Cinema World*.

18. *SLWN*, 7 August 1920.

19. This facet of the activities of Alphonso Lisk-Carew (c. 1887–1969), who opened a photographic studio in 1905 and then went into business with his brother, has not been studied. Viditz-Ward (1985) mentions it once in passing. *SLWN*, 12 August 1922; *The Freetown Cinema Theatrical Co. A Good Beginning*, 7 October 1922.

20. In 1936, there were an estimated 4,941 French, 1,567 other Europeans and 86,126 Africans in Dakar: that is, approximately 93,000 inhabitants (*Guide du Tourisme*, 1939).

21. The Bataclan was pulled down around 1950–55, and the Rialto around 1955–60.

22. *Courrier cinématographique de l'Ouest Africain Français*, 4 July 1936.

23. Girard went on to run several cinemas, including the Palace, and published *L'AOF-Ciné* in 1948. See interview with his granddaughter, Françoise Lemaire (email and phone, May to June 2013), Seck 2008, p. 27, p. 69; and the archives.

24. Archives Nationales de Côte d'Ivoire (ANCI), Dépôt A 48, 163, XIII-13–201/1648. Only a single edition appears to have been published: no. 1, 12 November 1937. Conveyed to the Governor by the Administrator-Mayor of Abidjan, Saint-Père, 15 November 1937.

25. Archives Nationales du Sénégal (ANS), 21G 189 Cinéma. The Governor of Upper-Volta's response, dated 18 March 1948, to the High Commissioner's circular, dated 10 March 1948.

26. *SLWN*, 14 June 1913; *The Colony and Provincial Reporter*, 30 September 1916.

27. CO 554/87/11, *Proposed Chain of Cinemas in West Africa 1931*. Request of 13 Mar. 1931. The Colonial Office refused to grant funding, deeming that the project was not financially sound.

28. CO 323/1122/3, Recommendation of the Federation of British Industry Scheme, 1931. The colonies' response to a CO survey on cinema, 5 Sept. 1931.

29. *SLWN*, 1 March 1913.

30. 'Educated natives' was a term designating those who had attended colonial schools for an extended period.

31. ANM 1D 62, response to the 1937 survey (the cinema is still attested in the 1932 report), Lieutenant-Governor F. Rougier's report, 24 January 1938.

32. Archives Nationales d'Outre-Mer (ANOM), Aff. Pol. 859, letter dated 24 January 1939, Brazzaville (cited by Martin 1995).

33. ANM 1D 62, response to a ministerial enquiry, dated 24 June 1932.

34. Ibid.

35. Archives Nationales du Burkina Faso (ANBF) 42V153, 'Correspondance relative à la séparation des places réservées aux Blancs et aux Noirs au cinéma Florida, 1948', a note by Governor M. G. Mourgues.

36. By-law of 15 February 1918 (*Journal Officiel Guinée*, 1 March 1918).

37. Archives Nationales de Guinée (ANG) 2 D362, Joint Committee Electricity Service (1930–39), d. 2. The 1939 *Guide du Tourisme en AOF* does not mention any cinematographic activity at this date.

38. Two prices applied for the matinee: 6 francs and 3 francs for children. See *Courrier cinématographique de l'Ouest Africain français*, 4 July 1936.

39. A. Londres perfectly depicts this characteristic, which differentiated them from other colonial subjects, in *Terre d'ébène* (1929).

40. ANM 1D 62, June 24 1932 report.

41. *Gold Coast Handbook*, the 1923, 1924, 1928 and 1937 editions.

42. Born in 1910, the author lived throughout the period under discussion.

43. 1937 Survey in ANM 1D 62 cinema, 1932–1938.

44. ANM, 1D 62, Koulouba, cited report, compiled by the Lieutenant-Governor on 24 January 1938.

45. A circular on film policy, 16 March 1932, ANOM, 1 Aff. Pol. 859. It may be noted that, unlike this survey in French West Africa, British official reports, while highly detailed concerning the cinemas themselves, said little about those who frequented them.

46. ANM, 1D 62, 1932 Survey.

47. ANOM FM 1 AFFPOL 859, Togo's response, dated 11 July 1932, to the 1932 survey, signed R. de Guise.

48. The 1932 and 1937 Surveys, in ANM, 1D 62.

49. Ibid.

50. ANS O 119 (31) Dépôt no. 13, École normale de jeunes filles de Rufisque,

1938–48. Letter dated 26 August 1941, addressed to Germaine Le Goff, head-mistress of the École Normale de Rufisque (1938–45).

51. Ibid.

52. Interview with X, born in 1947, secretary. Carried out in Conakry, 20 January 2005.

53. Interview with Moussa Kemoko Diakité, filmmaker (born 1940), Conakry, 21 October 2003; provided by political scientist Bernard Charles.

2. REGULATION, CONTROL AND CENSORSHIP IN THE INTERWAR YEARS

1. Such racial discourses have been amply analyzed. See, notably, Mudimbe 1988.

2. Sequential changes take place when, for example, a character exits a room without the audience seeing the door opening. This did not stop the censors from cutting certain scenes in order to limit the criminogenic impact of cinema; they frequently made interventions such as removing a scene in which a shot is fired to only show the fallen corpse.

3. Colonial Office (CO) 323/977/1, the governor's confidential report on film censorship (1927).

4. Archives Nationales d'Outre-Mer (ANOM) FM 1 AFFPOL 859. Togo report, 1932.

5. Archives Nationales du Mali (ANM) 1D 62, French Sudan report, 1932.

6. Ibid.

7. ANOM, 1 Aff. Pol. 859, circular on film policy, 16 March 1932.

8. Ibid.

9. Administrative report, February 1951, cited by Ramirez and Rolot 1985, p. 422.

10. In France, a 'commission in charge of cinematographic examination and control' was created on 16 June 1916.

11. ANOM, 1 Aff. Pol. 859, Gaston Joseph, report to the Ministry on the 'necessity of adopting a "film policy" in the Colonies', late 1931 to early 1932 (16 pages).

12. The survey carried out in 1932 requested a separate evaluation of 'silent films and synchronized films'.

13. CO 323/977/1, letter dated 8 January 1927.

14. CO 323/1051/3. The Committee was composed of administrators, former governors (including the governor of Mauritius and South Nigeria, colonies that adopted laws on cinema very early), and representatives of the film industry and the Trade Ministry.

15. Two American films that risked confusion over the identity of the soldiers portrayed were cited, namely *The Fleet Is In* and *The Big Parade*.

16. ANOM, 1 Aff. Pol. 859 (cited report, note 10), Joseph, report to the Ministry on the 'necessity of adopting a "film policy" in the Colonies'.

17. Ibid.
18. Ibid.
19. Ibid.
20. Ibid.
21. Ibid.
22. ANOM, 1 Aff. pol. 859, Chappedelaine, Minister of the Colonies, writing to the governor-generals, governors of the colonies, and the commissioners of the Republic in the territories under mandate, 16 March 1932, 'Adoption d'une "politique du film" aux colonies et dans les territoires sous mandat' (7 pages).
23. Ibid.
24. Ibid.
25. ANM, 1 D 62, letter from the Ministry dated 3 December 1937, and response from Lieutenant-Governor F. Rougier in the Sudan, dated 24 January 1938.
26. The tragic 1897 Bazar de la Charité fire in Paris led to the adoption of security regulations.
27. The general ruling of 28 September 1935 (FWA) specifically concerned 'inflammable or incombustible cinematographic films' and the need to fireproof the projection booth (ANOM, 1 Aff. Pol 542).
28. Ruling dated 28 June 1922.
29. Archives Nationales du Sénégal (ANS) 21G 189: letters dated 16, 18 and 26 March 1948.
30. ANS, 21 G 189, report to the governor of French Sudan, 27 June 1947.
31. ANOM FM 1 AFFPOL 859, Togo report 1932.
32. See *Blue Books*, *Gold Coast Gazette*, *Colony and Protectorate of Nigeria Gazette* and *Nigeria Gazette*.
33. Order 27 by the Governor, Gold Coast Colony, 1925, *Cinematograph Exhibitions Ord*, modified by order in council 5, 6, 8 and 41 of 1927; and Regulation 16 of 1927.
34. A confidential 1927 report, cited in CO 323/977/1.
35. Centre des Archives d'Outre-Mer (CAOM), FM 1AFFPOL/859, quoted in Joseph, report to the Ministry on the 'necessity of adopting a "film policy" in the Colonies', p. 4.
36. ANOM, 1 Aff. pol. 859, report on film policy, 16 March 1932 (quoted).
37. Joseph, Report to the minister on 'the need to adopt a "film policy" in the Colonies', p. 7.
38. 8 March 1934 Decree, Article 1.
39. Ibid., article 3.
40. *Commandants de cercle* (district officers) were administrators responsible for the colonial equivalents of France's departments.
41. AN Mali 1D 62, Cinéma 1932–38, censorship board reports, 1936.
42. In France in the 1920s, films were often judged by their screenplays.

43. ANM, 1D 62 Cinéma 1932–38, minutes dated 25 September 1936.

44. Decree dated 18 February 1928 (Article 6).

45. CO 323/1045/1 Films Censorship 1927–29, Report compiled by the Gold Coast Secretary for Native Affairs, London, 4 October 1929.

46. CO 323/977/1, confidential memorandum on film censorship, written by the governor, 1927.

47. Public Record Office (PRO), CO 323/978/4 Films, Censorship (1927). A report dated 26 October 1927, by the president of the censorship board, includes a letter about this movie.

48. This was also the case in the British colonies (*Colonial Cinema*, December 1942), where scenes of Chaplin mocking the police, as well as a sketch in which he dresses up as a woman, were deemed disruptive.

49. CO 323/1118/9, letter dated 28 July 1931.

50. This policy mainly targeted lower-class whites and women. Immigration was kept under surveillance, and deportation mechanisms put in place.

51. This question was discussed with regard to British East Africa (CO 323/1045/1 Film Censorship 1927–29); for Zanzibar, see Reinwald 2006, p. 99, and Fair 2018.

3. MOBILE CINEMA AND TRAVELLING ENTREPRENEURS: CINEMA IN THE VILLAGE (THE EARLY 1900s TO THE 1950s)

1. Archives Nationales d'Outre-Mer (ANOM), Aff. Pol. 542, d.3, 1934.

2. My research in the (very incomplete) Ivoirian archives did not bring to light any further information about him.

3. Cited in Retord 1986, p. 18; all of the following quotations from Borremans are taken from this account.

4. Archives Nationales du Sénégal (ANS), O 657 (31), 'CR de la tournée de la voiture cinématographique des Affaires sociales au Sénégal effectuée du 7.9. au 16.9.1955', MM Lompolo Koné and J.P. Poinsot, p. 9.

5. Information provided by historian Jean-Luc Martineau (INALCO, Paris), whose work focuses on southern Nigeria.

6. *Colonial Cinema*, March 1945, pp. 11–14.

7. Ibid.

8. President's Office to the Public Relations Department, Tongu Confederacy, Native Authority Council, Volo via Akuse, 9 August 1947. For online document, see https://cinemaintransit.wordpress.com, Jennifer Blaylock's blog on cinema in Ghana (last accessed 15 May 2019).

9. *Ghana Today*, 25 December 1957, cited by Tom Rice, 'Gold Coast Film Unit', Colonial Film, http://www.colonialfilm.org.uk/production-company/gold-coast-film-unit (last accessed 15 May 2019).

10. ANS, O 658 (31), a report by Touré Alsény, a specialist AMI nurse, and director and joint manager of the Forécariah Cultural Centre, 26 November 1954.

11. ANS, O 657 (31), quoted report, by M. M. Lompolo Koné and J. P. Poinsot, 1955.

12. ANS O 658 (31) report dated 21 November 1955.

13. ANS 21 G 193, Governor of Guinea to the High Commissioner, 27 September 1952.

14. Applications are, for the main part, conserved in ANS 21 G 198 (versement 174).

15. 'I own a van with a trailer. I reach a village. I set up the cinema and stay three to four days. [...]. The cinema has 150 seats.' See ANS, 21 G 198 (versement 174) Maestrati dossier, 1956.

16. Kayes Archives (letters dated October 1951); ANS 21 G 190 (report dated 14 September 1948) and 198 (letters dated October 1953). *Guid'AOF* 1958.

17. ANS 21 G 190, notes on Lequeux, 14 September 1948. The following quotations on Lequeux are from the same report.

18. ANS 21 G 198, request filed by Marcel Chahouar and Amiel Tolstoi, Neuchâtel, letter dated 4 March 1948.

19. Ibid., request filed by Jean Cornu, born Irma Pomazy.

20. Archives Nationales de Guinée (ANG) 2G 13, letter from the General Secretary in Guinea to district officers in Kissidougou and Guéckédou, 4 March 1952.

21. ANG 2G 16, letter from the district officer in Mamou, 1950.

22. ANS 21 G 198.

23. 'Pourquoi allons-nous au cinéma?', *Bingo*, August 1960, no. 91, pp. 34–35.

24. ANG 2G 13, administrator's report, 19 April 1947; ANS 21G 198, various 1947 letters.

25. From an interview with Khady Diallo, Raymond Borremans's assistant from 1983 until his death in 1988, Abidjan, 9 February 2017. See also: *Fraternité Matin*, 21–22 July 1984 (a long interview with Borremans).

26. Kayes Archives, 1F/1, Confidential report on general security and political information, dated 12 March 1951. Kayes had a population of 20,000 inhabitants, 340 of whom were European (*Guide bleu de l'Afrique de l'Ouest*, 1958).

27. Sivadier contacted me following the publication of *Fantômas sous le tropiques*, and sent me a copy of his entire archive. In addition to these archives I carried out a series of interviews with him, and he also wrote a 155-page, illustrated autobiographical account, half of which is about his mobile cinema. See Goerg 2016.

28. From Sivadier's autobiographical account, p. 85; see previous footnote.

29. Letter from the SECMA to Sivadier, 10 November 1959, from Sivadier's archive.

30. Letter from Sivadier to the SECMA, Bamako, 23 November 1959, from Sivadier's archive.

31. From Sivadier's autobiographical account, p. 99.

32. Letter, Kaolack, 4 February 1959, from Sivadier's archive.

33. FWA currency; stands for 'Côte Française d'Afrique'.

34. Letter, Matam, 10 April 1959, from Sikadier's archive.

35. Letter, Bamako, 6 November 1959, from Sivadier's archive.

36. Letter, Bamako, 23 November 1959, from Sivadier's archive.

4. A WINDOW ON THE WORLD

1. Archives Nationales de Côte d'Ivoire (ANCI), Dépôt A 48 163, XIII-13–201/1648.
2. Notably, the interviews with Sultan, Dieng, Diagne, and Fatou Sow.
3. Extract of a report, 4 October 1929, in Colonial Office (CO) 323/1045/1 Films Censorship 1927–29, p. 11.
4. Born in Dakar in 1941, the writer describes her first trip to the cinema in 1953.
5. Archives Nationales du Mali (ANM) 1D 62, Lieutenant-Govenor Ferdinand Rougier's response to the 1937 survey, Koulouba, 24 January 1938.
6. The author, who had already been to Dakar in 1928, later stayed in FWA from October 1932 to June 1935.
7. Circular on film policy, 16 March 1932, Archives Nationales d'Outre-Mer (ANOM), 1 Aff. Pol. 859.
8. Interview with Moïse Alassane Traoré about leisure activities in Ouagadougou in the 1930s, cited by Fourchard 2001, p. 204.
9. Public Records and Archives Administration Department (PRAAD) CSO/15/8/21 (archives provided by McFeely, whom I thank).
10. *Bulletin d'information et de renseignement* (Governorship General of French West Africa), no. 46, 24 January 1935.
11. *L'Étoile de l'AEF*, no. 47, 22 March 1934, p. 2.
12. There were still silent films in the Social Affairs cinema van tours in Senegal in 1955, which prompted angry protests (Archives Nationales du Sénégal [ANS], O 657).
13. His Civil Rights activism and his proximity to the USSR made him a key personality. His filmography was particularly rich, including: *Body and Soul* (1924), *The Emperor Jones* (1933), *Sanders of the River* (1935), *Song of Freedom* (1936), *Show Boat* (1936), *King Solomon's Mines* (1937).
14. ANOM, FM 1AFFPOL/859, Togo's reply to the survey launched in 1932, R. de Guise, 11 July 1932.
15. ANM 1D 62, response dated 24 June 1932.
16. French Sudan's response to the 1932 and 1937 surveys, in ANM 1D 62, Cinéma 1932–38.
17. Togo's response to the 1932 and 1937 surveys, dated 11 July 1932.
18. French Sudan's response to the 1932 and 1937 surveys, in ANM 1D 62, Cinéma 1932–38: direction des Affaires politiques et administratives.
19. Many studies have focused on colonial cinema and its racist prejudices, but few have focused on its actual distribution in Africa, or its local reception.
20. Public Record Office (PRO) CO 323/978/4, Films. 'Censorship' (letter from the governor, dated 26 October 1927).
21. CO 323/978/4 Film Censorship (1927), report dated 26 October 1927 by the Governor of Mauritius, head of the censorship board.

22. Sir Henry Hesketh Bell, a debate on cinema in Africa, cited in 'Tropical Africa & the Cinema. DANGER TO WHITE PRESTIGE. Censorship of Films', *Sunday Times*, 16 February 1930.

23. CO 323/1315/12, Films Quota legislation, 1935; CO 323/1356/1; Films Quota legislation, 1936.

24. This category existed in Nigeria as of 1923, and film imports were signaled as of 1924.

25. See the debate on India, whose national production managed to rival that of Hollywood (Jaikumar 2004).

26. Togo's response to the 1932 and 1937 surveys, dated 11 July 1932.

27. *Courrier cinématographique de l'Ouest Africain Français*, 4 July 1936.

5. THE SPREAD OF CINEMA (1945 TO THE INDEPENDENCE ERA)

1. *The Film in Colonial Development: A Report of a Conference*, London: British Film Institute, 1948, p. 16.

2. *West African Report*, George Vietheer, 3 December 1962, American Motion Picture Export Company Africa (AMPECA). I thank Gareth McFeely for sending me the report. Another source mentions slightly different figures, putting Nigeria at twenty-four in 1950, forty in 1959, and sixty-seven in 1963, and Gold Coast at ten, thirty-five, and fifty-nine in the same years (*United States Motion Picture Industry Reports*, 1950, 1959, 1963, quoted by Fair 2018, p.331, footnote 4.

3. Also see Forest 1995, p. 199. The figures vary, depending on the source (Rouch 1962a, Sadoul 1972, UNESCO 1961) and the criteria adopted (16 or 35mm, open-air or indoor, etc.).

4. Such as Lombard on Cotonou, 1953.

5. Archives Nationales du Sénégal (ANS) 21G 189, Cinéma. Response to the High Commission's survey on security regulations, dated 10 March 1948.

6. AMPECA report, 1962. No studies on cinema as a leisure activity in colonial Nigeria exist to date.

7. Only Dakar had over 100,000 inhabitants in 1950.

8. AMPECA report, 1962.

9. Ibid.

10. Information provided by interviews, the archives, and tourist guides.

11. Interview with her son, René, 2005; archives (Archives Nationales de Guinée (ANG) 376 W 20 d. 11).

12. ANS, 21G 189, 21 March 1950, governor of Ivory Coast to the High Commissioner of French West Africa.

13. Archives Nationales du Burkina Faso (ANBF), 3 V 72, 'Documentation sur la cinématographie dans le Territoire de la Haute Volta', 23 July 1955 (12 pages).

14. ANS, 21 G 189, list of cinemas in Dakar, mid-1950s.

15. Sagna Bakary Kéba, 25 years old, Dakar, in 'Pourquoi allons-nous au cinéma?', *Bingo*, August 1960, no. 91, pp. 34–35.

16. See also AMPECA report, 1962.

17. ANS 21G 189, 1947–48.

18. ANG 2G 16 (Kankan, file on the Sassine cinema); 2G 17 (Mamou, letter from the head of the province, dated 31 December 1951; minutes taken at the end of the enquiry, 18 January 1952).

19. ANS 21 G 190, letter to the high commissioner, 15 December 1955.

20. ANS 21 G 189; Seck 2008, p. 161.

21. ANS 21 G 193, Secretary General of the CINESYNDIC, Cl. Lacoste, Dakar, to the President of the federal Censorship Board, 9 February 1955.

22. Ibid., reply from the Censorship Board to Lacoste.

23. Enquiry into the Yacoubist community, Gagnoa, February 2017.

24. ANG 2G 16, complaints.

25. General decrees dated 22 March 1949 and 31 July 1950.

26. ANS 21 G 189; 21 G 203.

27. ANBF 3 V 72, file on incidents in cinemas during the rainy season, 1956–57 (Ouagadougou, Upper Volta).

28. F. Bouda, 'Vivre à l'air du temps', *Bingo*, no. 47, 1956.

29. Reinwald (2006) and Fair (2018) identify the same impact on social transformation in Zanzibar, although naturally other factors also came into play.

30. ANS 21 G 192, letter dated 23 February 1955.

31. ANS 21 G 192, letter by Maurice Jacquin, 25 April 1957.

32. 'Pourquoi allons-nous au cinéma?', *Bingo*, 1960.

33. Cited in Esther Eyra Doei, 'Why did all the old cinema houses die out?', Joy Online, 9 September 2014, https://www.myjoyonline.com/entertainment/2014/September–9th/why-did-all-the-old-cinema-houses-die-out.php (last accessed 20 May 2019).

34. ANS 21G 193 SECRET, Gustave Borgnis-Desbordes to the High Commissioner, 29 November 1949; object 'damaging/dangerous propaganda by the cinema' (concerning René Clement's *La Bataille du rail* (The Battle of the Rails, 1946).

35. ANBF, 42V133, note dated 18 March 1948.

6. THE INDEPENDENCE GENERATION: FILM CULTURE AND THE ANTI-COLONIAL STRUGGLE IN THE 1950s

1. Archives Nationales du Sénégal (ANS) 21G 193, SECRET, Gustave Borgnis-Desbordes to the High Commissioner, 29 November 1949; object 'damaging/dangerous propaganda by the cinema'.

2. Ibid.

3. ANS 21G 193, letter to the president of the Federal Censorship Board, 9 May 1958.

4. See also *West African Report*, George Vietheer, 3 December 1962, American Motion Picture Export Company Africa (AMPECA).

5. ANS 21G 192, Dakar, 7 March 1956.

6. See Rouch's *Moi, un Noir* (1959); among many books, see Colleyn 2009.

7. Before being stigmatized in Africa, westerns were first criticized in the United States (Powdermaker 1962; Akyeampong and Ambler 2002; Ambler 2007; Burns 2002a, p. 103; Genova 2004).

8. ANS 21G 190. The poster referred to the film *Bilâl mou'adhdhin al-rasoul* (Bilal, the Prophet's Muezzin) by Ahmed al-Toukhi, 1953, but was later banned due to Franco–Egyptian tensions.

9. ANS 21 G 192, note from the intelligence services, Gao (French Sudan), 27 August 1957.

10. 'Pourquoi allons-nous au cinéma?', *Bingo*, August 1960, no. 91, pp. 34–35.

11. ANS 21 G 192, Gao, 1957.

12. ANS 21 G 190; Seck 2008, p. 153, p. 172.

13. ANS 21G 199, circa 1958.

14. ANS 21G 199. Twenty-one films were banned on 12 February 1958, to which specific mentions were added (see, for example, Archives Nationales du Burkina Faso [ANBF] 3V 72). For a detailed study, see Goerg 2013.

15. Amadou Sow, 24 years old, accountant, in 'Pourquoi allons-nous au cinéma?', *Bingo*, 1960.

16. See also 'Boy Kumasenu', Colonial Film, http://www.colonialfilm.org.uk/node/332 (last accessed 20 May 2019).

17. A report written by Roger Bagage, director of the Belgian Congo and Ruanda-Urundi Information and Documentation Centre (CID) in Brussels, to the governor general of Léopoldville on 19 February 1951. Cited in Convents 2006, p. 95.

18. Archives Nationales de Guinée (ANG) 2G 2 IFAN dossier, Jean Brérault, Head of the Film Service, 11 July 1958.

19. ANS 18 G 215 (versement 60), dossier 614 GAC, letter from Sarr, 22 January 1957.

20. ANS VP (Vice-Presidency), 00461, 19-page document.

21. ANS 21G 193, Direction de la sûreté générale de l'AOF, 29 July 1947; 'Objet: État d'esprit de la population africaine' ('Object: State of Mind of the African Population').

22. Interview with Moussa Kemoko Diakité, filmmaker (born 1940), Conakry, 21 October 2003; provided by political scientist Bernard Charles.

23. ANS 21 G 109, letter dated 28 February 1941.

24. Ibid.

25. ANS 21 G 193, (undated, circa 1948) note concerning the 'Legality of the Federal Cinematographic Censorship Board'.

26. General decrees dated 6 November 1946, 15 December 1948, 20 June 1949, and 21 July 1954. For greater detail, see: Goerg 2009, 2012.

27. ANS 21 G 193, d. 4, letter dated 30 April 1949.

28. ANS 21 G 193, letter dated 27 September 1952.

29. ANS 21 G 193, Grand Council of French West Africa, Dakar, 9 June 1949.

30. Report by the Colonial Council on a planned decree on the control of cinematographic representations, 19 March 1954, cited in Convents 2006, p. 181.

31. 'We eliminate certain productions ourselves that are incompatible with the African clientele's level of mental maturity and ability to judge.' ANS, 21 G 192, Head of the SECMA to the governor of Senegal, 23 February 1955.

32. *The Film in Colonial Development: A Report of a Conference*, London: British Film Institute, 1948, p. 33.

33. The reason for the censorship of *Bengal Brigade* was clear: 'The theme of revolt against Colonial Power constitutes the essence of this film.' ANS 21G 199, Minutes of the Censorship Board, Dakar, 12 April 1957.

34. ANS 21 G 195, Minutes of the Censorship Board, Dakar, 31 July 1956.

35. ANG 2 G 17.

36. ANS 21 G 193, Division General Astier de Villates to the High Commissioner, 8 April 1950.

37. ANS 2 G 12, High Commissioner to the governors, 1 March 1955.

38. At the same time, the authorities attempted to regulate the colonizers' sexual morality and to present an ideal model of matrimony; see Lauro 2005; Stoler 2002.

39. ANG 2 G 17, letter dated 1 March 1951.

40. ANS 21 G 193, letter dated 31 January 1957.

41. ANG 2 G 16, list of films screened (undated, circa 1950).

42. ANS 21 G 193, 30 March 1955 to 14 June 1956.

43. ANS 21 G 193, Official gazette of parliamentary debates, 10 August 1948 (9 March session).

44. ANS 21 G 193, petition dated 19 November 1950, forwarded by the governor of Upper Volta to the governor general by post, 16 December 1950.

45. ANS 21 G 193, speech before the Grand Council of French West Africa, letter dated 17 May 1954. For Dar es Salaam, see Burton 2001.

46. ANS 21 G 195, Dakar, 'Banned films 1955' file.

47. ANS 21 G 193, motion dated 25 March 1954. Ibid. for the other colonies.

48. ANS 21 G 193, 21 July 1954 decree, article 2.

49. ANS 21 G 192, letter from the SECMA, 1955.

50. Mentioned by Colin Beale, Secretary of the Mission Society Organization, during the BFI conference, 1948.

51. PRO CO1027/102, Film Censorship Legislation Sierra Leone, law 10, 1958.

52. ANS, 21 G 193, letter dated 12 May 1954.

53. ANS 21G 193, letter dated 16 October 1954.

54. Bancel 2009, p. 119. ANS O 655, Maisons de jeunes 1954–56; ANS O 657, Centres culturels, 1956–57; ANS O 658, Centres culturels, 1954. The number of

cultural centres rose from twenty-eight in 1954 to 157 by the end of 1956, with an additional seven mobile cinema vans.

55. ANS 21G 193, letter dated 10 May 1954; ANS 18 G 215 dossier 241.

CONCLUSION

1. Without forgetting those that gained Independence earlier (Ghana in 1957, Guinea in 1958) or later (the Portuguese colonies in 1975, Zimbabwe in 1980, and Namibia in 1990).

2. Alsény René Gomez, *Camp Boiro. Parler ou périr*, Paris: L'Harmattan, 2007, p. 55. Arrested in November 1970, Gomez was incarcerated at Camp Boiro, where he was held for seven years.

3. Challenges to the hegemony of foreign circuits in the former French colonies have been widely studied; see Boughedir 2005; Debrix 1968; Diawara 1992, Chapter 7; Forest 2011; and Vieyra 1975. For more on American distributors in the former British colonies, see McFeely 2015, Chapter 4, 'The American Film Industry in Ghana, 1945–1965', and, notably, 'AMPECA's Early Operations: Forecasts Meet Reality, 1962–1964', p. 240, and 'Hollywood Settles In, 1960s', p. 254. Mention must also be made of the eviction of Lebanese traders and cinema operators in 1971. Cinema halls were nationalized (although their management remained private) in Zanzibar in 1964 and on the mainland in 1971, and distribution was put in the hands of the Tanzania Film Company Ltd in 1968 (Fair 2018). The first, and probably only, drive-in was opened in Dar es Salaam in 1966: see Fair 2013.

4. The rare films offering an alternative vision, such as René Vautier's *Afrique 50* (1950), or Chris Marker and Alain Resnais' *Les Statues meurent aussi* (Statues Also Die, 1953, 1954 Jean Vigo Prize), were banned in France and in French West Africa.

5. See McFeely 2015, Chapter 5, 'Managing Audience Enthusiasm: Elite and Administrative Anxieties, 1930s-1980s'; 'Official Concern Shifts, 1960–1970s', p. 303; and '"Gone are the Days"—The last boom and bust, 1970s-1980s', p. 307.

6. Film production in Ghana, Nigeria, and, more recently, Ivory Coast has been particularly prolific.

7. See Jean-Marie Teno, *Sacred Places*, Cameroon/France, 2009, for a documentary about video parlours in Ouagadougou.

8. In Burkina Faso, the impact of the Panafrican Film and Television Festival of Ouagadougou (FESPACO) is discernable in terms of state film policy, but in general cinemas there are little frequented.

SOURCES

Archival Sources

Numerous archival documents have been used for this book. Detailed references for these rich archives are given in the footnotes.

The research for this book took place across more than a decade—even longer if I take into account the previous period, when I was working on urban history in Guinea and Sierra Leone. The archival research has been carried out and the documentation has accumulated, therefore, over a long period. I first focused my attention on the main colonial archive funds (the PRO, London; the ANOM, Aix-en-Provence; and the ANS, Dakar). I then took advantage of conferences in various countries to visit national archives in Ivory Coast, Togo, Burkina Faso, and Congo-Brazzaville, supplementing archival research conducted in Guinea and Senegal.

Working on such a large geographic zone also required extended collaboration with other scholars working on similar topics or countries. Indeed, short trips do not allow one to visit all potential archival depots, and new documents also become available over time. Some colleagues kindly digitalized documents for me: Marie Rodet in Bamako and Kayes, and Susann Baller, Elsa Paris, and Mamadou Lô in Dakar. Others forwarded me their own material: Sophie Zimmermann for Togo and Gareth McFeely for Ghana. This collaboration made it possible to present an extensive survey of cinema in Western Africa. While it was not possible to conduct interviews personally in each and every country, I was able to access and draw on existing published ones.

Each colony has its own way not only of producing administrative material, but also of classifying it. This turns research into an adventure, with many good, and some bad, surprises: documents appear that one would not have expected to find in certain files, but anticipated documents also disappear without trace (such as answers to the 1932 enquiry in AOF). But this diversity in the nature and content of sources is what makes research worthwhile, multiplying the available human perspectives and factual information.

SOURCES

There is no 'cinema' category in the archive collections: the documents are classified by theme or period under the headings 'police and security', 'teaching', 'subsidies', 'general administration', and so on. The available material on cinema varies according to period. Generally scarce in the 1920s, when only a handful of colonial subjects were concerned, it is more plentiful when a special event or particular circumstances required the attention of the colonial powers, such as the transition to the talkies, or when political movements took advantage of the dark cinema space to express protest.

Despite their colonial bias, these official documents offer valuable information on film policy, the development of movie theatres, and distribution mechanisms. They can also be read 'against the grain', especially the sources on censorship, which give us important insights into the agency of colonized subjects. However, getting a sense of local film reception from such archival material and documentation remains difficult, making it necessary to refer to other oral or written sources such as novels, autobiographies, the press, and existing interviews.

Colonial archive funds

ANBF Archives Nationales du Burkina Faso (National Archives of Burkina Faso), Ouagadougou
ANCI Archives Nationales de Côte d'Ivoire (National Archives of Ivory Coast), Abidjan
ANG Archives Nationales de Guinée (National Archives of Guinea), Conakry
ANM Archives Nationales du Mali (National Archives of Mali), Bamako
ANOM Archives Nationales d'Outre-Mer (French National Archives, Overseas), Aix-en-Provence, France
ANS Archives Nationales du Sénégal (National Archives of Senegal), Dakar
PRAAD Public Records and Archives Administration Department, Accra, Ghana
PRO Public Record Office, London

ANBF Archives Nationales du Burkina Faso (National Archives of Burkina Faso), Ouagadougou

3 V 72 Cinematographic Activities 1948–58
32 V 143 on Nader Ciné in Ouagadougou

ANCI Archives Nationales de Côte d'Ivoire (National Archive of Ivory Coast), Abidjan

Dépôt A Box 13 file 563 Administrative Correspondence 1940–54
Box 18 file 580 Cinematographic Control
Box 55 file 1388 Public Safety 1934–35

SOURCES

Box 48 file 163 Newspapers (including on Cinema 1937)

ANG Archives Nationales de Guinée (National Archives of Guinea), Conakry

In addition to the sparse information found in the Conakry Municipality archives (2D), files about associations (2Z), and street plans and sketches of buildings (4P), the most informative series was the randomly classified (though mostly chronological) Political Affairs series (2G). Some documents added after Independence were also useful: W (post-1958): 376 W 20 file 11 on Mr Chediac's cinema in Kindia (1950s).

ANM Archives Nationales du Mali (National Archives of Mali), Bamako

1D 62 Cinema 1932–38, including:
– ind; Sudan's response to the 1932 colonial survey on cinema, 24 June 1932
– ind; Meetings of the Cinema Board of Control, 1936
Archives de cercle de Kayes (classification in progress)
1 F Public Safety, Political information
3 E Political Affairs; Movie Theatre Control

ANOM Archives Nationales d'Outre-Mer (National Overseas Archives), Aix-en-Provence, France

Fonds ministériels (FM), Political Affairs
FM 1 AFFPOL/859
FM 1 AFFPOL/542 (including file 3 on Cinema and sound recording, 1934–37):
This source includes the 8 March 1934 Decree 'concerning the organization of the control of cinematographic films, phonographic records, cinematographic film shoots and sound recordings in AOF' (also found in ANS 21G 188).
FM 1AFFPOL/859, various important documents, 1930s, including:
– ind; Gaston Joseph, report to the Ministry on the 'necessity of adopting a *film policy* in the Colonies', late 1931 to early 1932 (16 pages)
– ind; Circular on film policy, asking for a survey on cinema in FWA, by Chappedelaine, Secretary of State for the Colonies, 16 March 1932 (7 pages)
– ind; Togo response to the 1932 circular by Governor de Guise, 11 July 1932
FM 1AFFPOL/3672 Cultural Affairs, press, 1946–58
FM 1AFFPOL/2149 Cinema, 1948–58
FM 1AFFPOL/2117/d10, Cinema, 1948–51

ANS Archives Nationales du Sénégal (National Archives of Senegal), Dakar

18 G Grants for Culture

SOURCES

21 G Police and Public Safety

21 G 193 Board of Control and Censorship 1947–58, includes the 8 March 1934 censorship decree (file 3), also published in *Journal Officiel AOF*, 7 April 1934, pp. 252–53.

O Schools and Youth

VP (Vice-Presidency): 00461: Memorandum by Mamadou Sarr, 'Première histoire du cinéma et du théâtre africains' (19 pages)

PRAAD (Public Records and Archives Administration Department), Accra, Ghana

CSO/15/8/21

PRO Public Record Office (London)

CO 323 1927–38 including:

– ind; CO 323/977/1 (1927): Colonial Office Conference, Summary of Proceedings, London; Report of the Colonial Films Committee; Report by Gold Coast Governor Guggisberg

– ind; CO 323/1051/3 Films. Colonial Films Committee, 1929–30

Report of the Colonial Films Committee, July 1930 (27 pages)

CO 554/87/11 Proposed chain of cinemas in West Africa, 1931

CO 554/1160 Governors reports Sierra Leone 1954–56

CO1027/102 Films Censorship Legislation Sierra Leone, 1958

The press, Government reports, and semi-official publications have been of much use too.

Gold Coast Handbook, 1923, 1924, 1928 and 1937 editions

Blue Books, Gold Coast Gazette, Colony and Protectorate of Nigeria Gazette, and *Nigeria Gazette*, 1920s–1930s

Guid'AOF, Dakar, Agence de Distribution de Presse-Agence Havas AOF (1948, 1950, 1951, and 1955 editions)

Guide du Tourisme en AOF et au Territoire du Togo sous mandat français, 1939

Les Guides bleus, Afrique de l'ouest, AOF-Togo, Hachette, 1958

The British Library provided valuable documents such as:

The Film in Colonial Development. A Report of a Conference, the BFI (British Film Institute), March 1948, 53 pages

Colonial Cinema, Colonial Film Unit's quarterly magazine, 1942–55 (now online, University of St Andrews: http://cinemastandrews.org.uk/archive/colonial-cinema/)

UNESCO, *The Use of Mobile Cinema and Radio Vans in Fundamental Education*, Paris: 1949

SOURCES

Films and Other Sources

In order to make the documentary and fiction films produced during the colonial era available, certain countries and institutions have launched programmes to digitalize these old works.

Belgium

See the Tervuren Museum's 'Patrimoine d'Afrique centrale, Archives films' project:
Van Schuylenbergh, Patricia and Mathieu Zana Aziza Etambala (eds), *Patrimoine d'Afrique centrale. Archives Films. Congo, Rwanda, Burundi, 1912–1930*, Tervuren, Musée royal de l'Afrique centrale, 2010 (this work includes four DVDs).

United Kingdom

The British Film Institute promotes and conserves a wide range of films produced during the colonial period. See the 'Colonial Film. Moving images of the British Empire' project, http://www.colonialfilm.org.uk/.

France

Film production was more limited during the colonial period. There is no centralized policy to conserve the documentaries produced by different agencies—such as the Institut Pasteur and the Agence de la France d'Outre-Mer—the army, and various administrative services.
Certain film conservation sites may be mentioned, however:
L'ECPAD (Établissement de Communication et de Production Audiovisuelle de la Défense)
L'INA (Institut National de l'Audiovisuel)
The association Cinémémoire also collects private films belonging to families or film buffs (http://cinememoire.net/).

I would also like to mention the documentaries and docu-fictions of Jean Rouch:

Rouch, Jean, Marcel Griaule, Luc de Heusch, François Di Dio, and Germaine Dieterlin, *Jean Rouch. Une Aventure africaine. 1931 à 1984* (four DVDs), Paris, Éditions Montparnasse, 2010.
Jean Rouch 1956–1972, Paris, Éditions Montparnasse, 2005; a box set of 4 DVDs, presenting his 'fictional' turn from 1956 to 1972 (*Les Maîtres fous; Moi, un Noir; Jaguar; Un Lion nommé l'Américain; Petit à petit*).
Rouch, Jean, *Cocorico Monsieur Poulet* (1974), *Bataille sur le grand fleuve* (1950), *Cimetières dans la falaise* (1951) (1 DVD), Paris, Éditions Montparnasse, 2007.

SOURCES

Other sources include:

– ind; the first film by Senegal's Ousmane Sembène: *Borom Sarret*, 1963.
– ind; a documentary on video-parlours in Burkina Faso: Teno, Jean-Marie, *Lieux saints/Sacred Places*, 2009, Cameroon/France.

Interviews

In addition to drawing on already-published testimonials, I also carried out interviews in various countries. They give an idea of the atmosphere of film shows, and enrich the text without being cited on every point. They are explicitly mentioned when they add specific elements. The subject discussed being pleasant, most interviewees did not request to remain anonymous. Some are well-known intellectuals, others simple spectators.

Furthermore, I also interviewed certain filmmakers who grew up in the colonial period:

Gaston Kaboré, Burkinabè, born in 1951; interviewed in Paris, January 2008.

I also interviewed the Guinean author Tierno Monénembo in Conakry, in December 2012. This interview is complemented by the following publication: Monénembo, Tierno, 'Western à l'Africaine', interview with Taina Tervonen, in *Africultures*, no. 9, 1998.

Bakary, Kamian (1926–2016), Mali; PhD in Geography; Ouagadougou, 24 November 2008.

Barry, Bobo (1944–), Guinea; doctor; Conakry, 20 January 2005.

Barry, Sékoumar (1935–), Guinea; filmmaker, director of movie production in the 1980s; Conakry, 29 October 2003.

Chediac, René (1939/1942–), Guinea; manager of the Vox in Kindia; Kindia, 22 January 2005.

Coulibaly, Soumaïla (1941–), Ivory Coast; Bouaké, quartier Boukrou, 15 February 2017.

Diagne, Pathé (1934–), born in Saint-Louis, Senegal, he moved to Dakar in 1952; linguist and political scientist; Paris, April 2006.

Diakité, Moussa Kemoko, (1940–), Guinea; filmmaker; Conakry, 21 October 2003 and 27 January 2005.

Diallo, Khady, Ivory Coast; worked closely with Raymond Borremans, a former mobile cinema entrepreneur, from 1983 until Borremans's death in 1988; Abidjan, 9 February 2017.

Dieng, Amady Aly (1932–2015), Senegal; entered the École Nationale de la France d'Outre-Mer in 1957; active in the student pro-independence movement, the FEANF (Fédération des Étudiants d'Afrique Noire); PhD in Economy; Dakar, 7 May 2005.

Ghazi, Ahmed (1973–), Guinea; became manager of the Rogbane cinema (closed in 2006) after his father died in 2000; Conakry, 24 January 2005.

Ghussein, Isabelle (ca. 1938–), Avignon, France; arrived in Conakry in 1958 with her husband, a Lebano-Guinean; Conakry, 21 January 2005.

Hondo, Med (1936–2019), Atar, Mauritania, important filmmaker; made the well-known movie *Sarraounia* (1986); Strasbourg, 18 November 2008.

Iroko, Félix (1946–); History Professor at the University of Abomey-Calavi, Benin; Ouagadougou, 26 November 2008.

Lagache-Blanchet, Claude (early 1930s–), France; worked in Guinea, sporadically, from 1955 to 1959 as a journalist and a writer; Conakry, 21 January 2005 and Paris, 21 March 2005.

Monénembo, Tierno (1947–), Poredaka, Guinea; renowned writer; Conakry, December 2012.

Niane, Djibril Tamsir (1932–), Guinea; historian, essayist, and writer; Conakry, 16 June 2008.

Niang (1940s–2012), Guinea; his father was a Senegalese railroad worker, born in Saint-Louis, who settled down in Guinea; Niang grew up in Mamou but went to Saint-Louis for his studies in 1953; worked at the Public Works Department in Conakry; Conakry, 21 January 2005.

Owono, Nguema, François (mid-1940s–), Gabon; grew up in Libreville and went to high school in Brazzaville; Aix-en-Provence, 5 May 2010.

Sivadier, Jean-Paul (1929–), France; owned a mobile cinema in the late 1950s based in Bamako; Le Vieux Moulin, Neuville-sur-Sarthe, 19 November 2015 (as well as extensive correspondence through phone calls and emails).

Sow, Ciré (1954–), Guinea; movie fan in the 1960s to 70s; Conakry, 17 June 2008.

Sow, Fatou (1941–), Dakar, Senegal; sociologist; Paris, 5 July 2007.

Sultan, Gabriel, known as Doctor Sultan (1917–2018), Guinea; Lebano-Guinean doctor; student at the William Ponty teacher training school in Dakar from 1931; came back to Conakry in 1947; worked in Kankan and Conakry; Conakry, 25 January 2005.

Thioub, Ibrahima (1955–), Senegal; Professor of History, Rector of Cheikh Anta Diop University (UCAD), Dakar (2014–); Amsterdam, 24 August 2010.

Walter, Pierre (1921–unknown), France; engineer, and his wife; they lived in Guinea from 1949 to 1953; Strasbourg, 18 January 2006.

X (1947–), Guinea; secretary; Conakry, 20 January 2005.

Yacoubist community (Ivory Coast), followers of Yacouba Sylla, a Muslim leader and entrepreneur who founded cinemas in the 1950s; collective interviews at Gagnoa, Oumé, Daloa, and Adzopé in February 2017.

BIBLIOGRAPHY

Akyeampong, Emmanuel, and Charles Ambler, 'Leisure in African History: an Introduction', *The International Journal of African Historical Studies*, vol. 35, no. 1, 2002, pp. 1–16.

Allen, Robert C., 'From Exhibition to Reception: Reflections on the Audience in Film History', *Screen*, vol. 31, no. 4, 1990, pp. 347–56.

Ambler, Charles, 'Projecting the Modern Colonial State: Mobile Cinema in Kenya', in Lee Grieveson and Colin MacCabe (eds), *Film and the End of Empire*, London: Palgrave, 2011, pp. 199–224.

———, 'Cowboy Modern: African Audiences, Hollywood Films, and Visions of the West', in Richard Maltby, Melvyn Stokes and Robert C. Allen (eds), *Going to the Movies: Hollywood and the Social Experience of the Cinema*, Exeter: Exeter University Press, 2007, pp. 348–63.

———, 'Popular Films and Colonial Audiences in Central Africa', in Melvyn Stokes and Richard Maltby (eds), *Hollywood Abroad: Audiences and Cultural Exchange*, London: BFI Publishing, 2004, Chapter 9.

———, 'Popular Films and Colonial Audiences: The Movies in Northern Rhodesia', *The American Historical Review*, vol. 106, no. 1, 2001, pp. 81–105.

Anthony, Farid Raymond, *Sawpit Boy*, self-published, 1980.

Armbrust, Walter, *Mass Culture and Modernism in Egypt*, Cambridge: Cambridge University Press, 1996.

Armes, Roy, *Dictionary of African Filmmakers*, Bloomington: Indiana University Press, 2008.

Bâ, Amadou Hampâté, 'Le dit du cinéma africain', *Catalogue: Films ethnographiques sur l'Afrique noire*, Paris: UNESCO, 1967, pp. 9–19.

Bachy, Victor, 'Les Cinémas noirs d'Afrique', *Cinémaction*, no. 26, Paris: L'Harmattan, 1983.

———, *Le Cinéma en Côte d'Ivoire*, Brussels: Organisation catholique international du cinéma et de l'audiovisuel (OCIC), 1982.

Balandier, Georges, *Sociologie des Brazzavilles noires*, Paris: Presses de la FNSP, 1985 [1st ed. 1955].

Balogun, Françoise, *The Cinema in Nigeria*, Enugu: Delta, 1987.

Bancel, Nicolas, 'Les centres culturels en AOF (1953–1960). Un projet de contrôle sociopolitique des jeunes élites', in Laurent Fourchard, Odile Goerg and Muriel Gomez-Perez (eds), *Lieux de sociabilité urbaine en Afrique*, Paris: L'Harmattan, 2009, pp. 109–132.

Barlet, Olivier, *Les cinémas d'Afrique des années 2000. Perspectives critiques*, Paris: L'Harmattan, 2012.

———, *Les cinémas d'Afrique noire, le regard en question*, Paris: L'Harmattan, 1996.

Barrot, Pierre (ed.), *Nollywood: The Video Phenomenon in Nigeria*, Ibadan: HEBN; Bloomington: Indiana University Press, 2008.

Bazenguissa-Ganga, Rémy, 'Les *Ninja*, les *Cobra* et les *Zoulou* crèvent l'écran à Brazzaville: le rôle des médias et la construction des identités de violence politique', *Canadian Journal of African Studies*, vol. 33, nos 2–3, 1999, pp. 329–61.

Bickford-Smith, Vivian and Richard Mendelsohn (eds), *Black and White in Colour: African History on Screen*, Oxford: James Currey; Athens: Ohio University Press; Cape Town: Double Storey, 2007.

Bickford-Smith, Vivian, 'How Urban South Africa life was represented in film and films consumed in South African cities—in the 1950s', Workshop, Urban Living in the Twentieth Century, 2000.

Blanchon, Karine, *Les cinémas de Madagascar: 1937–2007*, Paris: L'Harmattan, 2009.

Blaylock, Jennifer, 'Peter Morton-Williams: Anthropology & Mobile Cinema', https://cinemaintransit.wordpress.com/2011/01/11/peter-morton-williams-anthropology-mobile-cinema/, January 2011.

Bloom, Peter J., *French Colonial Documentary: Mythologies of Humanitarianism*, Minneapolis: University of Minnesota Press, 2008.

Bosséno, Christian-Marc, 'Le répertoire du grand écran. Le cinéma "par ailleurs"', Jean-Pierre Rioux and Jean-François Sirinelli (eds), *La Culture de masse en France*, Paris: Fayard, 2002.

———, *La prochaine séance. Les Français et leurs cinés*, Paris: Gallimard, 1996.

Boughedir, Férid, 'Cinémas nationaux et politiques cinématographiques en Afrique noire: "Du rêve Sud-Sud à la défense de la diversité culturelle"', *Afriques 50: Singularités d'un cinéma pluriel*, Paris: L'Harmattan, 2005, pp. 161–71.

———, *Le Cinéma africain de A à Z*, Brussels: Organisation catholique international du cinéma et de l'audiovisuel (OCIC), 1987.

Boulanger, Pierre, *Le Cinéma colonial: de 'L'Atlantide' à 'Lawrence d'Arabie'*, Paris: Seghers, 1975.

Bourgeois, Henri, *Walipana, Carnets d'un fils de l'école de la République au service d'un Empire qui se mourait*, Paris: H. Bourgeois, 1997.

Burgess, Thomas, 'Cinema, Bell Bottoms, and Miniskirts: Struggles over Youth and

Citizenship in Revolutionary Zanzibar', *International Journal of African Historical Studies*, vol. 35, nos 2–3, 2002, pp. 287–313.

Burns, James, *Cinema and Society in the British Empire, 1895–1940 (Britain and the World)*, London: Palgrave Macmillan, 2013.

———, 'John Wayne on the Zambezi: Cinema, Empire, and the American Western in British Central Africa', *The International Journal of African Historical Studies*, vol. 35, no. 1, 2002a, pp. 103–17.

———, *Flickering Shadows: Cinema and Identity in Colonial Zimbabwe*, Athens: Ohio University Press, 2002b.

Burthe d'Annelet, André, *À travers l'Afrique française*, Paris: Firmin-Didot et Compagnie, ca. 1932–33.

Burton, Andrew, 'Urchins, Loafers and the Cult of the Cowboy: Urbanization and Delinquency in Dar es Salaam, 1919–61', *The Journal of African History*, vol. 42, no. 2, 2001, pp. 199–216.

Carlier, Omar, 'Le cinéma en Algérie à l'entre-deux-guerres: de la percée en ville européenne à l'émergence d'un public "indigène"', in Morgan Corriou, (ed.), *Publics et spectacle cinématographique en situation coloniale*, Tunis: IRMC-CERES, *Cahiers du CERES*, no. 5, 2012, pp. 37–67.

Casciato, Maristella, 'Une "place au soleil": Le patrimoine colonial italien de la ville d'Asmara en Erythrée', in Bernard Toulier and Marc Pabois (eds), *Architecture coloniale et Patrimoine: les expériences européennes*, Paris: INP/SOMOGY, 2006.

Chaplain, Renaud, 'Les cinémas dans la ville. La diffusion du spectacle cinématographique dans l'agglomération lyonnaise (1896–1945)', PhD, University Lumière-Lyon 2, 2007.

Chomentowski, Gabrielle, 'Implanter le socialisme par le cinéma? La diffusion des films soviétiques en Afrique au début des années 1960', *Socialismes africains/ Socialismes en Afrique*, Maria-Benadita Basto, Françoise Blum, Pierre Guidi et al. (eds), Paris: Publications de la Sorbonne (forthcoming, 2019).

———, 'L'expérience soviétique des cinémas africains au lendemain des indépendances', *Le Temps des médias*, no. 26, 2016, pp. 111–25.

Chowdhry, Prem, *Colonial India and the Making of Empire Cinema: Image, Ideology, and Identity*, Manchester: Manchester University Press, 2000.

Colleyn, Jean-Paul (ed.), *Jean Rouch, cinéma et anthropologie*, Paris: INA, 2009.

Collins, John, 'A century of changing locations of Ghanaian commercial popular entertainment venues', in Laurent Fourchard, Odile Goerg, and Muriel Gomez-Perez (eds), *Lieux de sociabilité urbaine en Afrique*, Paris: L'Harmattan, 2009, pp. 225–52.

Condé, Maryse, *La vie sans fards*, Paris: JC Lattès, 2012.

Convents, Guido, *Images et démocratie. Les Congolais face au cinéma et à l'audiovisuel. Une histoire politico-culturelle du Congo des Belges jusqu'à la république démocratique du Congo (1896–2006)*, Kessel-Lo: Afrika Filmfestival, 2006.

Coplan, David, *In Township Tonight. Musique et théâtre dans les villes d'Afrique du Sud*, Paris: Karthala-Credu, 1992.

Corriou, Morgan, 'Un nouveau loisir en situation coloniale: le cinéma dans la Tunisie du Protectorat (1896–1956)', PhD, University Paris-Diderot, 2011.

———, '"Le choix entre l'Orient et l'Occident"? Les Tunisiens et le cinéma dans les dernières années du protectorat français (1946–1956)', in Romain Bertrand, Hélène Blais and Emmanuelle Sibeud (eds), *Cultures d'Empires. Échanges et affrontements culturels en situation coloniale*, Paris: Karthala, 2015, pp. 171–96.

———, 'Hourras, "hou hou" et tohu-bohu dans les cinémas de Tunisie à l'époque du protectorat', in Omar Carlier (ed.), *Images du Maghreb, Images au Maghreb (XIXe-XXe siècles). Une révolution du visuel?*, Paris: L'Harmattan, 2010, pp. 203–36.

Cousturier, Lucie, *Mes inconnus chez eux. Mon amie Fatou citadine*, Paris: L'Harmattan, 2003 [1st ed. F. Rieder et Cie, 1925].

D'Anfreville de la Salle, Léon, *Sur la côte d'Afrique*, Paris: Larose, 1912.

Dadié, Bernard, *Climbié*, African Writers Series, London: Heinemann, 1971 [1st ed. 1966, Seghers, written in 1953].

Debrix, Jean-René, 'Le Cinéma Africain', *Afrique contemporaine*, no. 38–39, 1968, pp. 7–12; no. 40, pp. 2–6.

De Heusch, Luc, *Rencontres internationales: le cinéma et l'Afrique au sud du Sahara*, General Report, Brussels, Exposition Universelle et Internationale, 24–26 July 1958.

Diallo, Nafissatou, *De Tilène au Plateau. Une enfance dakaroise*, Dakar: NEA-Sénégal, 1997.

Diawara, Manthia, *African Film: New Forms of Aesthetics and Politics*, Munich: Prestel, 2010.

———, *African Cinema: Politics and Culture*, Bloomington: Indiana University Press, 1992.

Diop, Birago, *La Plume raboutée*, Paris: Présence africaine; Dakar: NEA, 1978.

Drieu, Cloé (ed.), *Écrans d'Orient, Propagande, innovation et résistance dans les cinémas de Turquie, d'Iran et d'Asie centrale (1897–1945)*, Paris: IISM-Karthala, 2014.

Fair, Laura, *Reel Pleasures: Cinema Audiences and Entrepreneurs in Twentieth-Century Urban Tanzania*, Athens: Ohio University Press, 2018.

———, 'Drive-In Socialism: Debating Modernities and Development in Dar es Salaam, Tanzania', *American Historical Review*, vol. 118, no. 4, October 2013, pp. 1077–104.

———, '"They stole the show!": Indian films in coastal Tanzania, 1950s–1980s', *Journal of African Media Studies*, vol. 2, no. 1, 2010, pp. 91–106.

———, 'Making Love in the Indian Ocean: Hindi Films, Zanzibari Audiences, and the Construction of Romance in the 1950s and 1960s', *Love in Africa*, in Jennifer Cole and Lynn M. Thomas (eds), Chicago: University of Chicago Press, 2009, pp. 58–82.

———, 'Hollywood Hegemony? Hardly: Audience Preferences in Zanzibar, 1950s-1970s', *ZIFF Journal*, vol. 1, no. 1, 2004, pp. 52–58.

Forest, Claude (ed.) 'L'industrie du cinéma en Afrique. Introduction thématique', *Afrique contemporaine*, no. 238, 2011, pp. 59–73.

———, *Les Dernières Séances: cent ans d'exploitation des salles de cinéma*, Paris: CNRS Éditions, 1995.

Fouhba, Honoré, *Les salles de cinéma au Nord-Cameroun: des implantations aux transformations*, Yaoundé: Ifrikiya, 2016.

Fourchard, Laurent, *De la ville coloniale à la cour africaine. Espaces, pouvoirs et sociétés à Ouagadougou et à Bobo-Dioulasso (Haute-Volta), fin XIXème siècle–1960*, Paris: L'Harmattan, 2001.

Furhmann, Wolfgang, *Imperial Projections: Screening the German Colonies*, New York; Oxford: Berghahn Books, 2015.

Gangnat, Émilie, Annie Lenoble-Bart, and Jean-François Zorn (eds), *Mission et Cinéma. Films missionnaires et Missionnaires au cinéma*, Paris: Karthala, 2013.

Gehrts, Meg, *Une actrice de cinéma dans la brousse du Nord-Togo (1913–1914)*, Chroniques anciennes du Togo no. 6, Lomé: Haho, Presses de l'UB; Paris: Karthala, 1996 [*A Camera Actress in the Wilds of Togoland: The Adventures, Observations and Experiences of a Cinematograph Actress in West African Forests Whilst Collecting Films Depicting Native Life and when Posing as the White Woman in Anglo-African Cinematgraph Dramas*, London: Seeley, Service and Co., 1915].

Genova, James E., 'Cinema and the Struggle to (De)colonize the Mind in French/Francophone West Africa (1950s–1960s)', *The Journal of the Midwest Modern Language Association*, vol. 39, no. 1, 2006, pp. 50–62.

———, *Colonial Ambivalence, Cultural Authenticity, and the Limitations of Mimicry in French-Ruled West Africa, 1914–1956*, New York: Peter Lang, 2004.

Ginio, Ruth, 'La politique antijuive de Vichy en Afrique occidentale française', *Archives Juives*, 2003, no. 1, pp. 109–118.

Goerg, Odile, 'Le soufi, le cinéma et la mémoire. Les salles de Cheikh Yacouba Sylla (Côte d'Ivoire)', *Canadian Journal of African Studies*, vol. 53, 2019, pp. 1–25.

———, 'Les cinémas de Cheikh Yacouba Sylla. Entre discours communautaire et lieux de mémoire ivoiriens', *Afrique contemporaine*, vol. 3, nos 263–64, 2017, pp. 271–74.

———, '"Les nègres, ils t'emmerdent!" Rires, applaudissements et protestations: Les formes de visibilité de publics africains en Afrique coloniale', in *Regarder des films en Afriques*, Patricia Caillé and Claude Forest (eds), Villeneuve d'Ascq: Presses universitaires du Septentrion, 2017, pp. 43–62.

———, 'En route sur les pistes du Mali avec Jean-Paul Sivadier. Le *Circuit Cinéma Africain* à la fin des années 1950', *Images & Mémoires*, no. 48, 2016, pp. 13–19.

———, 'Des cowboys dans la savane. Cinéma et hybridation culturelle en contexte colonial', *Afrika Zamani*, nos 20 & 21, 2012–2013, pp. 69–94.

———, 'Les films arabes, une menace pour l'Empire? La politique des films arabes à la veille des indépendances en Afrique Occidentale Française', *Outre Mers*, nos 380–81, 2013, pp. 287–312.

———, 'Entre infantilisation et répression coloniale. Censure cinématographique en AOF. "Grands enfants" et protection de la jeunesse', *Cahiers d'Etudes Africaines*, no. 205, 2012, pp. 165–98.

Gomery, Douglas, *Shared Pleasures: A History of Movie Presentation in the United States*, London: BFI Publishing, 1992.

Gomez, Alsény René, *Camp Boiro. Parler ou périr*, Paris: L'Harmattan, 2007.

Gondola, Ch. Didier, *Tropical Cowboys: Westerns, Violence, and Masculinity in Kinshasa*, Bloomington: Indiana University Press, 2016.

———, 'Le culte du cowboy et les figures du masculin à Kinshasa dans les années 1950', *Cahiers d'Etudes Africaines*, nos 209–10, 2013, pp. 173–99.

———, 'Tropical Cowboys. Westerns, Violence, and Masculinity among the Young Bills of Kinshasa', *Histoire & Afrique*, no. 7, 2009, pp. 76–98.

Grieveson, Lee and Colin MacCabe (eds), *Empire and Film*, London: Palgrave Macmillan/BFI, 2011a.

Grieveson, Lee and Colin MacCabe (eds), *Film at the end of Empire*, London: BFI/Palgrave Macmillan, 2011b.

Gugler, Josef, *African Film: Re-Imagining a Continent*, Oxford: James Currey, 2003.

Gutberlet, Marie-Hélène, *Auf Reisen. Afrikanisches Kino*, Frankfurt am Main: Stroemfeld, 2004.

Haffner, Pierre, 'Comment Dakar fonda le cinéma d'Afrique noire. Développement urbain, développement cinématographique et démocratie', in Daus Ronald (ed.), *Grossstadtliteratur*, Frankfurt am Main: Vervuert Verlag, 1992, pp. 185–95.

———, 'Nations nègres et cinéma', *Notre librairie. Cinémas d'Afrique*, no. 49, 2002, p. 149.

———, *Essai sur les fondements du cinéma africain*, Dakar; Abidjan: NEA, 1978.

Haynes, Jonathan, *Nollywood: The Creation of Nigerian Film Genres*, Chicago: University of Chicago Press, 2016.

———, *Nigerian Video Films*, Athens: Ohio University Press, 2000.

Hennebelle, Guy, 'Les cinémas africains en 1972', *L'Afrique littéraire et artistique*, no. 20, 1972.

Jaikumar, Priya, 'Hollywood and the Multiple Constituencies of Colonial India', in Melvyn Stokes and Richard Maltby (eds), *Hollywood Abroad: Audiences and Cultural Exchange*, London: BFI Publishing, 2004, pp. 78–97.

Jancovich, Mark, Lucy Faire, and Sarah Stubbings, *The Place of the Audience: Cultural Geographies of Film Consumption*, London: BFI Publishing, 2003.

Kerr, David, 'The Best of Both Worlds? Colonial Film Policy and Practice in Northern Rhodesia and Nyasaland', *Critical Arts*, vol. 7, nos 1–2, 1993, pp. 11–42.

Kipré, Pierre, *Villes de Côte d'Ivoire 1893–1940*, vol. 2, Abidjan; Dakar; Lomé: NEA, 1985.

Lacolley, Albert, *Le Cinéma dans les territoires d'Outre-Mer*, ENFOM thesis, Paris: 1946

Lagrée, Michel, 'L'encyclique Vigilanti cura sur le cinéma (1936)', Achille Ratti Pape Pie XI, Rome: École Française de Rome, 1996, pp. 839–53.

Larkin, Brian, *Signal and Noise: Media, Infrastructure, and Urban Culture in Nigeria*, Durham; London: Duke University Press, 2008.

——, 'The Materiality of Cinema Theaters in Northern Nigeria', *Media Worlds: Anthropology on New Terrain*, in Faye D. Ginsburg, Lila Abu-Lughod, and Brian Larkin (eds), Berkeley; Los Angeles; London: University of California Press, 2002, pp. 319–36.

——, 'Theaters of the Profane: Cinema and Colonial Urbanism', *Visual Anthropology Review*, vol. 14, no. 2, 1998, pp. 46–62.

Lauro, Amandine, *Coloniaux, ménagères et prostituées au Congo belge 1885–1930*, Loverval: Labor, 2005.

Leiris, Michel, *L'Afrique fantôme*, Paris: Gallimard, 1981 [1st ed. 1934].

Lidji, Ahui François, 'L'Évolution des habitudes de consommation en Côte d'Ivoire de 1945 à 1980', PhD, University Paris I, 1998.

Lombard, Jacques, 'Cotonou, ville africaine', *Études dahoméennes*, Cotonou: IFAN, Gouvernement du Dahomey, vol. 10, 1953.

Londres, Albert, *Terre d'ébène*, Paris: Le serpent à plumes, 1994 [1st ed. 1929, Albin Michel].

Low, Rachael, *The History of British Film, Vol. 4, 1918–1929*, London: Routledge, 1997 [1st ed. 1971].

Mahir, Şaul and Ralph A. Austen (eds), *Viewing African cinema in the Twenty-First Century: Art Films and the Nollywood Video Revolution*, Athens: Ohio University Press, 2010.

Maltby, Richard, Melvyn Stokes, and Robert C. Allen (eds), *Going to the Movies: Hollywood and the Social Experience of the Cinema*, Exeter: Exeter University Press, 2007.

Marguerat Yves and T. Pelei (eds), *Si Lomé m'était contée...*, Lomé: Presses universitaires du Bénin, 1992.

Martin, Phyllis, *Leisure and Society in Colonial Brazzaville*, Cambridge: Cambridge University Press, 1995.

McFeely, Gareth '"Gone are the days": A Social and Business History of Cinema-going in Gold Coast/Ghana, 1910–1982', PhD. Boston University, 2015.

Méker, Maurice, *Le Temps colonial. Itinéraire africain d'un naïf du colonialisme à la cooperation, 1931–1960*, Abidjan: NEA, 1980.

Meyer, Birgit, 'Popular Ghanaian Cinema and "African Heritage"', *Africa Today*, vol. 46, no. 2, 1999, pp. 93–114.

——, *Sensational Movies: Video, Vision, and Christianity in Ghana*, Berkeley: University of California Press, 2015.

Monénembo, Tierno, 'Western à l'Africaine', interview with Taina Tervonen, *Africultures*, no. 9, 1998.

———, *Cinéma*, Paris: Seuil, 1997.

Montebello, Fabrice, *Le Cinéma en France depuis les années 1930*, Paris: Colin, 2005.

Moorman, Marissa, 'Of Westerns, Women, and War: Re-Situating Angolan Cinema and the Nation', *Research in African Literatures*, vol. 32, no. 3, 2001, pp. 103–22.

Mudimbe, Valentin, *Invention of Africa: Gnosis, Philosophy and the Order of Knowledge*, Bloomington: Indiana University Press, 1988.

Murphy, David and Patrick Williams, *Postcolonial African Cinema: Ten Directors*, Manchester: Manchester University Press, 2007.

Nasson, Bill, '"She Preferred Living in a Cave with Harry the Snake-Catcher": Towards an Oral History of Popular Leisure and Class Expression in District Six, Cape Town, c. 1920s–1950s', in Philip Bonner, Isabel Hofmeyr, Deborah James, and Tom Lodge (eds), *Holding Their Ground: Class, Locality and Culture in Nineteenth and Twentieth-Century South Africa*, Johannesburg: Witwatersrand University Press, 1989, pp. 285–309.

Ndiltah, Patrick, *Les Écrans noirs de N'Djaména. Les ciné-clubs comme réponse à la fermeture des salles traditionnelles en Afrique: le cas du Tchad*, Paris: L'Harmattan, 2015.

NFVCB [National Film and Video Censors Board], *The Challenges of Film and Video Censorship in Nigeria*, Lagos: NFVCB, 1996.

Notcutt, L. A. and G. C. Latham, *The African and the Cinema*, London: Edinburgh House Press, 1937.

Okome, Onookome and Jonathan Haynes, *Cinema and Social Change in West Africa*, Jos: Nigerian Film Corporation (NFC), 1997 [1st ed. 1995].

Olufunke, Adeboye, 'A Church in a Cinema Hall?', *Journal of Religion in Africa*, vol. 42, no. 2, 2012, pp. 145–71.

Ouattara, Ibrahima, 'Festivités et loisirs à Bouaké de 1914 à 1990', PhD, University of Bouaké (Ivory Coast), 2018.

Pfaff, Françoise, *Focus on African Films*, Bloomington: Indiana University Press, 2004.

———, *Twenty-Five Black African Filmmakers: A Critical Study, with Filmography and Bio-Bibliography*, Westport: Greenwood Press, 1988.

———, 'Hollywood's Image of Africa', Images of Africa in the New World/Images de l'Afrique dans le Nouveau Monde, *Commonwealth Essays and Studies*, University Sorbonne Nouvelle, no. 5, 1981–82, pp. 97–116.

Phelps, Guy, *Film Censorship in Britain*, London: Gollancz, 1975.

Pommier, Pierre, *Cinéma et Développement en Afrique Noire Francophone*, Paris: A. Pedone, 1974.

Powdermaker, Hortense, *Copper Town: Changing Africa; the Human Situation on the Rhodesian Copperbelt*, New York: Harper & Row, 1962.

Ramirez, Francis and Christian Rolot, *Histoire du cinéma au Zaire, au Rwanda et au Burundi*, Bruxelles-Tervuren: Musée Royal de l'Afrique Centrale de Tervuren, 1985.

Reinwald, Brigitte, 'Tonight at the Empire. Cinema and Urbanity in Zanzibar, 1920s to 1960s', *Afrique & Histoire*, no. 5, 2006, pp. 81–109.

Retord, Georges L. A., 'Les premières projections cinématographiques en Côte d'Ivoire', *Le cinéma en Côte d'Ivoire, Communication Audiovisuelle*, no. 6, CERAV, Abidjan, 1986, pp. 11–31.

Reynolds, Glenn, *Colonial Cinema in Africa: Origins, Images, Audiences*, Jefferson, NC: McFarland & Company, 2015.

Rice, Tom, '"Are You Proud to Be British?": Mobile Film Shows, Local Voices and the Demise of the British Empire in Africa', *Historical Journal of Film, Radio and Television*, vol. 36, no. 3, 2016, pp. 331–51.

———, 'Exhibiting Africa: British Instructional Films and The Empire Series, 1925–1928', Lee Grieveson and Colin MacCabe (eds), *Empire and Film*, London: BFI/Palgrave Macmillan, 2011, pp. 115–34.

———, 'Gold Coast Film Unit', Colonial Film, http://www.colonialfilm.org.uk/production-company/gold-coast-film-unit, June 2010.

Robertson, James C., *The British Board of Film Censors: Film Censorship in Britain, 1896–1950*, London: Croom Helm, 1985.

———, *The Hidden Cinema: British Film Censorship in Action, 1913–72*, London: Routledge, 1993.

Rouch, Jean, 'Situation et tendances actuelles du cinéma africain' (27 pages, roundtable, Venice, 1961), UNESCO, 1962a [longer version published in *Catalogue. Films ethnographiques sur l'Afrique noire*, UNESCO, 1967, pp. 374–408], http://unesdoc.unesco.org/images/0018/001842/184262fb.pdf

———, 'The awakening of African Cinema', *Courier*, UNESCO, March 1962b, pp. 10–15.

———, 'L'Africain devant le film ethnographique', *Rencontres internationales: le cinéma et l'Afrique au sud du Sahara*, General Report, Brussels, Exposition Universelle et Internationale, 1958, pp. 92–94.

Ruelle, Catherine (ed.), *Afrique 50. Singularités d'un cinéma pluriel*, Paris: L'Harmattan, 2005.

Sadji, Abdoulaye, *Maïmouna*, Paris: Présence Africaine, 1958.

Sadoul, Georges (ed.), *Les Cinémas des pays arabes*, Beyrouth: Centre Interarabe du Cinéma et de la Télévision, 1966.

———, *Histoire du cinéma mondial*, Paris: Flammarion, 1972 [1st ed. 1949].

Schmidt, Nancy J., 'Focus on: African Filmmaking Country by Country', *African Studies Review*, vol. 28, no. 1, 1985, pp. 111–14.

Seck, Djibril, 'Le loisir cinématographique à Dakar, 1926–1974', PhD, UCAD, Dakar, 2008.

———, 'Le loisir cinématographique à Dakar, 1945–1960', Master's dissertation, UCAD, Dakar, 2003.

Sembène, Ousmane, 'L'image cinématographique et la poésie en Afrique', Rencontre

Internationale des Poètes, Berlin, December 1964, p. 165; quoted by Vieyra, *Sembène Ousmane, cinéaste*, Paris: Présence africaine, 1972, pp. 1651–73.

———, 'La Leçon du cinéma d'Ousmane Sembène', Cannes Film Festival, http://africultures.com/la-lecon-de-cinema-dousmane-sembene-au-festival-de-cannes-2005-3854/, 2005.

Shafik, Viola, *Arab Cinema: History and Cultural Identity*, Le Caire: The American University in Cairo Press, 2007 [1st ed. 1998].

Slavin, David Henry, *Colonial Cinema and Imperial France, 1919–1939: White Blind Spots, Male Fantasies, Settler Myths*, Baltimore; London: Johns Hopkins University Press, 2001.

Smyth, Rosaleen, 'The Feature Film in Tanzania', *African Affairs*, vol. 88, no. 352, 1989, pp. 389–96.

———, 'Movies and Mandarins: The Official Film and British Colonial Africa', *British Cinema History*, James Curran and Vincent Porter (eds), London: Weidenfeld & Nicholson, 1983a, pp. 129–43.

———, 'The Central African Film Unit's Images of Empire, 1948–1963', *Historical Journal of Film, Radio and Television*, vol. 3, no. 2, 1983b, pp. 131–47.

———, 'The Development of British Colonial Film Policy, 1927–1939, with Special Reference to East and Central Africa', *The Journal of African History*, vol. 20, no. 3, 1979, pp. 437–50.

Stokes, Melvyn and Richard Maltby (eds), *Hollywood Abroad: Audiences and Cultural Exchange*, London: BFI Publishing, 2004.

Stoler, Ann L., *Carnal Knowledge and Imperial Power: Race and the Intimate in Colonial Rule*, Berkeley: University of California Press, 2002.

Thackway, Melissa, *African Shoots Back: Alternative Perspectives in Sub-Saharan Francophone African Film*, Bloomington: Indiana University Press; London: James Currey, 2003.

Thioub, Ibrahima, 'Savoirs interdits en contexte colonial. La politique culturelle de la France en Afrique de l'Ouest', in Chantal Chanson-Jabeur and Odile Goerg (eds), '*Mama Africa*'. *Hommage à Catherine Coquery-Vidrovitch*, Paris: L'Harmattan, 2005, pp. 75–97.

Ukadike, Nwachukwu Frank, *Black African Cinema*, Berkeley: California University Press, 1994.

UNESCO, *Basic Facts and Figures: International Statistics Relating to Education, Culture and Mass Communications*, Paris: UNESCO, 1961.

———, *The Use of Mobile Cinema and Radio Vans in Fundamental Education*, Paris: UNESCO, 1949.

Vaughan, J. Koyinde, 'Africa South of the Sahara and the Cinema', *Présence africaine*, vol. 3, nos 14–15, 1957, pp. 210–21.

Viditz-Ward, Vera, 'Alphonso Lisk-Carew: Creole Photographer', *African Arts*, Los Angeles: California, 1985, vol. 19, no. 1, pp. 46–51.

Vieyra, Paulin, 'Responsabilités du cinéma dans la formation d'une conscience nationale africaine', *Présence Africaine*, nos 27–28, 1959, pp. 303–13.

———, 'Propos sur le cinéma africain', *Présence africaine*, vol. 5, no. 22, 1958a, pp. 106–11.

———, 'Discussion' and 'Suggestions pour le développement du cinéma en A.O.F.', *Rencontres internationales: le cinéma et l'Afrique au sud du Sahara*, General Report, Brussels, Exposition Universelle et Internationale, 1958b, pp. 15–16; pp. 95–97.

———, *Le Cinéma africain des origines à 1973*, Paris: Présence africaine, 1975.

Villers, Roland, *Le Cinéma et ses merveilles*, Paris: Librairie Bernardin-Bechet, 1930.

Wassef, Magda (ed.), *Egypte. 100 ans de cinéma*, Paris: Plume-Institut du Monde Arabe, 1995.

Weulersse, Jacques, *Noirs et Blancs. À travers l'Afrique nouvelle: de Dakar au Cap*, Paris: Éditions du Comité des travaux historiques et scientifiques, 1994 [1st ed. 1931].

Zimmermann, Sophie, 'Le Développement du cinéma comme loisir et lieu de sociabilité au Togo (années 1910–2007)', Master's dissertation, University Paris-Diderot, 2008.

INDEX

INDEX